SAPPORO SNOW FESTIVAL

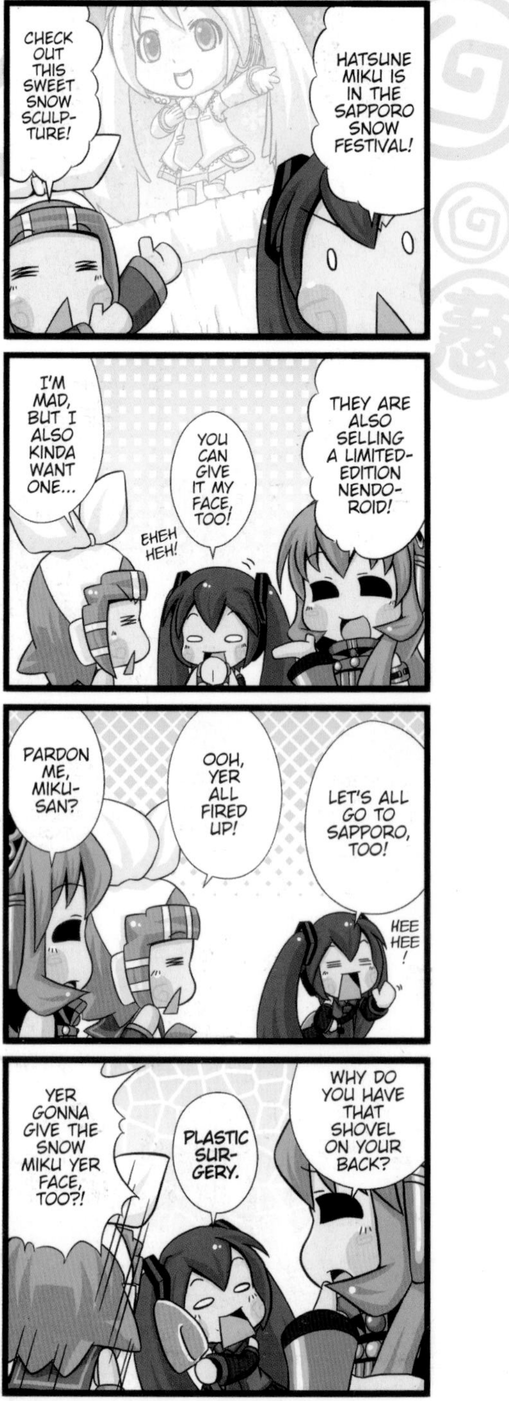
HATSUNE MIKU IS IN THE SAPPORO SNOW FESTIVAL!
CHECK OUT THIS SWEET SNOW SCULP-TURE!
THEY ARE ALSO SELLING A LIMITED-EDITION NENDO-ROID!
YOU CAN GIVE IT MY FACE, TOO!
EHEH HEH!
I'M MAD, BUT I ALSO KINDA WANT ONE...
LET'S ALL GO TO SAPPORO, TOO!
HEE HEE!
OOH, YER ALL FIRED UP!
PARDON ME, MIKU-SAN?
WHY DO YOU HAVE THAT SHOVEL ON YOUR BACK?
PLASTIC SUR-GERY.
YER GONNA GIVE THE SNOW MIKU YER FACE, TOO?!

PORSCHE GETS SERIOUS

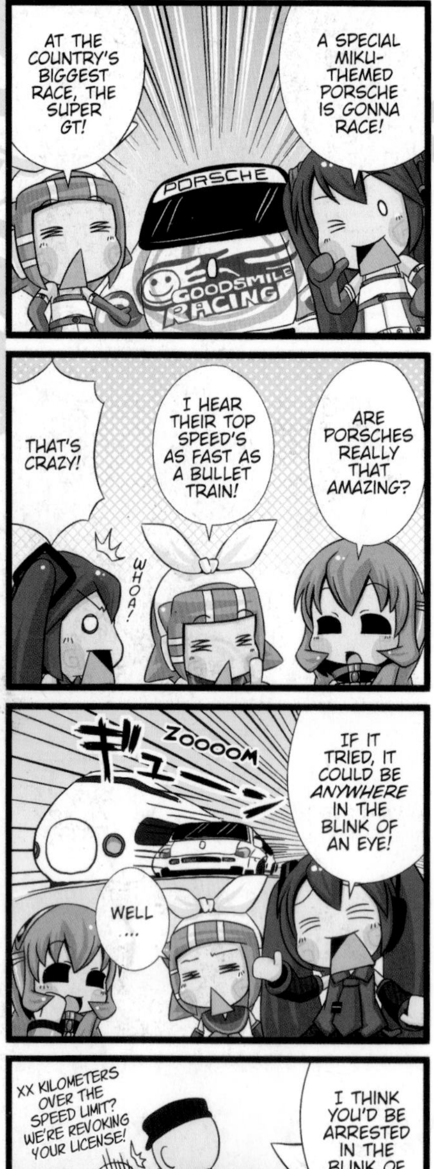
A SPECIAL MIKU-THEMED PORSCHE IS GONNA RACE!
AT THE COUNTRY'S BIGGEST RACE, THE SUPER GT!
PORSCHE
GOODSMILE RACING
ARE PORSCHES REALLY THAT AMAZING?
I HEAR THEIR TOP SPEED'S AS FAST AS A BULLET TRAIN!
WHOA!
THAT'S CRAZY!
IF IT TRIED, IT COULD BE *ANYWHERE* IN THE BLINK OF AN EYE!
ZOOOOM
WELL ....
I THINK YOU'D BE ARRESTED IN THE BLINK OF AN EYE...
XX KILOMETERS OVER THE SPEED LIMIT? WE'RE REVOKING YOUR LICENSE!

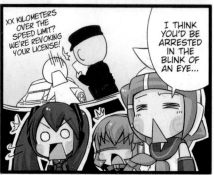

PROJECT DIVA ARCADE

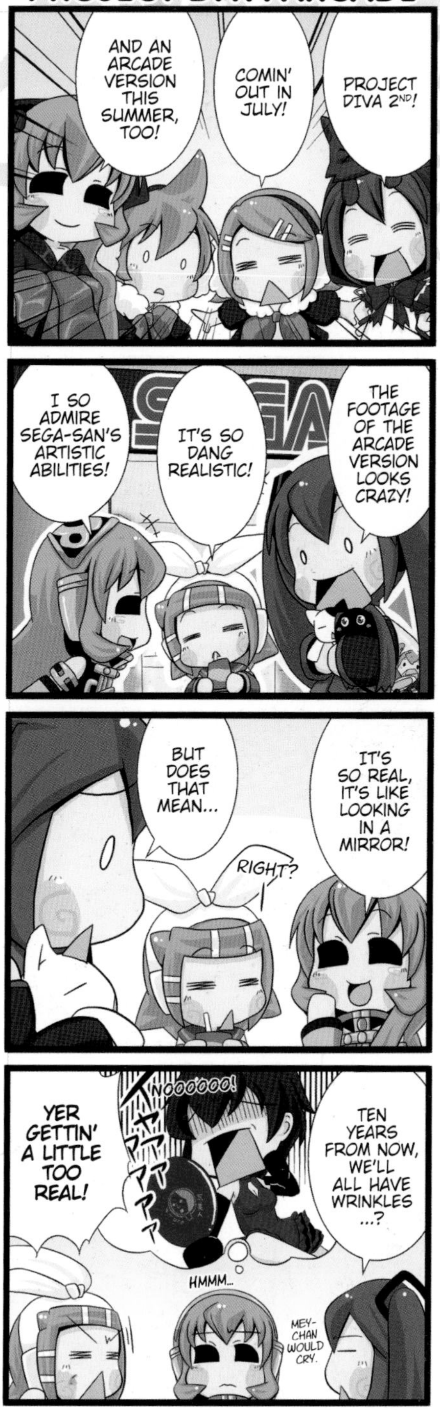
PROJECT DIVA 2ND!
COMIN' OUT IN JULY!
AND AN ARCADE VERSION THIS SUMMER, TOO!
THE FOOTAGE OF THE ARCADE VERSION LOOKS CRAZY!
IT'S SO DANG REALISTIC!
I SO ADMIRE SEGA-SAN'S ARTISTIC ABILITIES!
IT'S SO REAL, IT'S LIKE LOOKING IN A MIRROR!
BUT DOES THAT MEAN...
RIGHT?
TEN YEARS FROM NOW, WE'LL ALL HAVE WRINKLES...?
NOOOOOOO!
イヤァァァ
アァァァ
YER GETTIN' A LITTLE TOO REAL!
HMMM...
MEY-CHAN WOULD CRY.

DREAMY THEATER

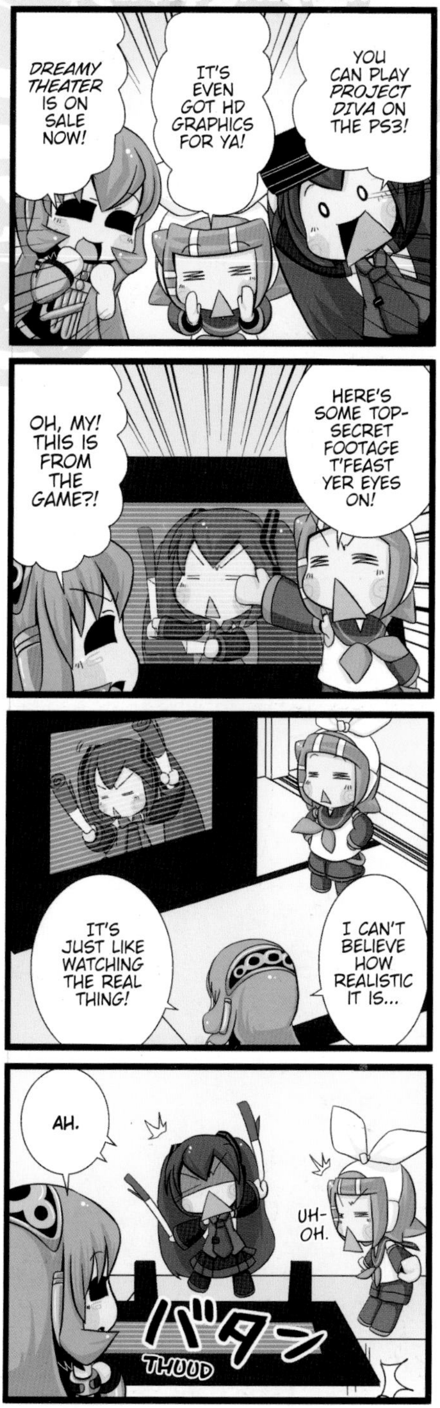
YOU CAN PLAY PROJECT DIVA ON THE PS3!
IT'S EVEN GOT HD GRAPHICS FOR YA!
DREAMY THEATER IS ON SALE NOW!
HERE'S SOME TOP-SECRET FOOTAGE T'FEAST YER EYES ON!
OH, MY! THIS IS FROM THE GAME?!
I CAN'T BELIEVE HOW REALISTIC IT IS...
IT'S JUST LIKE WATCHING THE REAL THING!
UH-OH.
AH.
バタン
THUUD

DUET

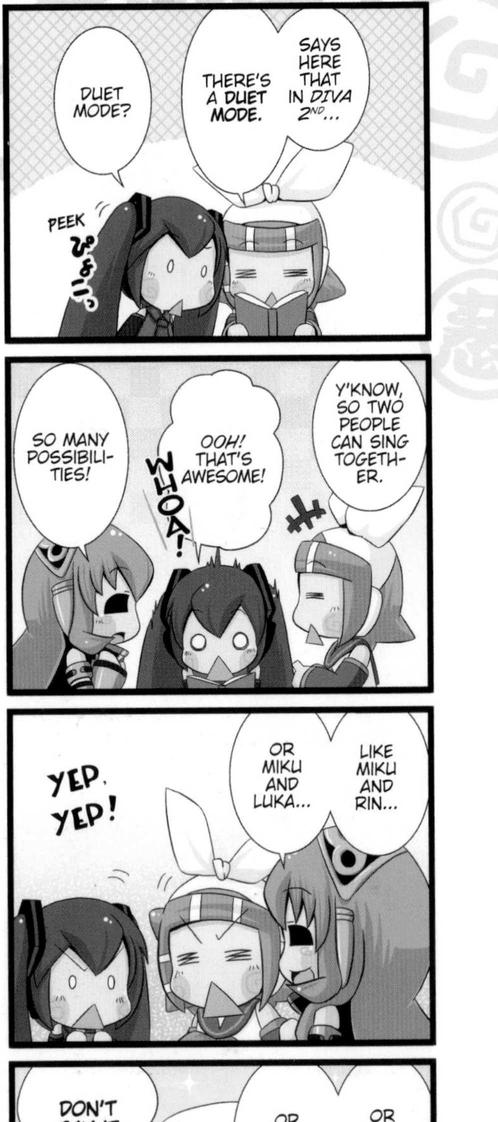
SAYS HERE THAT IN *DIVA 2ND*...
THERE'S A **DUET MODE.**
DUET MODE?
PEEK
ぴょこっ
Y'KNOW, SO TWO PEOPLE CAN SING TOGETH-ER.
OOH! THAT'S AWESOME!
WHOA!
SO MANY POSSIBILI-TIES!
LIKE MIKU AND RIN...
OR MIKU AND LUKA...
YEP, YEP!
OR RIN x LEN...
OR KAITO x LEN!
DON'T SAY IT LIKE THAT, Y'FREAK!
FOR SO MANY REASONS!
FWIP

NEW MODULE

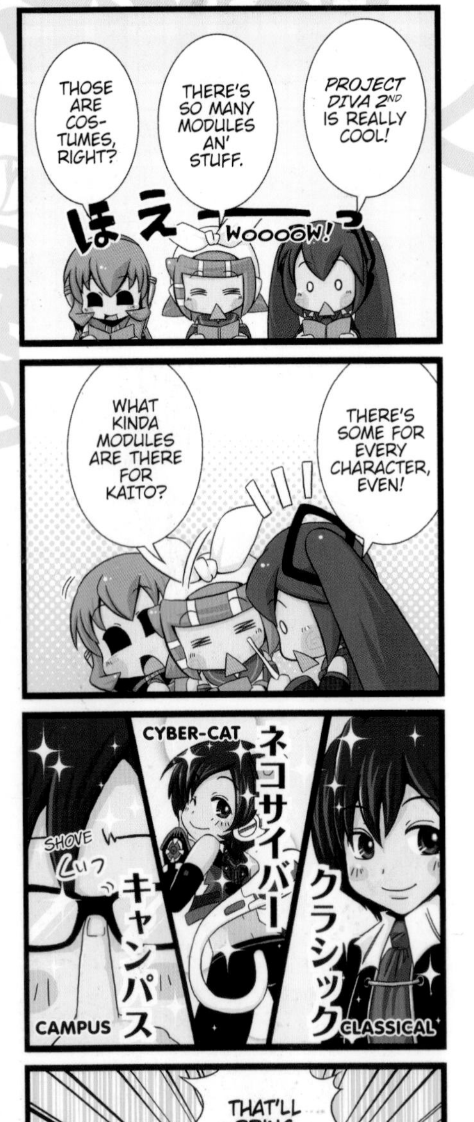
PROJECT DIVA 2ND IS REALLY COOL!
THERE'S SO MANY MODULES AN' STUFF.
THOSE ARE COS-TUMES, RIGHT?
ほえーーーっ
WOOOOOW!
THERE'S SOME FOR EVERY CHARACTER, EVEN!
WHAT KINDA MODULES ARE THERE FOR KAITO?
クラシック
CLASSICAL
ネコサイバー
CYBER-CAT
キャンパス
CAMPUS
SHOVE
くいっ
WAAAAAAAH!
THAT'LL BRING IN THE FEMALE FANS!!
?

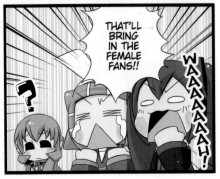

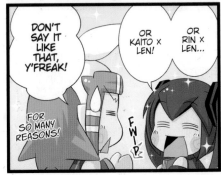

SWIMSUIT MODULES

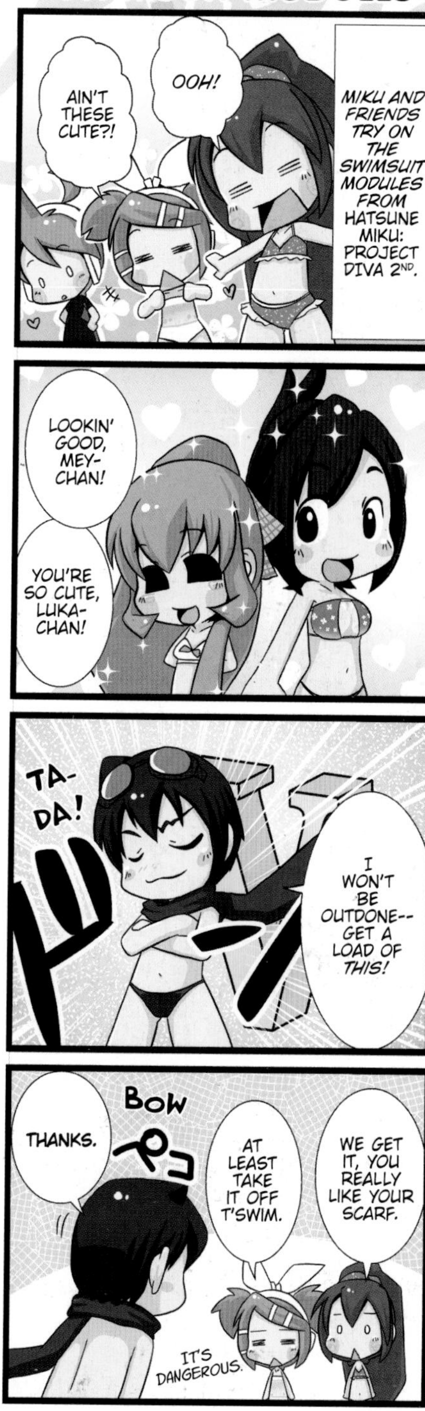
MIKU AND FRIENDS TRY ON THE SWIMSUIT MODULES FROM HATSUNE MIKU: PROJECT DIVA 2ND.
OOH!
AIN'T THESE CUTE?!
LOOKIN' GOOD, MEY-CHAN!
YOU'RE SO CUTE, LUKA-CHAN!
I WON'T BE OUTDONE--GET A LOAD OF THIS!
TA-DA!
WE GET IT, YOU REALLY LIKE YOUR SCARF.
AT LEAST TAKE IT OFF T'SWIM.
BOW
THANKS.
IT'S DANGEROUS.

OUTLINE CHANNEL

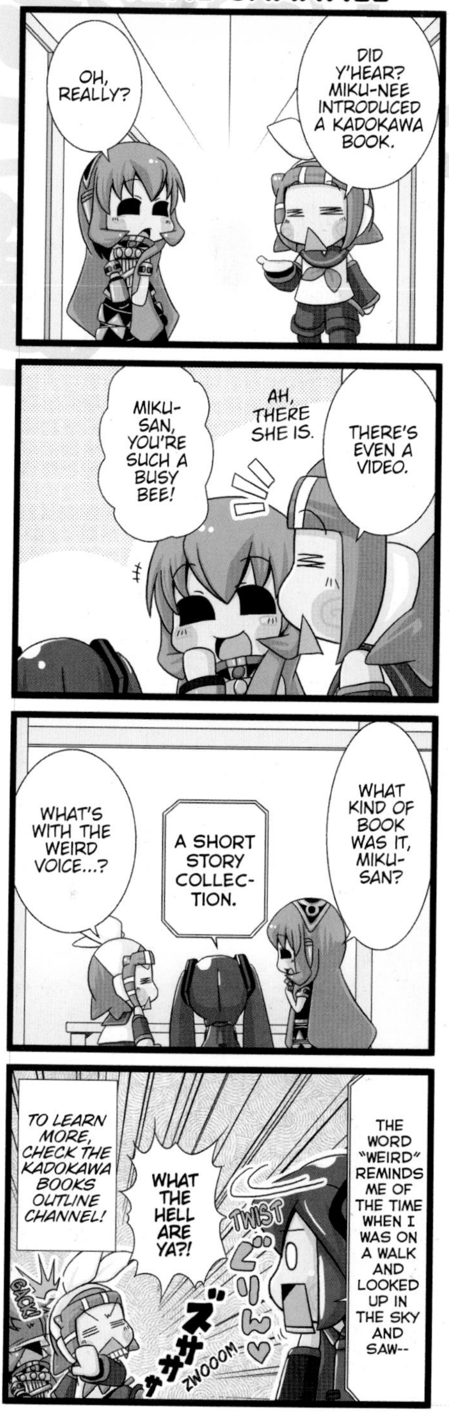
DID Y'HEAR? MIKU-NEE INTRODUCED A KADOKAWA BOOK.
OH, REALLY?
THERE'S EVEN A VIDEO.
AH, THERE SHE IS.
MIKU-SAN, YOU'RE SUCH A BUSY BEE!
WHAT KIND OF BOOK WAS IT, MIKU-SAN?
A SHORT STORY COLLECTION.
WHAT'S WITH THE WEIRD VOICE...?
THE WORD "WEIRD" REMINDS ME OF THE TIME WHEN I WAS ON A WALK AND LOOKED UP IN THE SKY AND SAW--
TWIST
ZWOOOM
WHAT THE HELL ARE YA?!
TO LEARN MORE, CHECK THE KADOKAWA BOOKS OUTLINE CHANNEL!
GACK!

ROCK-PAPER-SCISSORS

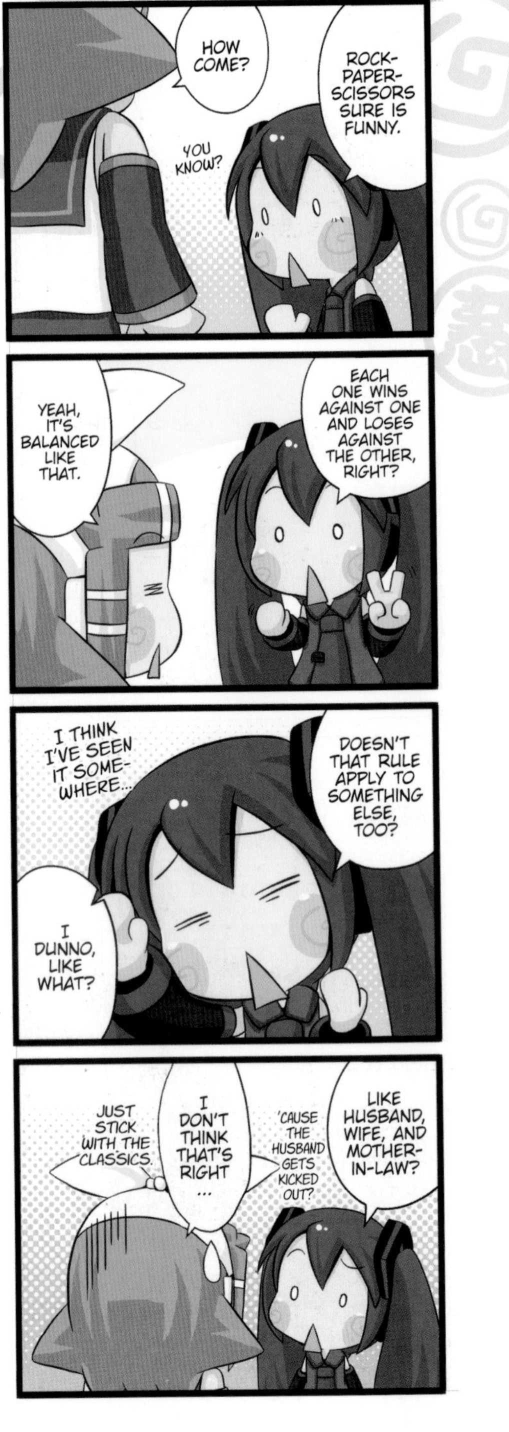
ROCK-PAPER-SCISSORS SURE IS FUNNY.
YOU KNOW?
HOW COME?
EACH ONE WINS AGAINST ONE AND LOSES AGAINST THE OTHER, RIGHT?
YEAH, IT'S BALANCED LIKE THAT.
DOESN'T THAT RULE APPLY TO SOMETHING ELSE, TOO?
I THINK I'VE SEEN IT SOME-WHERE...
I DUNNO, LIKE WHAT?
LIKE HUSBAND, WIFE, AND MOTHER-IN-LAW?
'CAUSE THE HUSBAND GETS KICKED OUT?
I DON'T THINK THAT'S RIGHT...
JUST STICK WITH THE CLASSICS.

HALLOWEEN

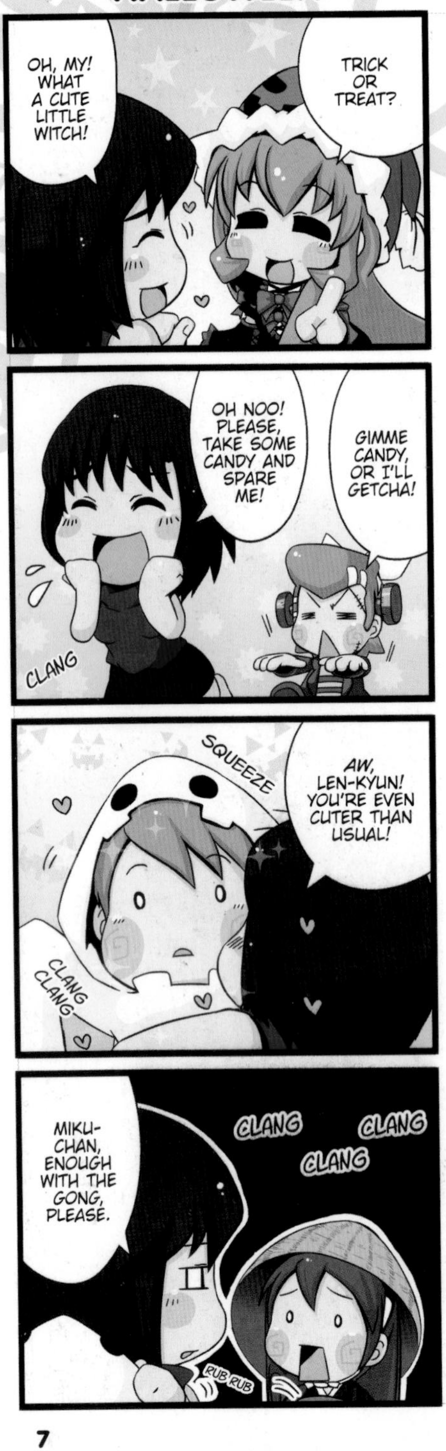
TRICK OR TREAT?
OH, MY! WHAT A CUTE LITTLE WITCH!
GIMME CANDY, OR I'LL GETCHA!
OH NOO! PLEASE, TAKE SOME CANDY AND SPARE ME!
CLANG
AW, LEN-KYUN! YOU'RE EVEN CUTER THAN USUAL!
SQUEEZE
CLANG CLANG
CLANG
CLANG
CLANG
MIKU-CHAN, ENOUGH WITH THE GONG, PLEASE.
RUB RUB

CAN'T WIN

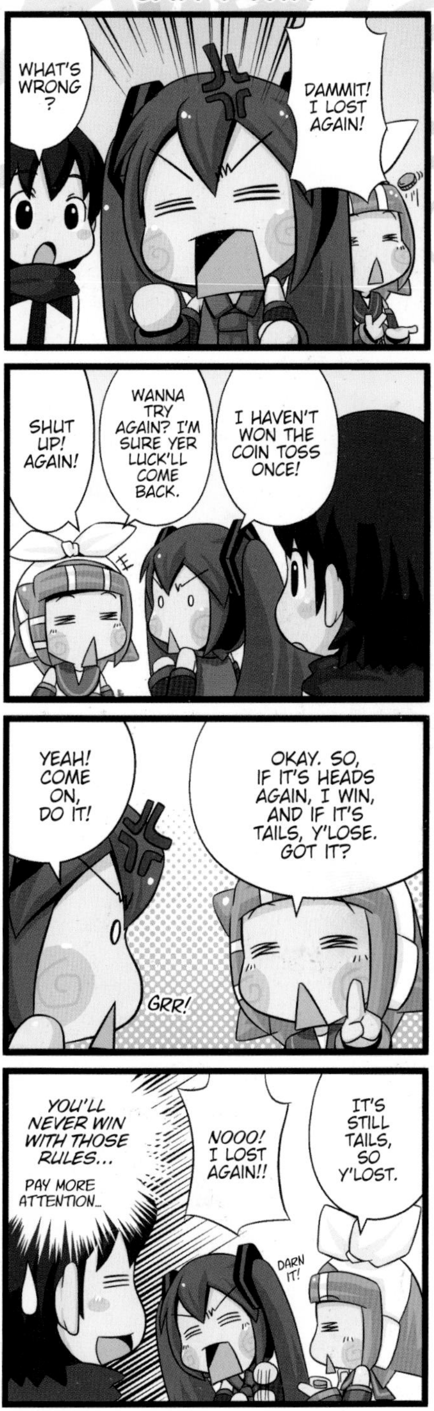
DAMMIT! I LOST AGAIN!
WHAT'S WRONG?
I HAVEN'T WON THE COIN TOSS ONCE!
WANNA TRY AGAIN? I'M SURE YER LUCK'LL COME BACK.
SHUT UP! AGAIN!
OKAY. SO, IF IT'S HEADS AGAIN, I WIN, AND IF IT'S TAILS, Y'LOSE. GOT IT?
YEAH! COME ON, DO IT!
GRR!
IT'S STILL TAILS, SO Y'LOST.
NOOO! I LOST AGAIN!!
DARN IT!
YOU'LL NEVER WIN WITH THOSE RULES...
PAY MORE ATTENTION...

KIDS

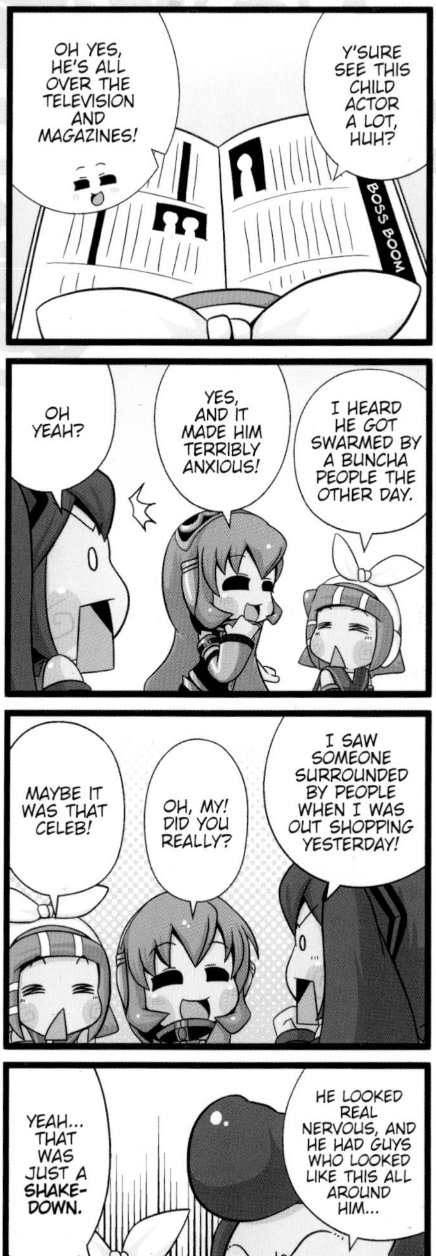
Y'SURE SEE THIS CHILD ACTOR A LOT, HUH?
BOSS BOOM
OH YES, HE'S ALL OVER THE TELEVISION AND MAGAZINES!
I HEARD HE GOT SWARMED BY A BUNCHA PEOPLE THE OTHER DAY.
YES, AND IT MADE HIM TERRIBLY ANXIOUS!
OH YEAH?
I SAW SOMEONE SURROUNDED BY PEOPLE WHEN I WAS OUT SHOPPING YESTERDAY!
OH, MY! DID YOU REALLY?
MAYBE IT WAS THAT CELEB!
HE LOOKED REAL NERVOUS, AND HE HAD GUYS WHO LOOKED LIKE THIS ALL AROUND HIM...
YEAH... THAT WAS JUST A SHAKE-DOWN.

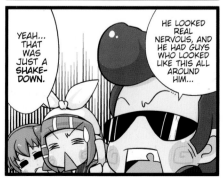

PARENTS

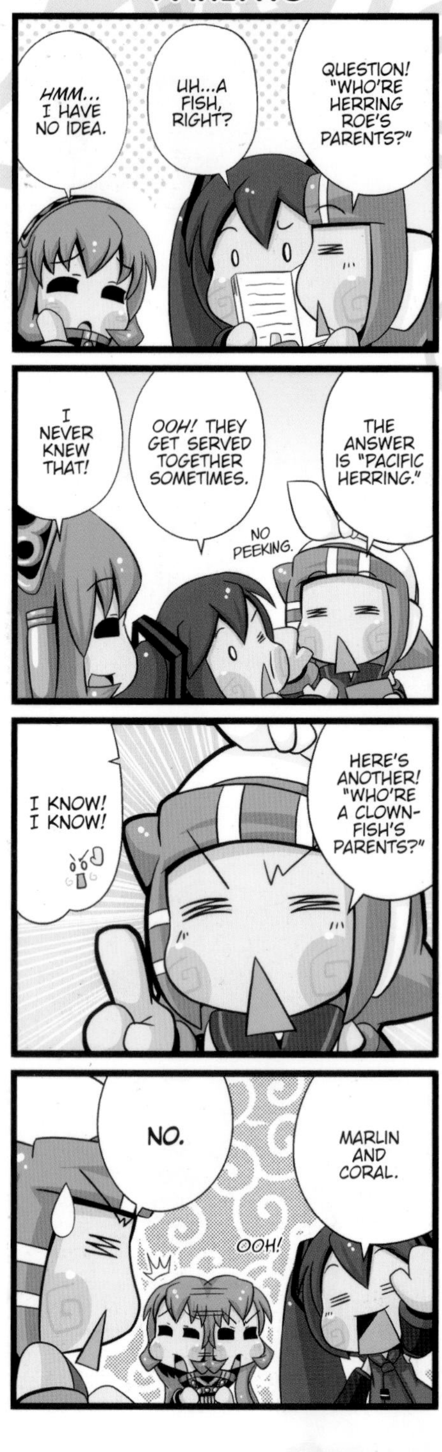
QUESTION! "WHO'RE HERRING ROE'S PARENTS?"
UH...A FISH, RIGHT?
HMM... I HAVE NO IDEA.
THE ANSWER IS "PACIFIC HERRING."
OOH! THEY GET SERVED TOGETHER SOMETIMES.
NO PEEKING.
I NEVER KNEW THAT!
HERE'S ANOTHER! "WHO'RE A CLOWNFISH'S PARENTS?"
I KNOW! I KNOW!
MARLIN AND CORAL.
OOH!
NO.

HACHUNE HEADS FOR VICTORY

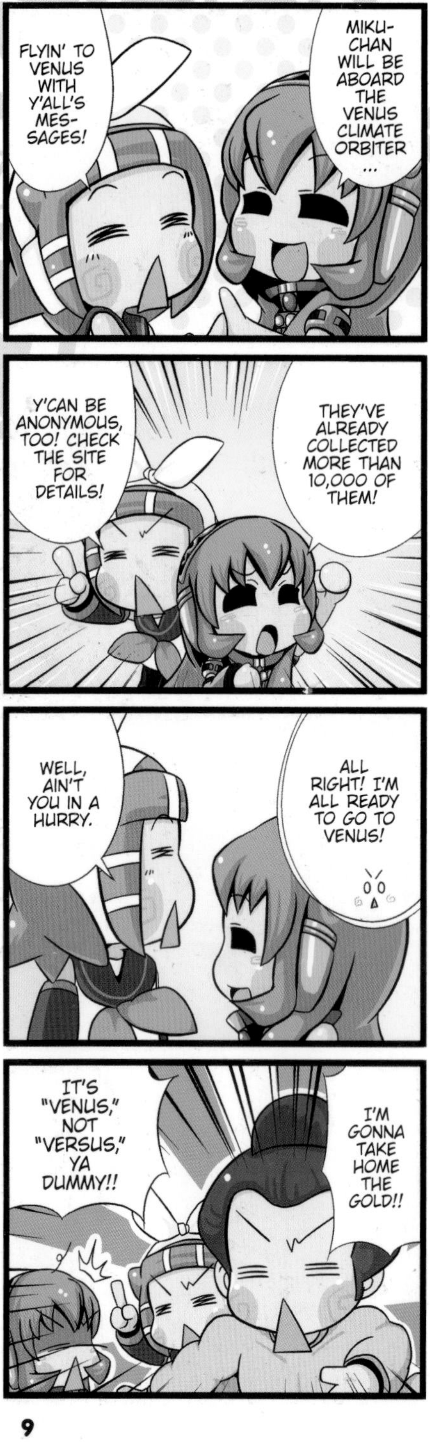
MIKU-CHAN WILL BE ABOARD THE VENUS CLIMATE ORBITER...
FLYIN' TO VENUS WITH Y'ALL'S MESSAGES!
THEY'VE ALREADY COLLECTED MORE THAN 10,000 OF THEM!
Y'CAN BE ANONYMOUS, TOO! CHECK THE SITE FOR DETAILS!
ALL RIGHT! I'M ALL READY TO GO TO VENUS!
WELL, AIN'T YOU IN A HURRY.
I'M GONNA TAKE HOME THE GOLD!!
IT'S "VENUS," NOT "VERSUS," YA DUMMY!!

NEW YEAR'S SHRINE VISIT

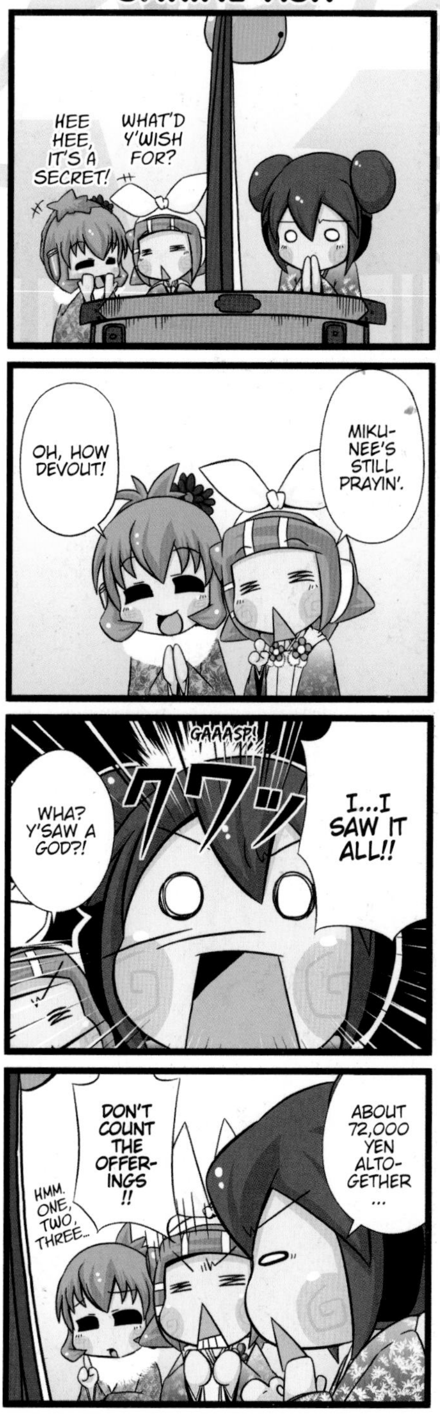
WHAT'D Y'WISH FOR?
HEE HEE, IT'S A SECRET!
MIKU-NEE'S STILL PRAYIN'.
OH, HOW DEVOUT!
GAAASP!
クワッ
I...I SAW IT ALL!!
WHA? Y'SAW A GOD?!
ABOUT 72,000 YEN ALTOGETHER ...
DON'T COUNT THE OFFERINGS !!
HMM. ONE, TWO, THREE...

BACK TO BED

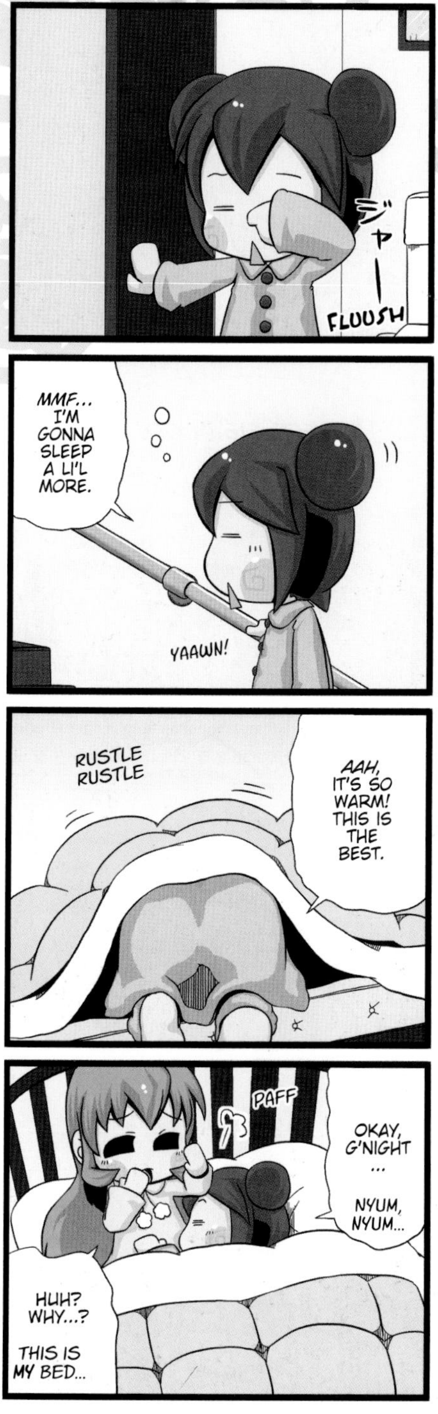
ジャー
FLUUSH
MMF... I'M GONNA SLEEP A LI'L MORE.
YAAWN!
AAH, IT'S SO WARM! THIS IS THE BEST.
RUSTLE RUSTLE
PAFF
OKAY, G'NIGHT ... NYUM, NYUM...
HUH? WHY...?
THIS IS MY BED...

FORTUNE ROLL

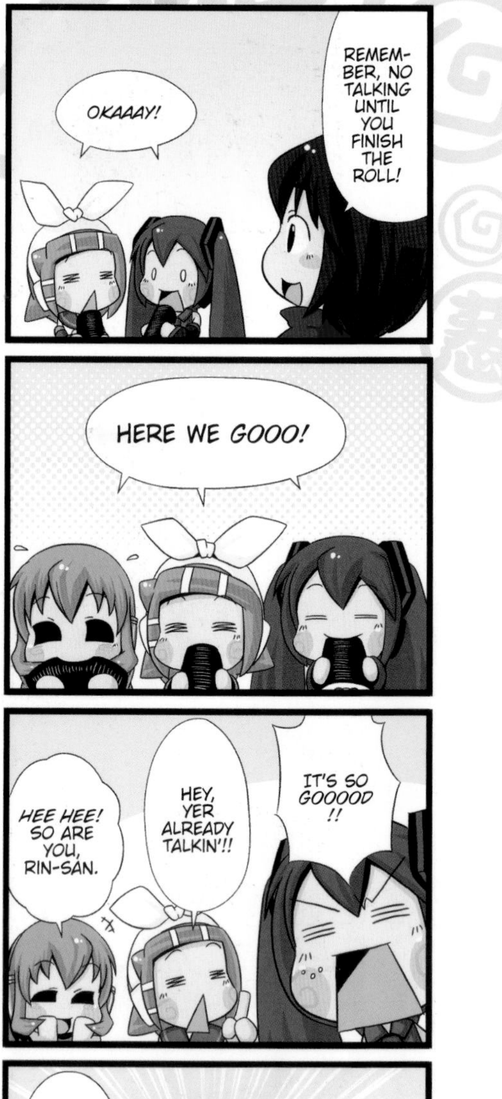
REMEMBER, NO TALKING UNTIL YOU FINISH THE ROLL!
OKAAAY!
HERE WE GOOO!
IT'S SO GOOOOD!!
HEY, YER ALREADY TALKIN'!!
HEE HEE! SO ARE YOU, RIN-SAN.
YOU'RE ALL OUT!

SPECIALIST

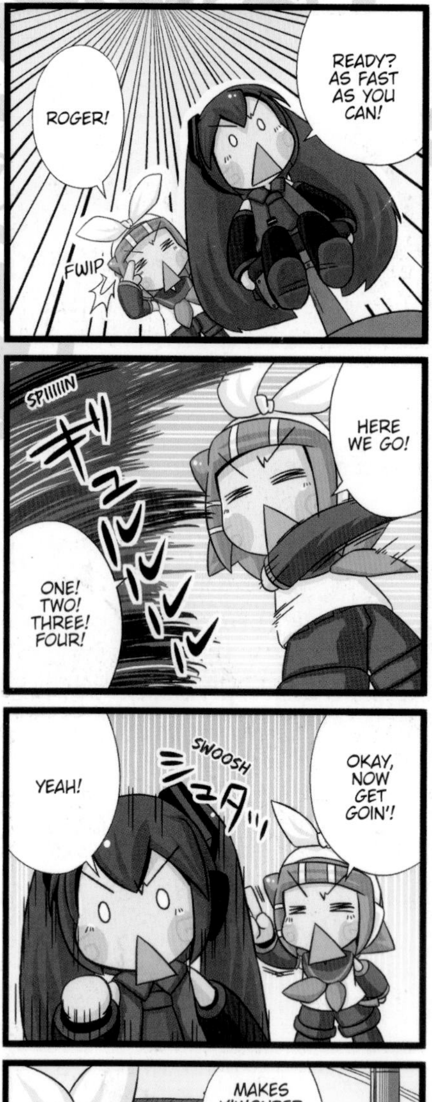
READY? AS FAST AS YOU CAN!
ROGER!
FWIP
HERE WE GO!
SPIIIIIN
ONE! TWO! THREE! FOUR!
OKAY, NOW GET GOIN'!
SWOOSH
YEAH!
MAKES Y'WONDER HOW FIGURE SKATERS DO IT, HUH?
GONK
SWAAY
WOBBLE WOBBLE

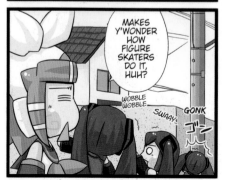

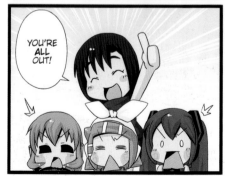

KOALA

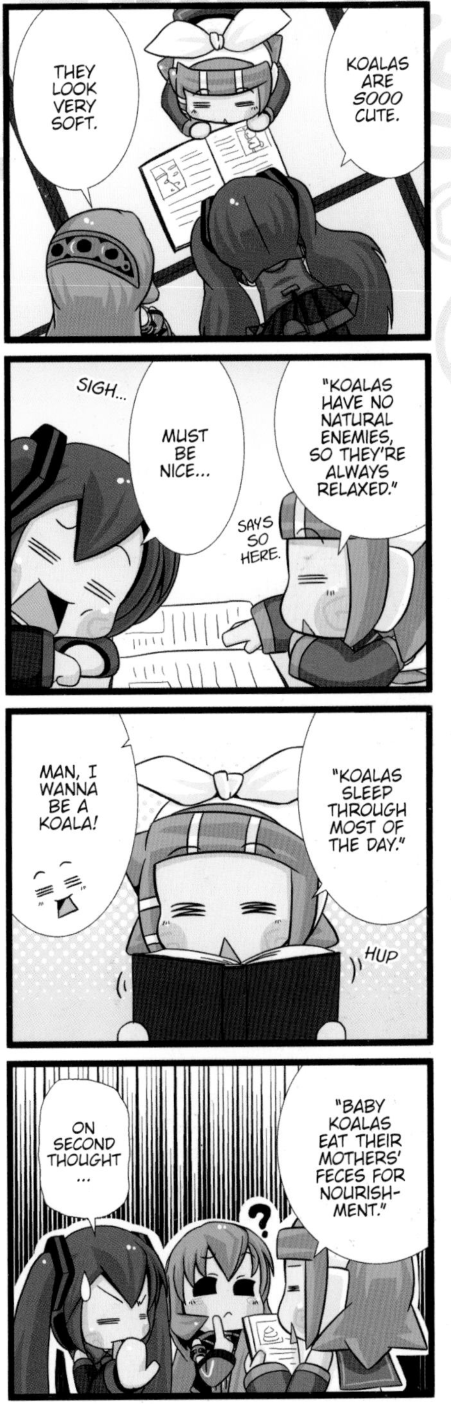
KOALAS ARE SOOO CUTE.
THEY LOOK VERY SOFT.
"KOALAS HAVE NO NATURAL ENEMIES, SO THEY'RE ALWAYS RELAXED."
SAYS SO HERE.
MUST BE NICE...
SIGH...
"KOALAS SLEEP THROUGH MOST OF THE DAY."
HUP
MAN, I WANNA BE A KOALA!
"BABY KOALAS EAT THEIR MOTHERS' FECES FOR NOURISHMENT."
?
ON SECOND THOUGHT ...

SOMETHING ON YOUR FACE

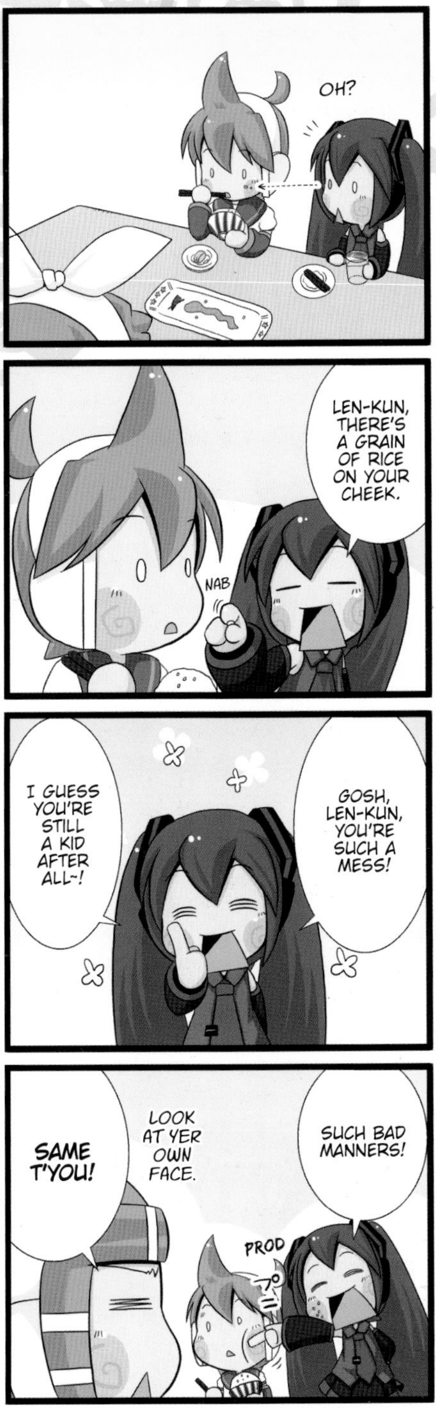
OH?
LEN-KUN, THERE'S A GRAIN OF RICE ON YOUR CHEEK.
NAB
GOSH, LEN-KUN, YOU'RE SUCH A MESS!
I GUESS YOU'RE STILL A KID AFTER ALL~!
SUCH BAD MANNERS!
PROD
LOOK AT YER OWN FACE.
SAME T'YOU!

COLLABORATION GALLERY

ALL THE HACHUNE MIKU COLLABORATION ILLUSTRATIONS AND COMICS SO FAR!

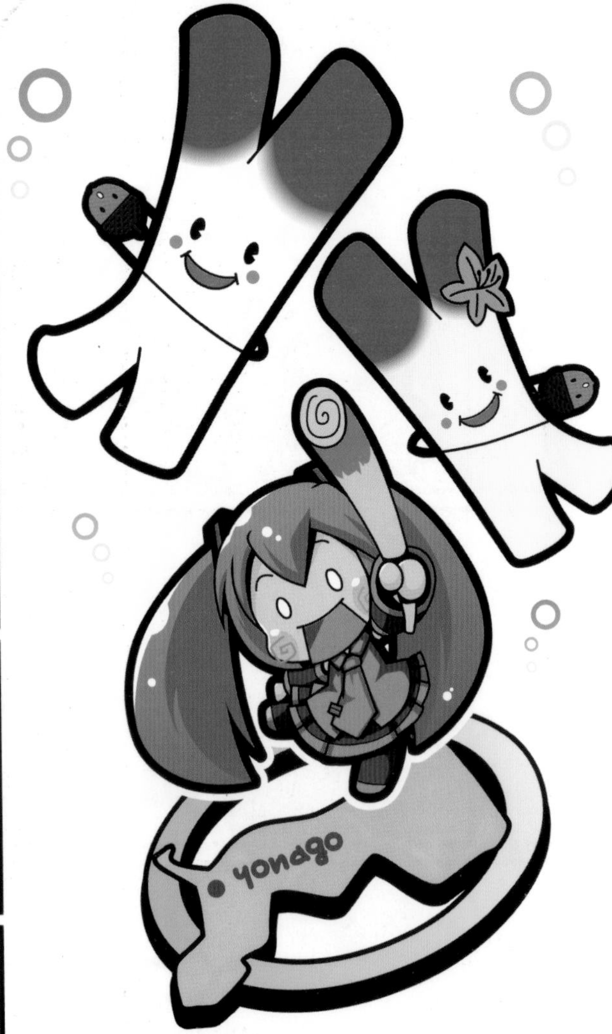
yonago

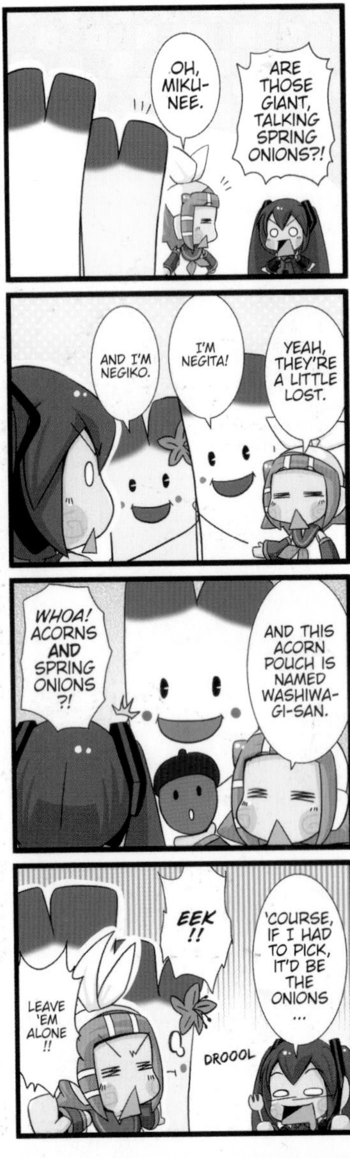
ARE THOSE GIANT, TALKING SPRING ONIONS?!
OH, MIKU-NEE.
YEAH, THEY'RE A LITTLE LOST.
I'M NEGITA!
AND I'M NEGIKO.
AND THIS ACORN POUCH IS NAMED WASHIWAGI-SAN.
WHOA! ACORNS AND SPRING ONIONS ?!
'COURSE, IF I HAD TO PICK, IT'D BE THE ONIONS ...
EEK !!
DROOOL
LEAVE 'EM ALONE !!

● Collab illustration (above) and comic (left) are with the Yonegiz, the mascot characters of Yonago in Tottori Prefecture.

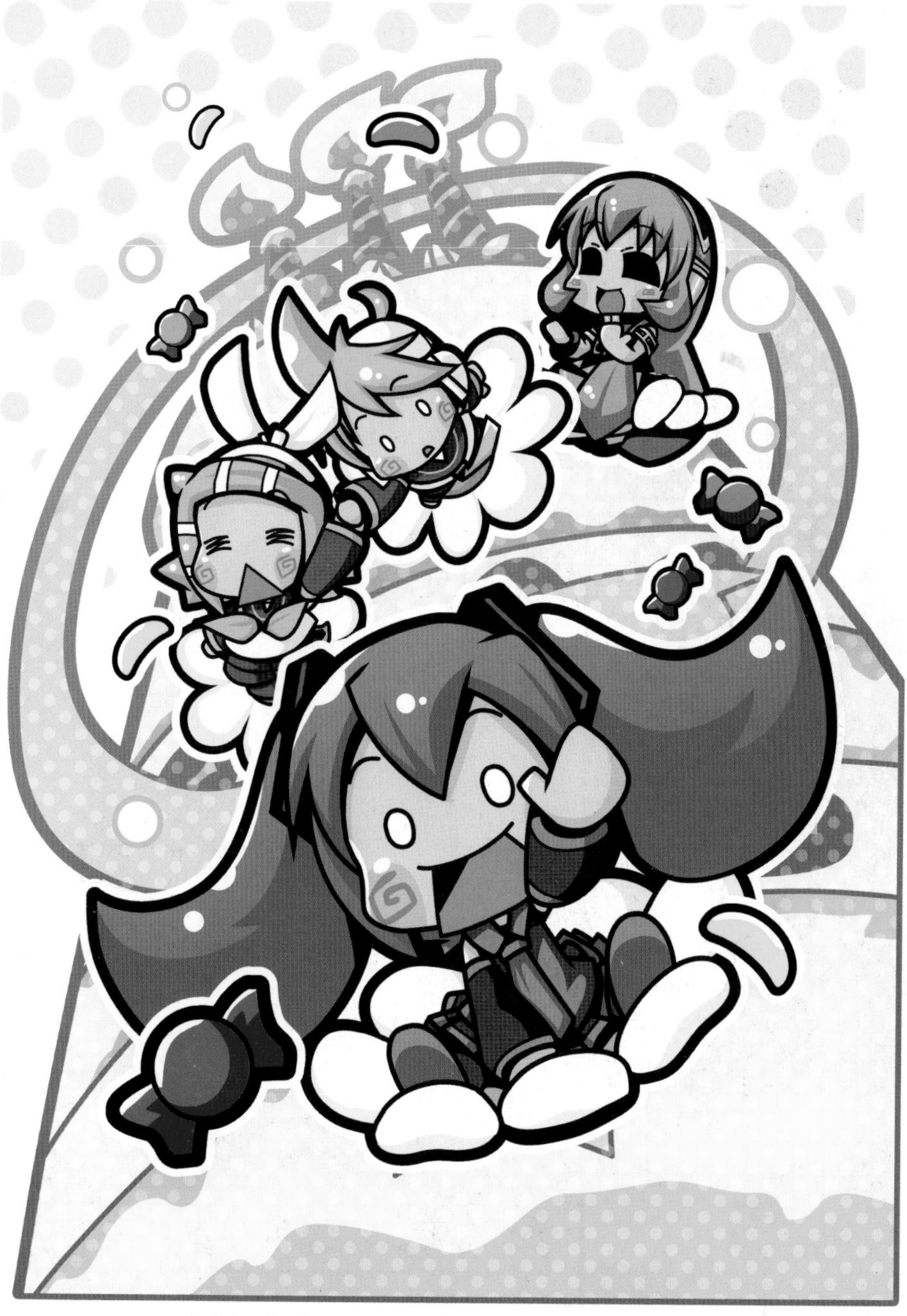

Animate Hatsune Miku Fair 3RD Anniversary Birthday Card Illustration.

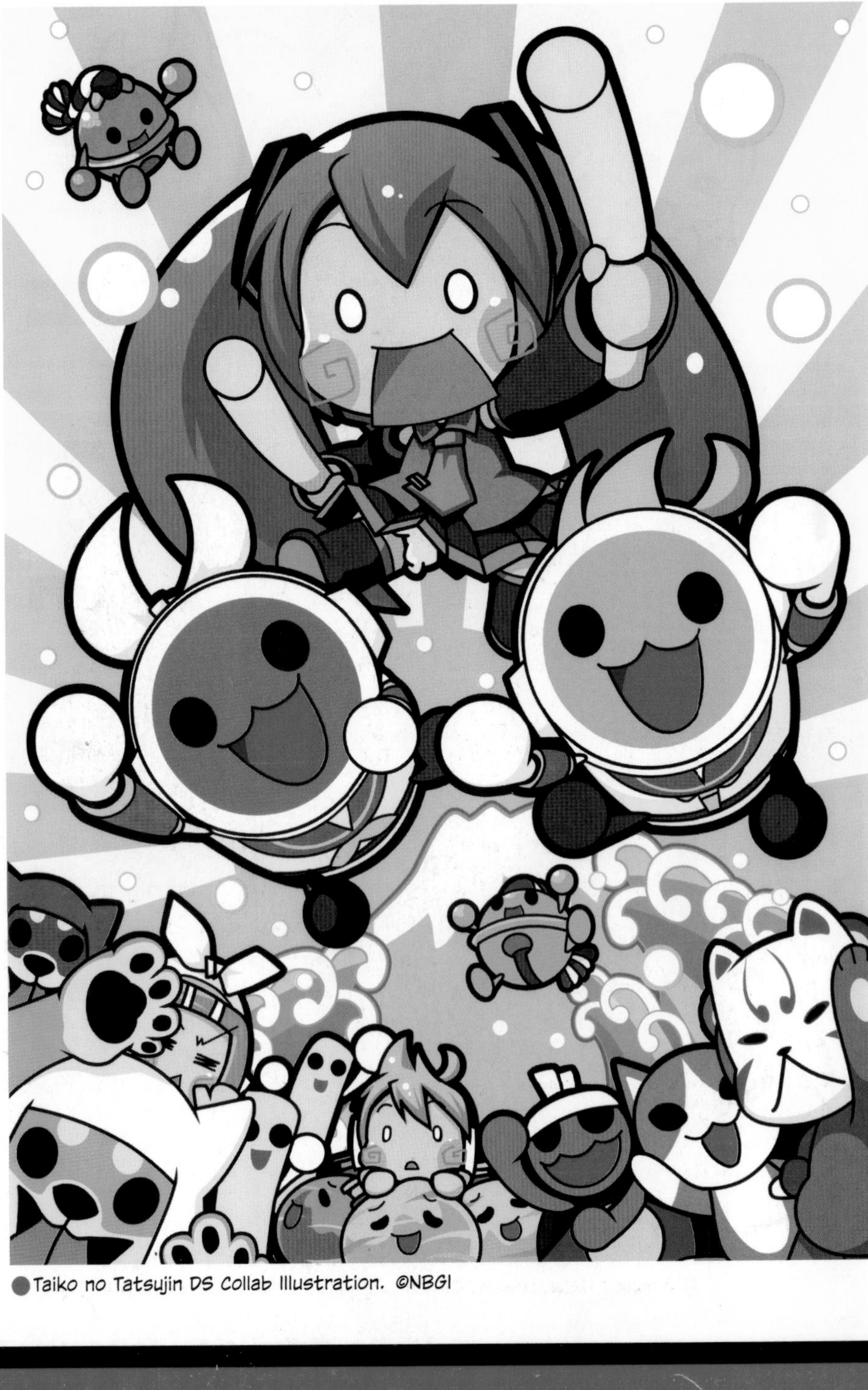

●Taiko no Tatsujin DS Collab Illustration. ©NBGI

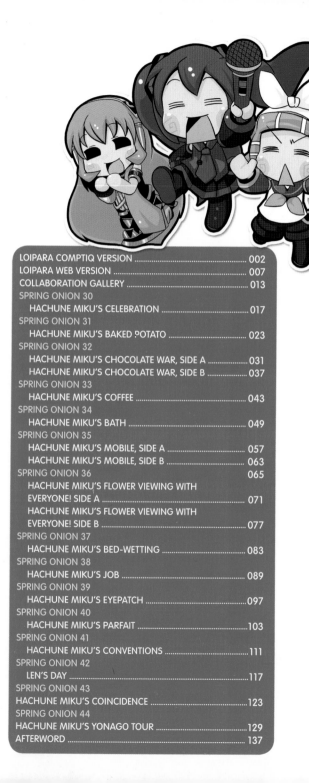

CONTENTS

SPRING ONION 30:

HACHUNE MIKU'S CELEBRATION

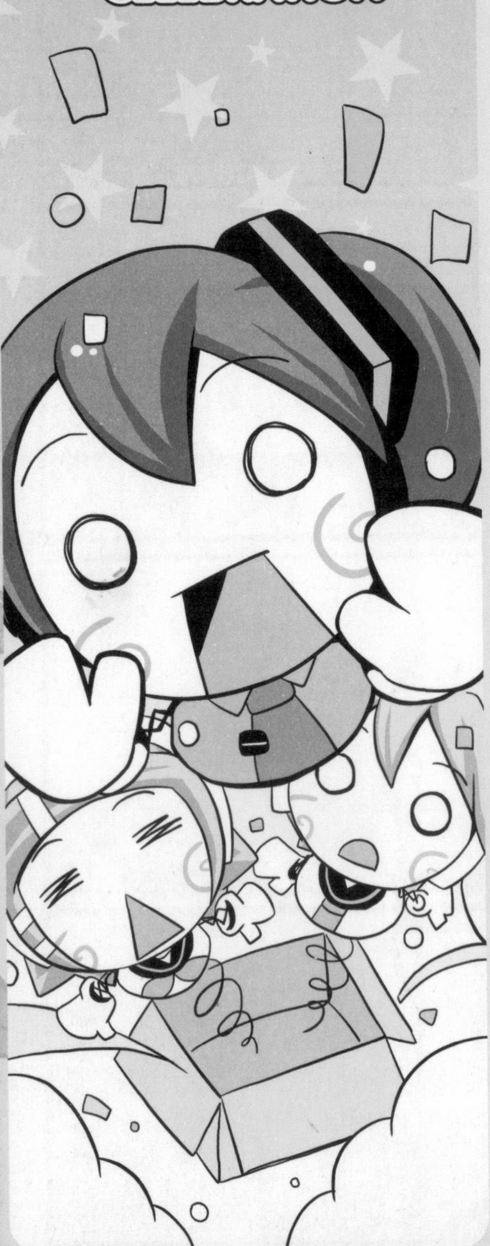

LIGHTNING SPEED

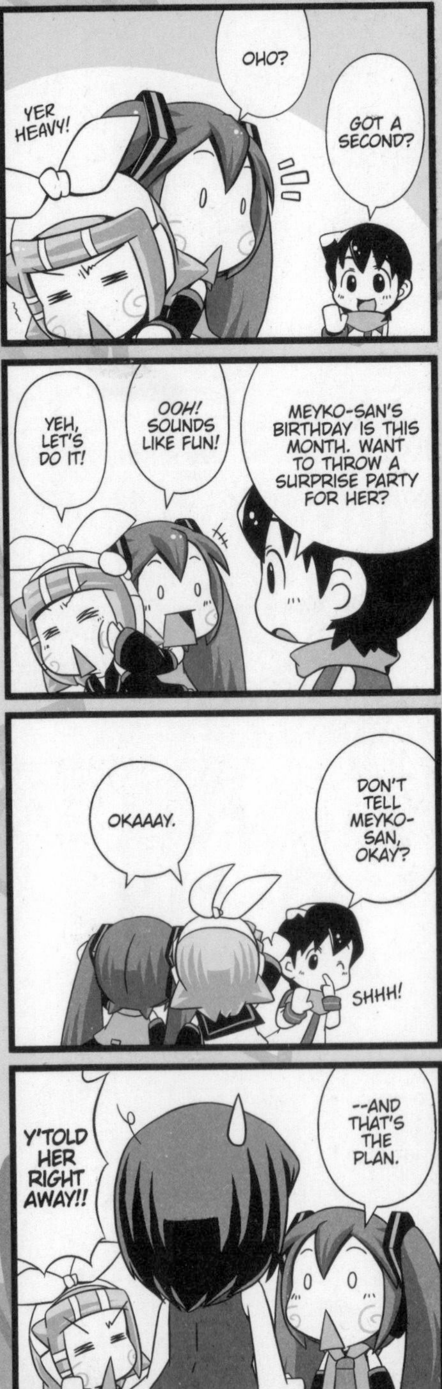
GOT A SECOND?
OHO?
YER HEAVY!
MEYKO-SAN'S BIRTHDAY IS THIS MONTH. WANT TO THROW A SURPRISE PARTY FOR HER?
OOH! SOUNDS LIKE FUN!
YEH, LET'S DO IT!
DON'T TELL MEYKO-SAN, OKAY?
SHHH!
OKAAAY.
--AND THAT'S THE PLAN.
Y'TOLD HER RIGHT AWAY!!

MODESTY

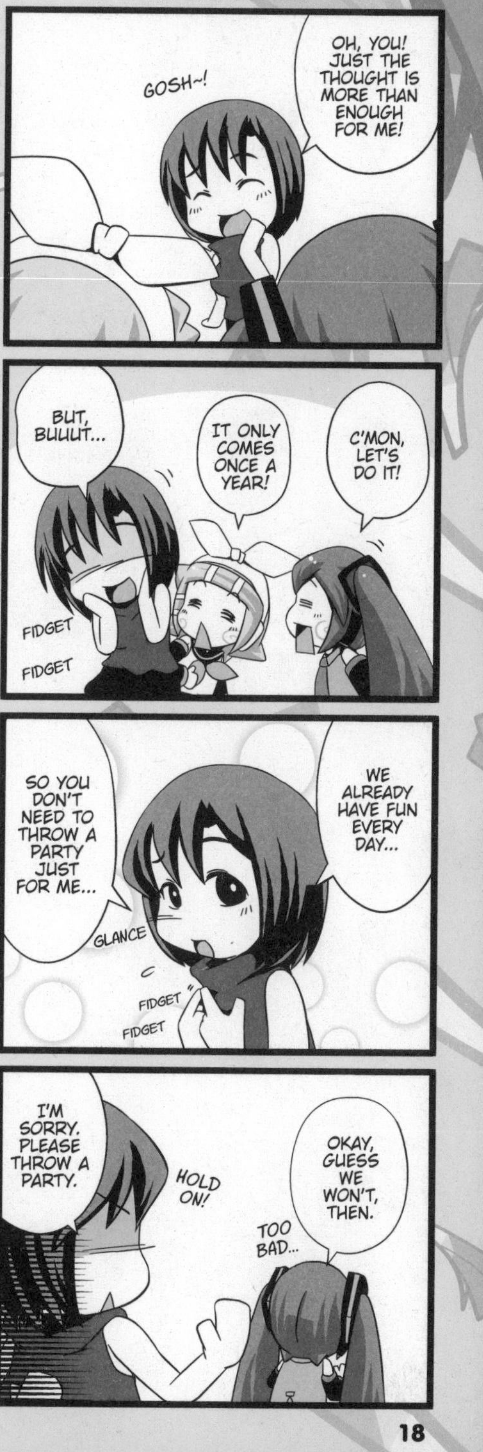
OH, YOU! JUST THE THOUGHT IS MORE THAN ENOUGH FOR ME!
GOSH~!
C'MON, LET'S DO IT!
IT ONLY COMES ONCE A YEAR!
BUT, BUUUT...
FIDGET
FIDGET
WE ALREADY HAVE FUN EVERY DAY...
SO YOU DON'T NEED TO THROW A PARTY JUST FOR ME...
GLANCE
FIDGET
FIDGET
OKAY, GUESS WE WON'T, THEN.
TOO BAD...
HOLD ON!
I'M SORRY. PLEASE THROW A PARTY.

BRIGHT RED

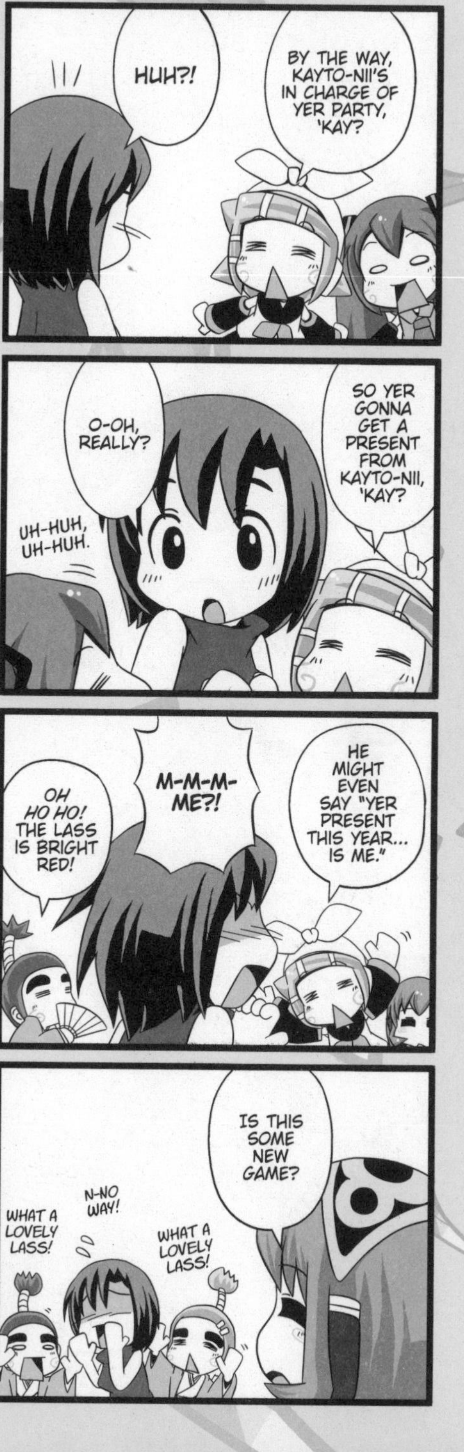
BY THE WAY, KAYTO-NII'S IN CHARGE OF YER PARTY, 'KAY?
HUH?!
SO YER GONNA GET A PRESENT FROM KAYTO-NII, 'KAY?
O-OH, REALLY?
UH-HUH, UH-HUH.
HE MIGHT EVEN SAY "YER PRESENT THIS YEAR... IS ME."
M-M-M-ME?!
OH HO HO! THE LASS IS BRIGHT RED!
IS THIS SOME NEW GAME?
WHAT A LOVELY LASS!
N-NO WAY!
WHAT A LOVELY LASS!

SCALE

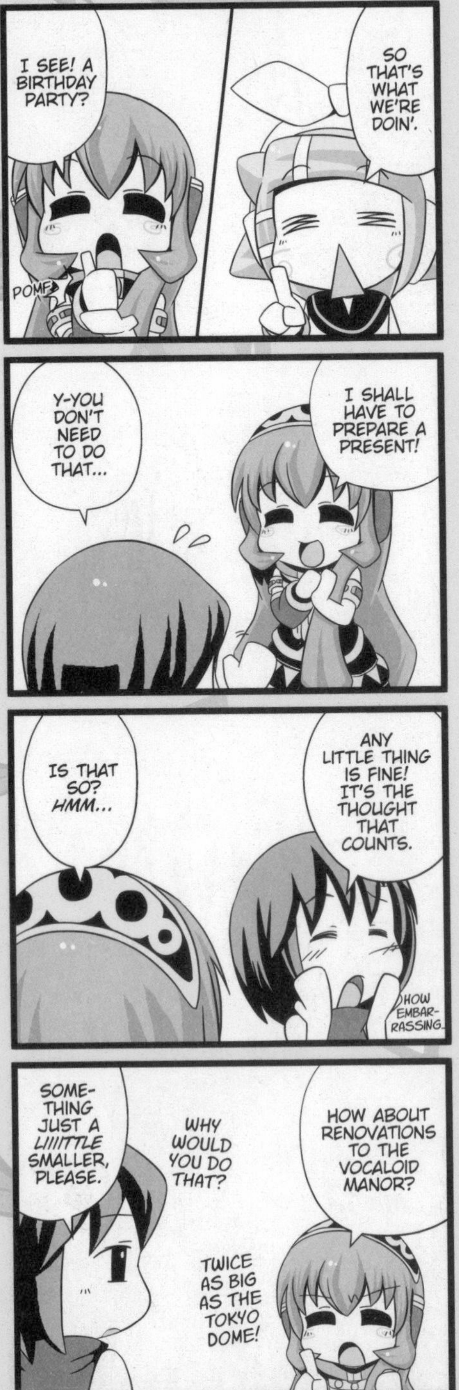
SO THAT'S WHAT WE'RE DOIN'.
I SEE! A BIRTHDAY PARTY?
POMF
I SHALL HAVE TO PREPARE A PRESENT!
Y-YOU DON'T NEED TO DO THAT...
ANY LITTLE THING IS FINE! IT'S THE THOUGHT THAT COUNTS.
IS THAT SO? HMM...
HOW EMBARRASSING
HOW ABOUT RENOVATIONS TO THE VOCALOID MANOR?
TWICE AS BIG AS THE TOKYO DOME!
WHY WOULD YOU DO THAT?
SOMETHING JUST A LIIIITTLE SMALLER, PLEASE.

SIMILARITIES

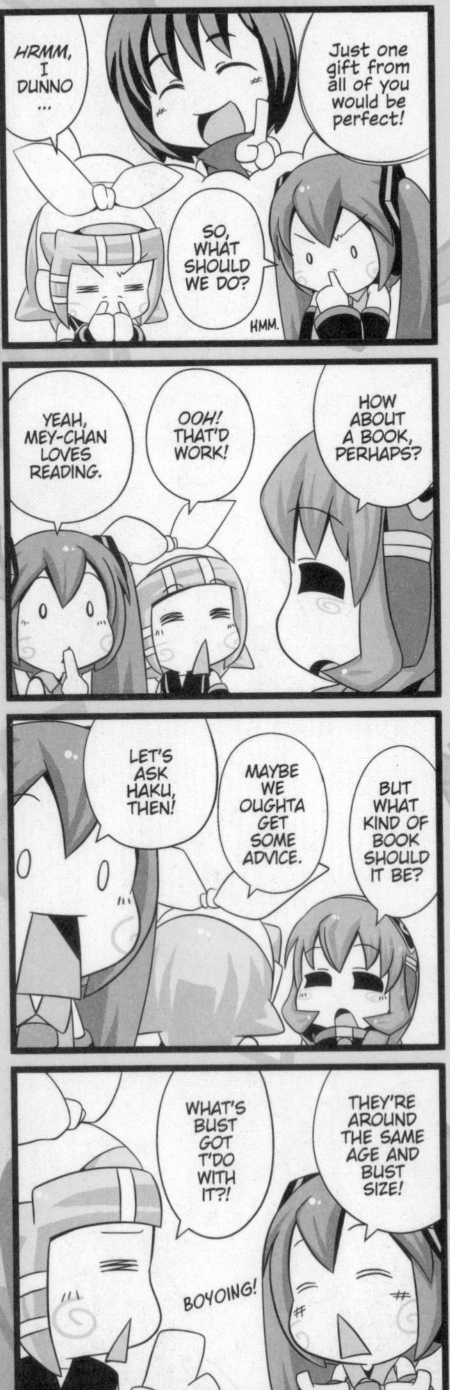
Just one gift from all of you would be perfect!
SO, WHAT SHOULD WE DO?
HMM.
HRMM, I DUNNO ...
HOW ABOUT A BOOK, PERHAPS?
OOH! THAT'D WORK!
YEAH, MEY-CHAN LOVES READING.
BUT WHAT KIND OF BOOK SHOULD IT BE?
MAYBE WE OUGHTA GET SOME ADVICE.
LET'S ASK HAKU, THEN!
THEY'RE AROUND THE SAME AGE AND BUST SIZE!
WHAT'S BUST GOT T'DO WITH IT?!
BOYOING!

UNEXPECTED

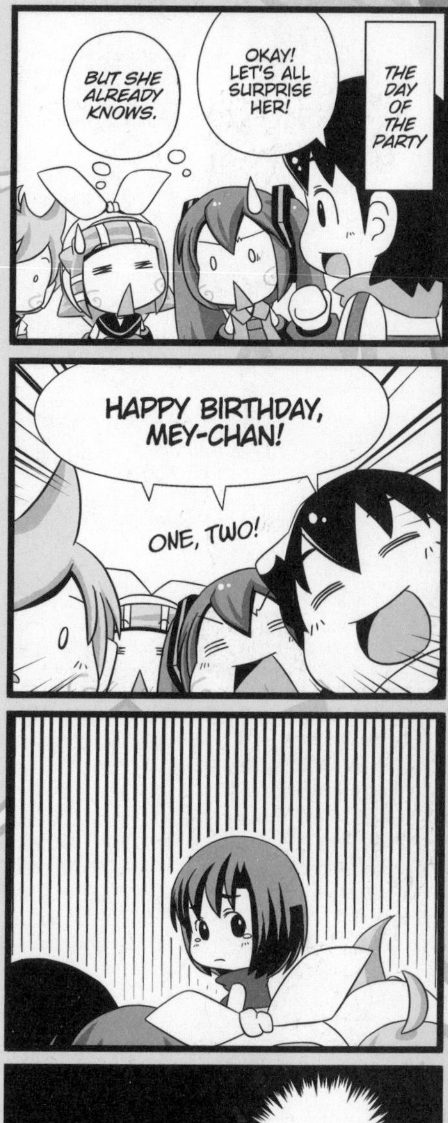
THE DAY OF THE PARTY
OKAY! LET'S ALL SURPRISE HER!
BUT SHE ALREADY KNOWS.
HAPPY BIRTHDAY, MEY-CHAN!
ONE, TWO!
HUH ...?!
SNIFFLE

WHOOPS

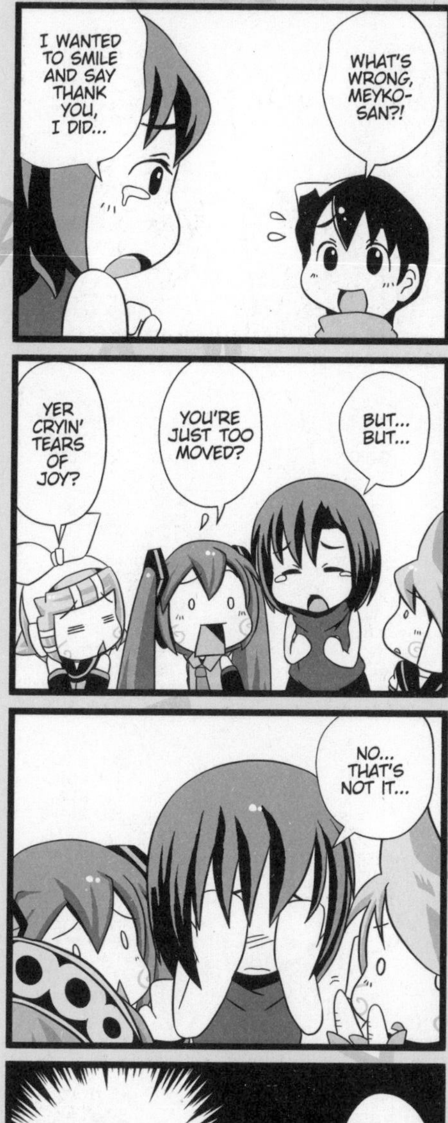
WHAT'S WRONG, MEYKO-SAN?!
I WANTED TO SMILE AND SAY THANK YOU, I DID...
BUT... BUT...
YOU'RE JUST TOO MOVED?
YER CRYIN' TEARS OF JOY?
NO... THAT'S NOT IT...
MY BIRTH-DAY...WAS YESTER-DAY...
WE MADE A HUGE MISTAKE!!

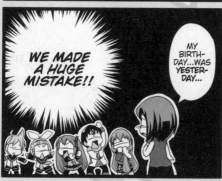

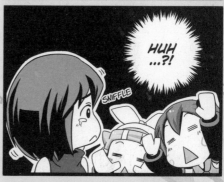

ON A WAGON

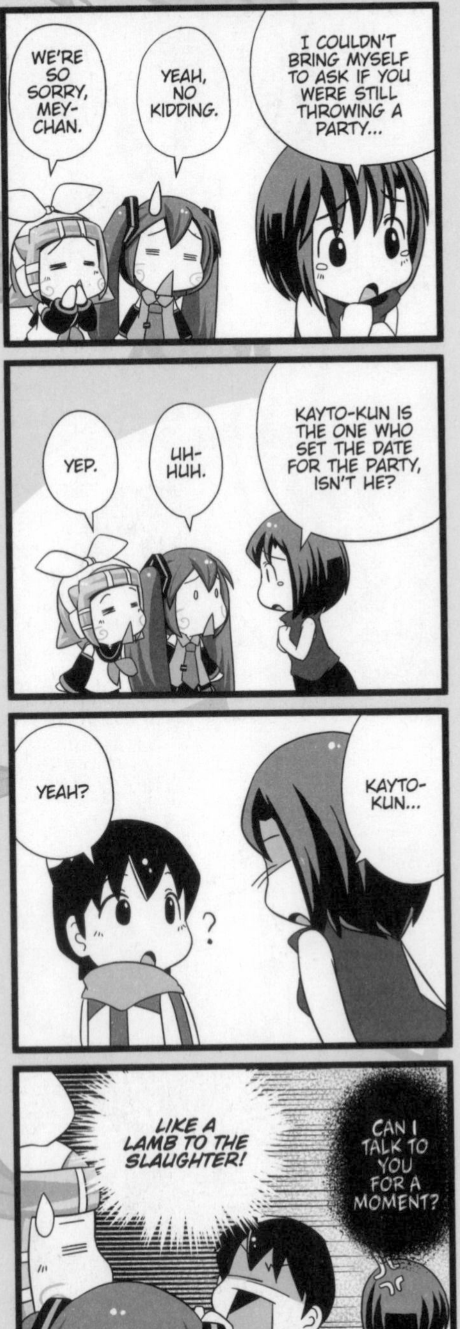
I COULDN'T BRING MYSELF TO ASK IF YOU WERE STILL THROWING A PARTY...
YEAH, NO KIDDING.
WE'RE SO SORRY, MEY-CHAN.
KAYTO-KUN IS THE ONE WHO SET THE DATE FOR THE PARTY, ISN'T HE?
UH-HUH.
YEP.
KAYTO-KUN...
YEAH?
CAN I TALK TO YOU FOR A MOMENT?
LIKE A LAMB TO THE SLAUGHTER!

GOOD ENOUGH

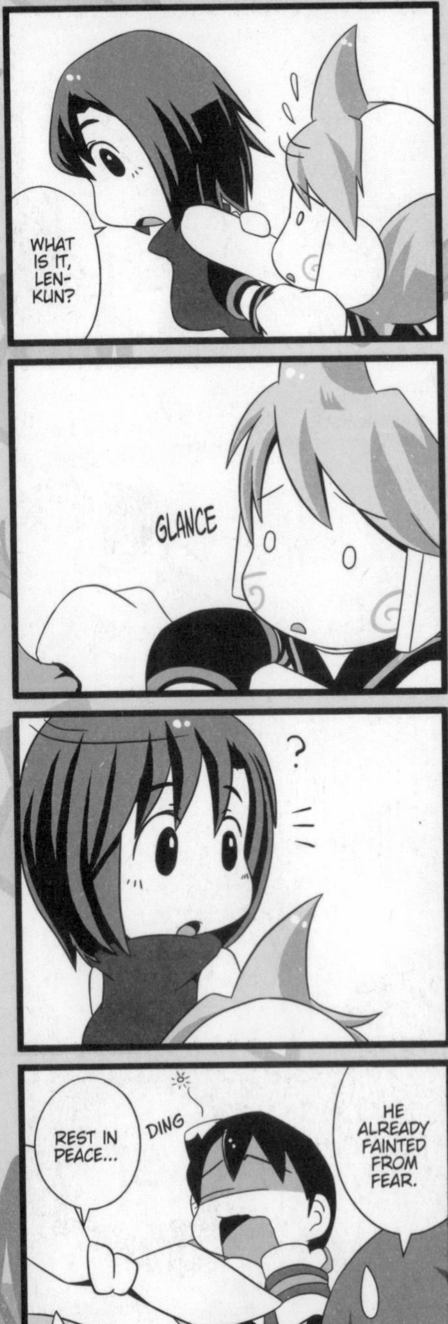
WHAT IS IT, LEN-KUN?
GLANCE
HE ALREADY FAINTED FROM FEAR.
DING
REST IN PEACE...

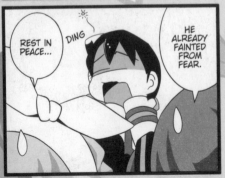

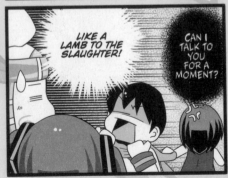

NAIL

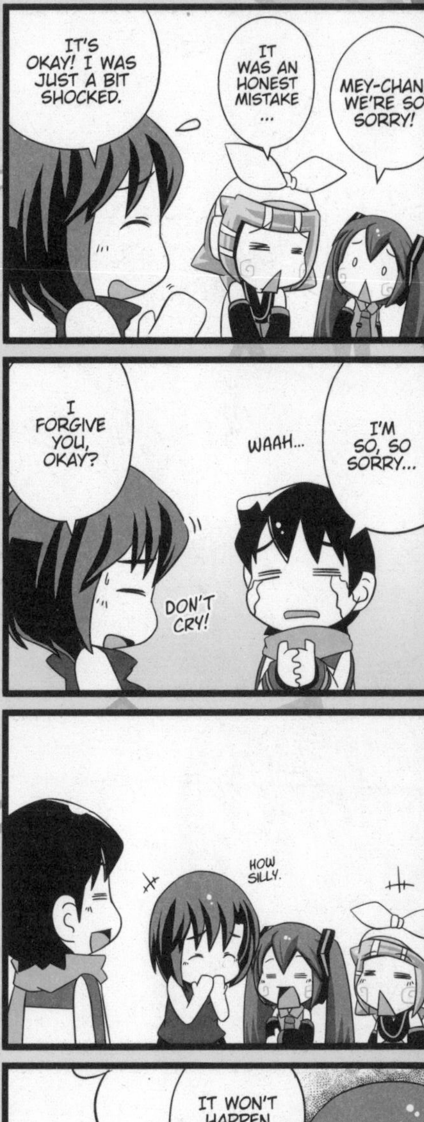

MEY-CHAN, WE'RE SO SORRY!
IT WAS AN HONEST MISTAKE ...
IT'S OKAY! I WAS JUST A BIT SHOCKED.
I'M SO, SO SORRY...
WAAH...
I FORGIVE YOU, OKAY?
DON'T CRY!
HOW SILLY.
IT WON'T HAPPEN AGAIN... RIGHT?
YES, MA'AM !!
FLINCH

PRESENT

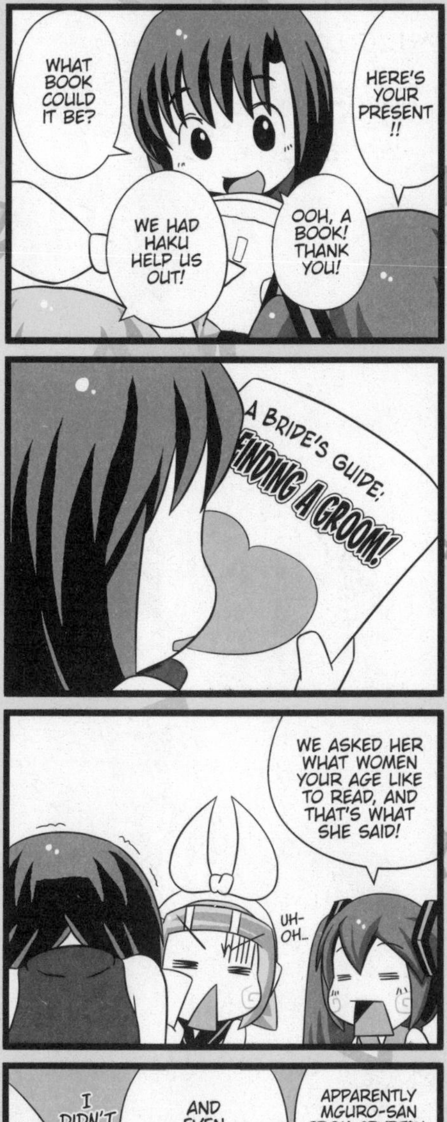

HERE'S YOUR PRESENT !!
OOH, A BOOK! THANK YOU!
WHAT BOOK COULD IT BE?
WE HAD HAKU HELP US OUT!
A BRIDE'S GUIDE: FINDING A GROOM!
WE ASKED HER WHAT WOMEN YOUR AGE LIKE TO READ, AND THAT'S WHAT SHE SAID!
UH-OH...
APPARENTLY MGURO-SAN FROM CRYPT*N, MIKATAN-SAN FROM GOOD SM*LE...
AND EVEN STA-SAN FROM C*MP ACE READ IT!
I DIDN'T KNOW, 'KAY?
HOO BOY...

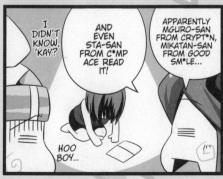

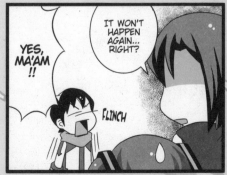

SPRING ONION 31:
HACHUNE MIKU'S BAKED POTATO

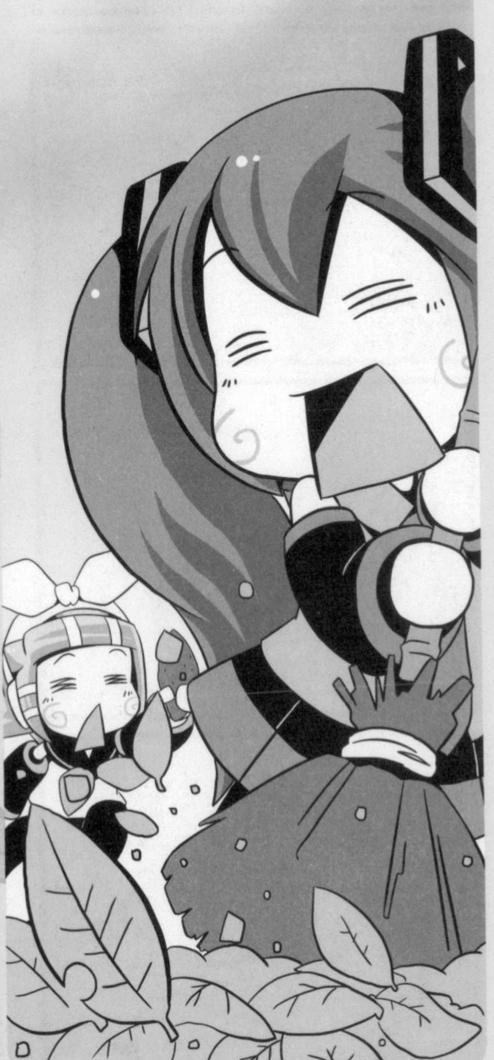

QUIET!

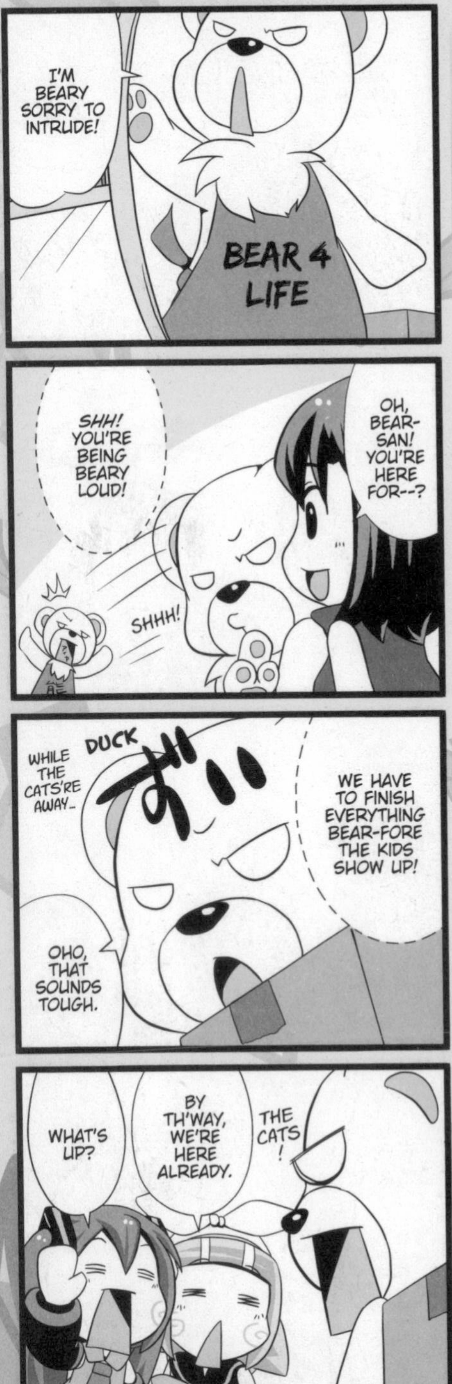
I'M BEARY SORRY TO INTRUDE!
BEAR 4 LIFE
OH, BEAR-SAN! YOU'RE HERE FOR--?
SHH! YOU'RE BEING BEARY LOUD!
SHHH!
WE HAVE TO FINISH EVERYTHING BEAR-FORE THE KIDS SHOW UP!
DUCK
WHILE THE CATS'RE AWAY...
OHO, THAT SOUNDS TOUGH.
THE CATS!
BY TH'WAY, WE'RE HERE ALREADY.
WHAT'S UP?

DOWN IN FLAMES

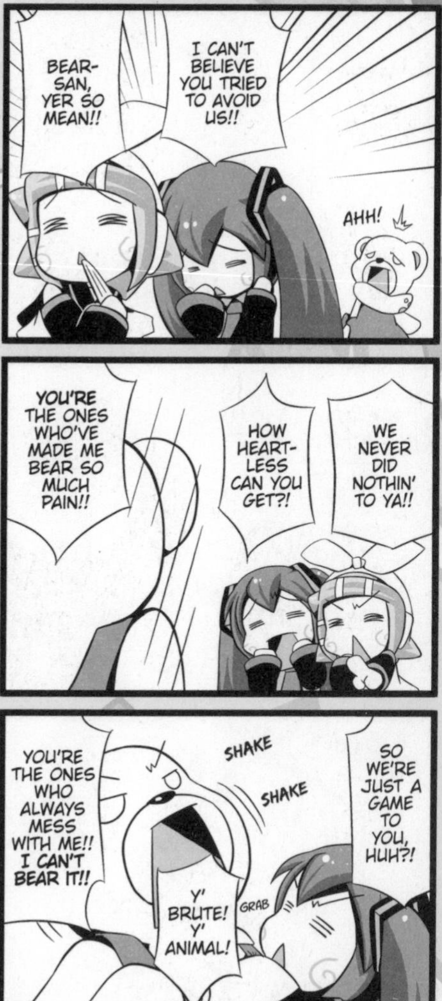
I CAN'T BELIEVE YOU TRIED TO AVOID US!!
BEAR-SAN, YER SO MEAN!!
AHH!
WE NEVER DID NOTHIN' TO YA!!
HOW HEARTLESS CAN YOU GET?!
YOU'RE THE ONES WHO'VE MADE ME BEAR SO MUCH PAIN!!
SO WE'RE JUST A GAME TO YOU, HUH?!
SHAKE
SHAKE
YOU'RE THE ONES WHO ALWAYS MESS WITH ME!! I CAN'T BEAR IT!!
GRAB
Y' BRUTE! Y' ANIMAL!
OUR LOVE BURNED SO BRIGHT-LY!!
HOT ENOUGH TO BURN YA!!
I'M THE ONE WHO GOT BURNED, THANK YOU BEARY MUCH!!

FUN

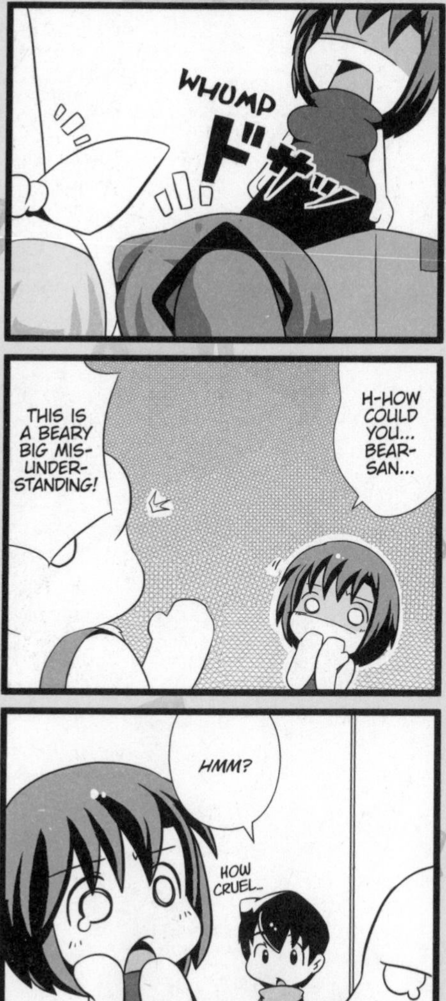
WHUMP
ドサッ
H-HOW COULD YOU... BEAR-SAN...
THIS IS A BEARY BIG MIS-UNDER-STANDING!
HMM?
HOW CRUEL...
LOOKS LIKE YOU'RE ALL HAVING FUN.
BEAR EXACTLY DID YOU GET THAT IDEA?!
HIS NEXT VICTIM?!

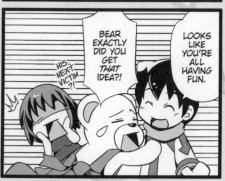

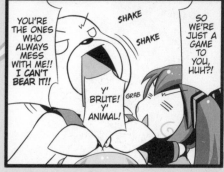

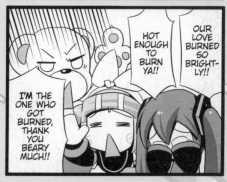

WORDS

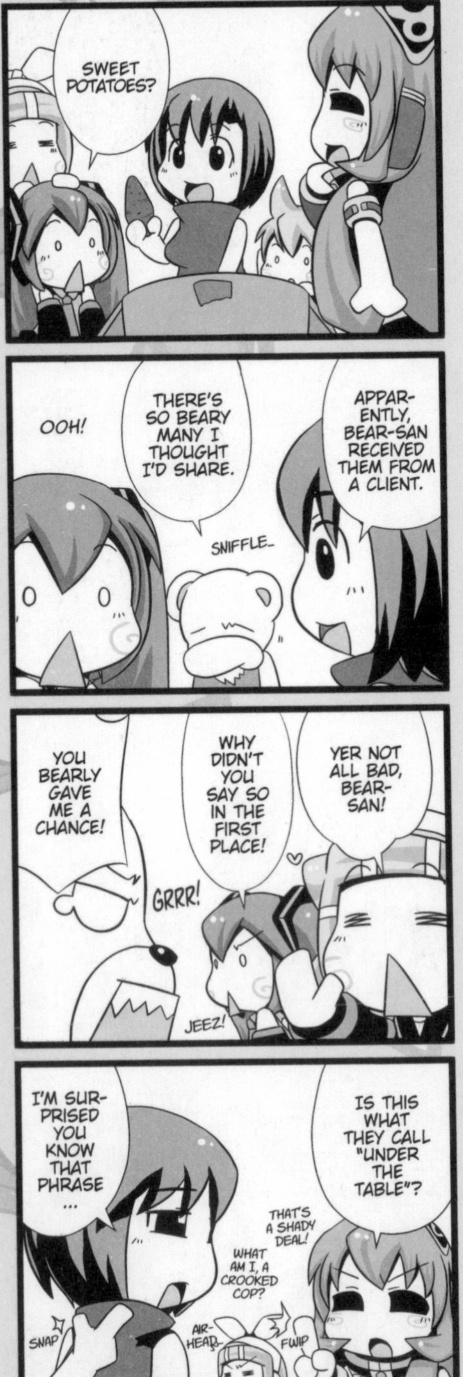

SWEET POTATOES?
APPARENTLY, BEAR-SAN RECEIVED THEM FROM A CLIENT.
THERE'S SO BEARY MANY I THOUGHT I'D SHARE.
OOH!
SNIFFLE...
YER NOT ALL BAD, BEAR-SAN!
WHY DIDN'T YOU SAY SO IN THE FIRST PLACE!
YOU BEARLY GAVE ME A CHANCE!
GRRR!
JEEZ!
IS THIS WHAT THEY CALL "UNDER THE TABLE"?
THAT'S A SHADY DEAL!
WHAT AM I, A CROOKED COP?
I'M SURPRISED YOU KNOW THAT PHRASE...
FWIP
AIR-HEAD...
SNAP

NOW?

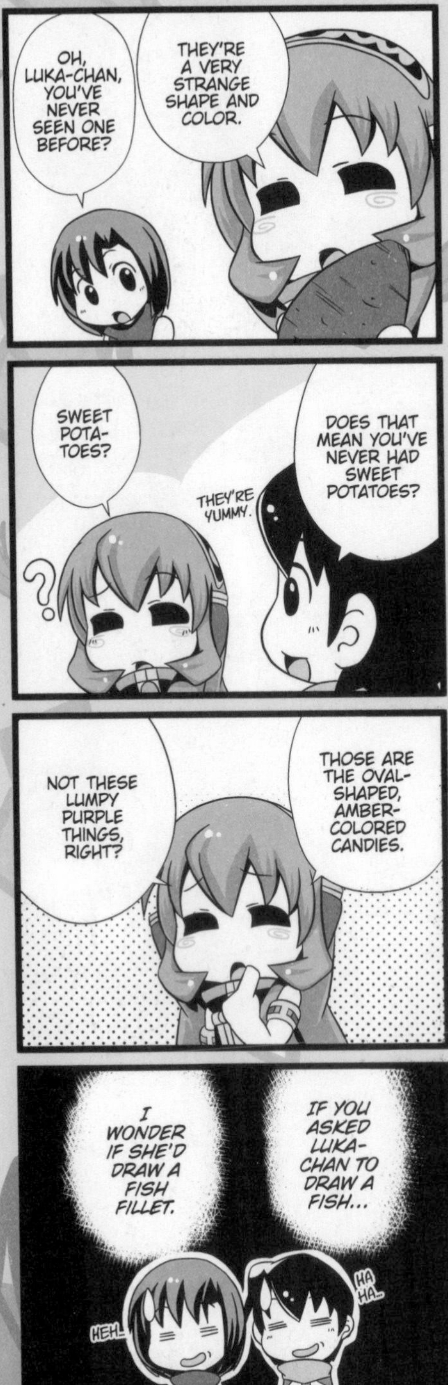

THEY'RE A VERY STRANGE SHAPE AND COLOR.
OH, LUKA-CHAN, YOU'VE NEVER SEEN ONE BEFORE?
DOES THAT MEAN YOU'VE NEVER HAD SWEET POTATOES?
THEY'RE YUMMY.
SWEET POTATOES?
THOSE ARE THE OVAL-SHAPED, AMBER-COLORED CANDIES.
NOT THESE LUMPY PURPLE THINGS, RIGHT?
IF YOU ASKED LUKA-CHAN TO DRAW A FISH...
I WONDER IF SHE'D DRAW A FISH FILLET.
HA HA...
HEH...

ASSIGNMENTS

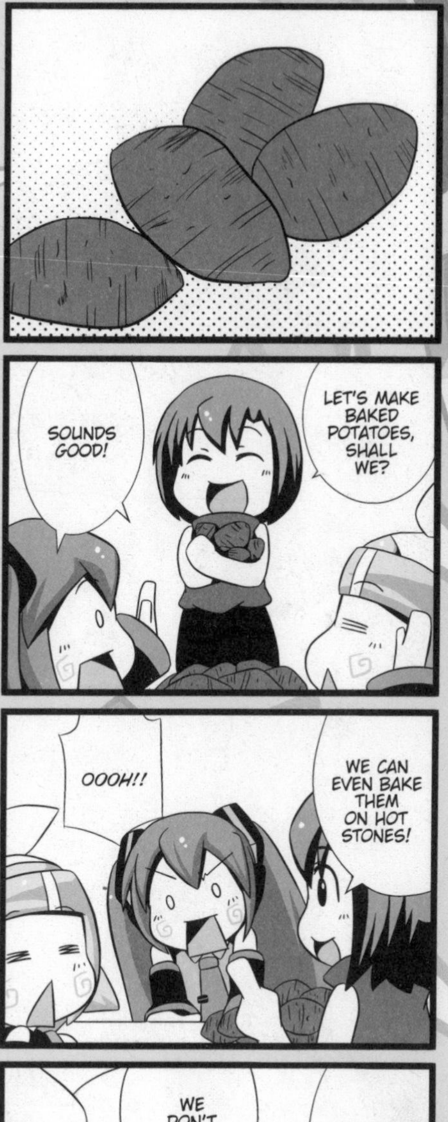
LET'S MAKE BAKED POTATOES, SHALL WE?
SOUNDS GOOD!
WE CAN EVEN BAKE THEM ON HOT STONES!
OOOH!!
I'LL SING THE "HOT POTATO" SONG, THEN!
WE DON'T NEED Y'TO.
AH HA HA!

QUITE SO

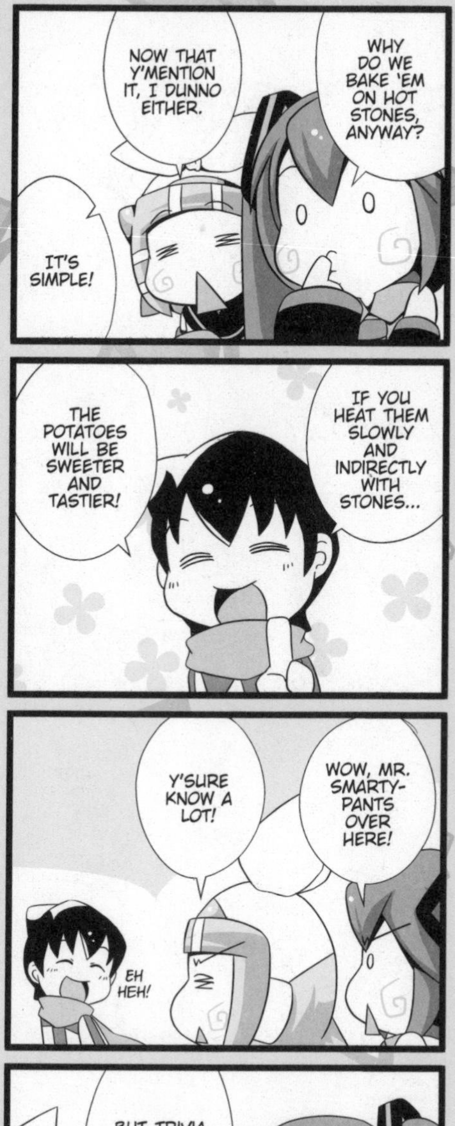
WHY DO WE BAKE 'EM ON HOT STONES, ANYWAY?
NOW THAT Y'MENTION IT, I DUNNO EITHER.
IT'S SIMPLE!
IF YOU HEAT THEM SLOWLY AND INDIRECTLY WITH STONES...
THE POTATOES WILL BE SWEETER AND TASTIER!
WOW, MR. SMARTY-PANTS OVER HERE!
Y'SURE KNOW A LOT!
EH HEH!
BUT TRIVIA WON'T PUT FOOD ON THE TABLE, YOU KNOW!

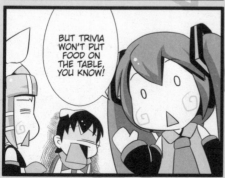

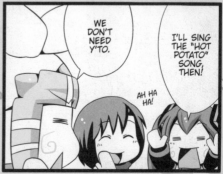

POOT

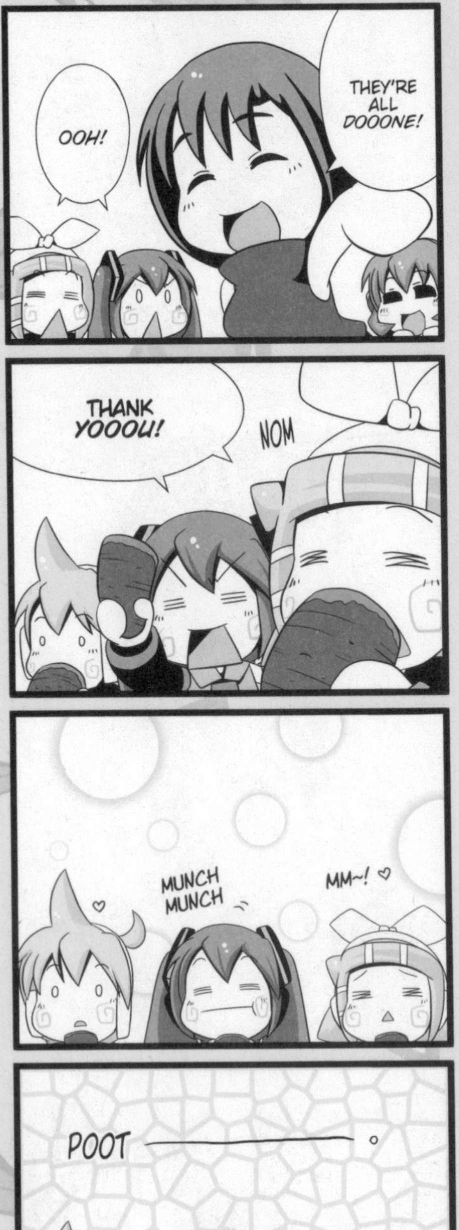
THEY'RE ALL DOOONE!
OOH!
NOM
THANK YOOOU!
MM~! ♡
MUNCH MUNCH
POOT
PFBBT!

STARE

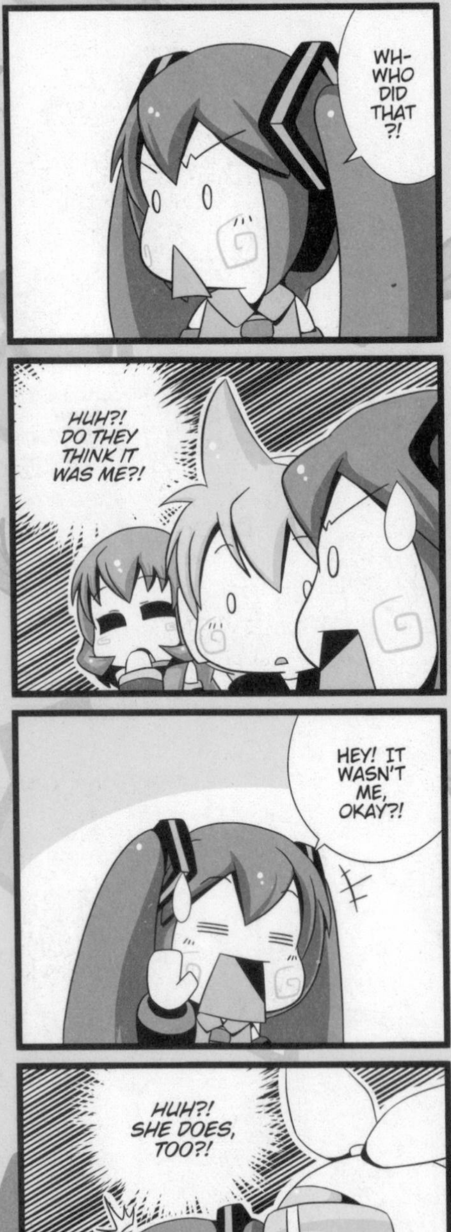
WH- WHO DID THAT?!
HUH?! DO THEY THINK IT WAS ME?!
HEY! IT WASN'T ME, OKAY?!
HUH?! SHE DOES, TOO?!

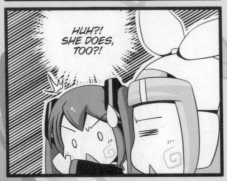

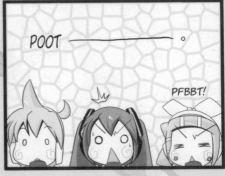

TOO LOVABLE

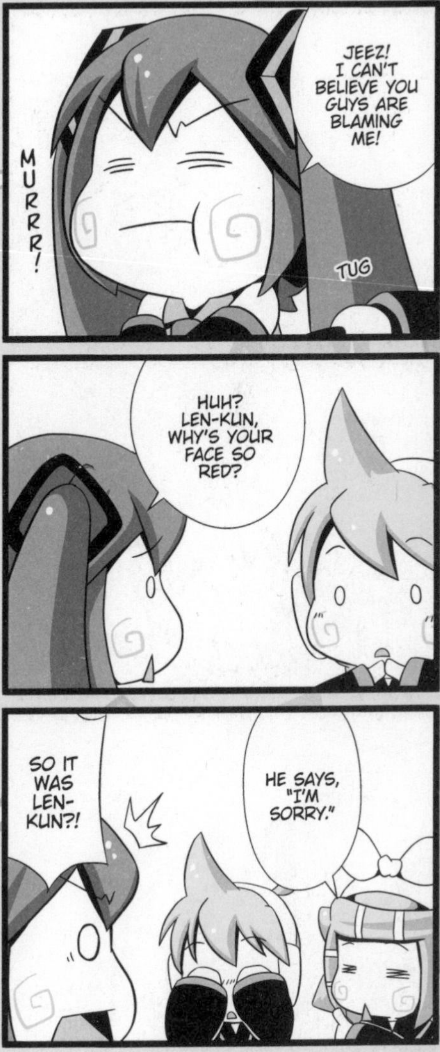
JEEZ! I CAN'T BELIEVE YOU GUYS ARE BLAMING ME!
MURRR!
TUG
HUH? LEN-KUN, WHY'S YOUR FACE SO RED?
HE SAYS, "I'M SORRY."
SO IT WAS LEN-KUN?!
AW, JEEZ! YOU'RE TOO CUTE, LEN-KUN!
OH, I CAN'T GET MAD AT THAT FACE!
HE'S GETTING OFF EASY!!

THE TIME IS NOW

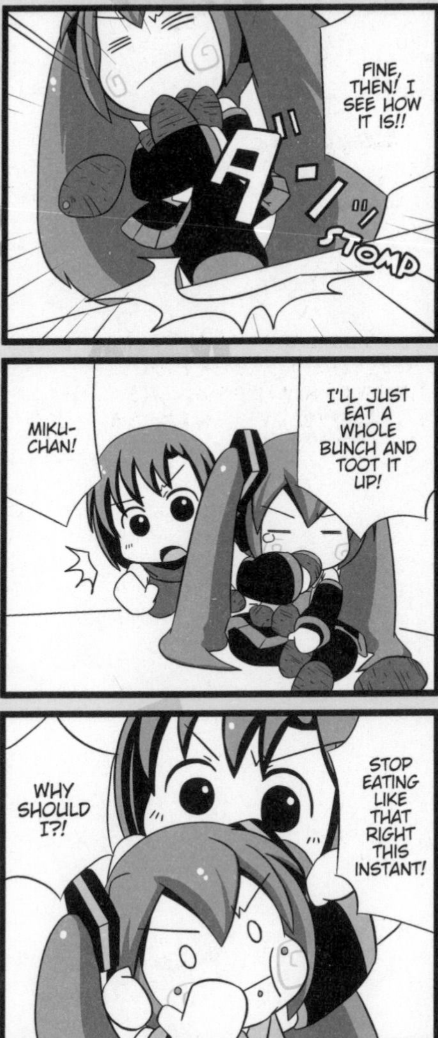
FINE, THEN! I SEE HOW IT IS!!
STOMP
I'LL JUST EAT A WHOLE BUNCH AND TOOT IT UP!
MIKU-CHAN!
STOP EATING LIKE THAT RIGHT THIS INSTANT!
WHY SHOULD I?!
GUH?! MMF...
TALK ABOUT LEARNIN' FROM EXPERI-ENCE!
YOU'RE GOING TO CHOKE!

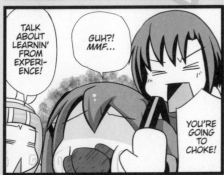

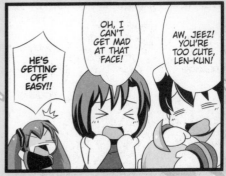

MOBILE VERSION LoiPara! BAND EDITION #1

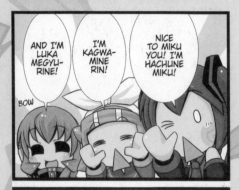

**A SPECIAL EPISODE PUBLISHED ON THE OFFICIAL COMPTIQ MOBILE SITE!
AFTER READING A CERTAIN MANGA, MIKU AND FRIENDS DECIDED TO FORM A BAND?!**

NICE TO MIKU YOU! I'M HACHUNE MIKU!
I'M KAGWA-MINE RIN!
AND I'M LUKA MEGYU-RINE!
BOW
WE'RE BREAKING INTO THE MOBILE SCENE!!
Y'ALL BETTER SUPPORT US!! PLEASE!
'KAY MIKU-NEE, YOU'RE REPPIN' US. SHOW 'EM WHAT WE GOT!
YOU GOT IT! HMM, LET ME SEE...
SWISH
AHEM!
HEE HEE!
ドーン
TA-DA!
THANKS FOR READING!! THAT'S ALL, FOLKS!!
DON'T JUST END IT, YA DUMMY!!

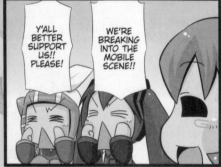

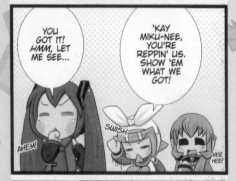

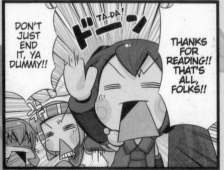

MOBILE VERSION

LoiPara!

BAND EDITION

#2

MOBILE VERSION

HEY, THIS IS RANDOM, BUT DO YOU WANNA START A BAND?
THAT'S RANDOM AR-RIGHT!
WHAT-CHA READIN'?
K-YON!
I MEAN, SHOULDN'T WE DO SOMETHING VOCALO-ISH ONCE IN A WHILE?
ISH ...?
I GUESS WE SHOULD BE MAKIN' SOME MUSIC...
THAT SOUNDS LIKE FUN!
WHAT INSTRU-MENTS WILL WE PLAY?
HMM, LEMME SEE...
FOR STARTERS, MAYBE A PIPE ORGAN...
TWIRL
FOR SO MANY REASONS.
NO WAY.
GRIN

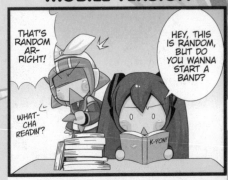

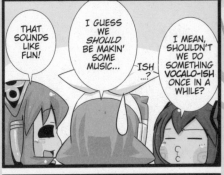

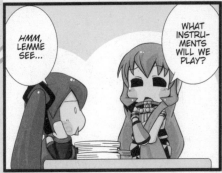

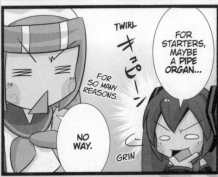

SPRING ONION 32:

HACHUNE MIKU'S CHOCOLATE WAR SIDE A

MISUNDERSTANDING

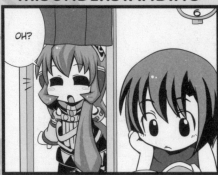

OH?
WHAT ARE YOU READING SO INTENTLY?
JUST DOING A LITTLE RESEARCH.
HEE HEE. NO NEED TO WORRY!
HMM?
YOUR SKIN IS STILL QUITE LOVELY!
WHAT EXACTLY DO YOU THINK IS GOING ON?

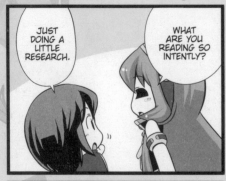

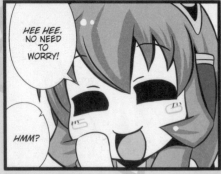

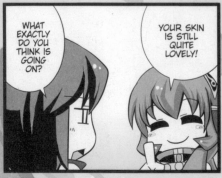

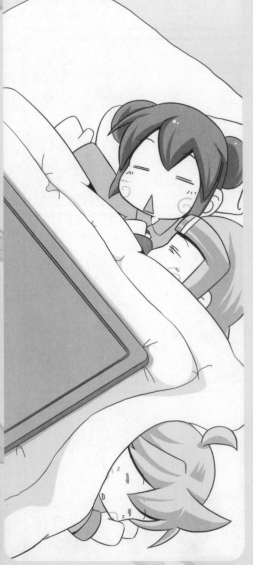

REGRETTABLE

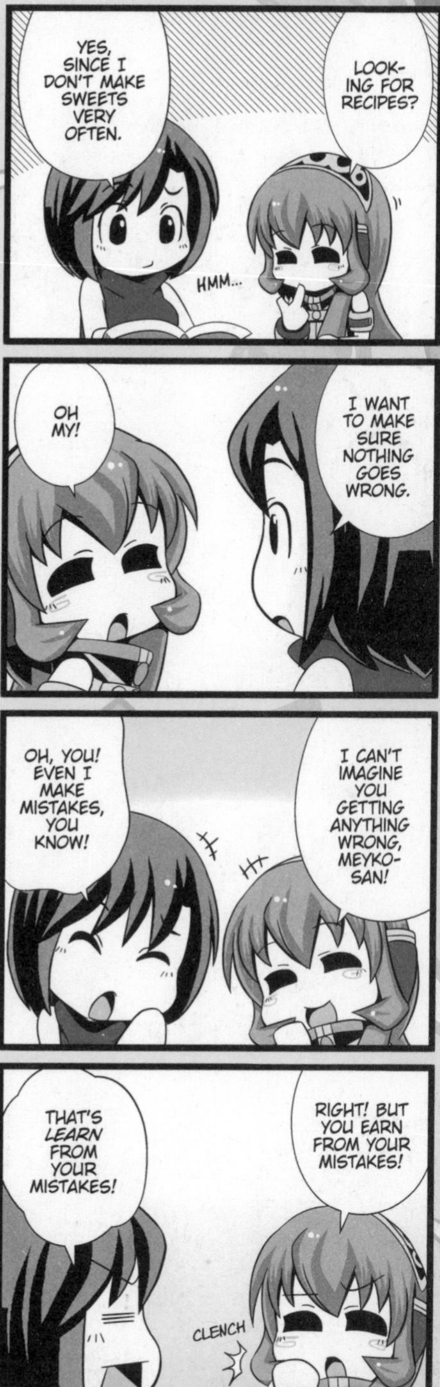
LOOKING FOR RECIPES?
YES, SINCE I DON'T MAKE SWEETS VERY OFTEN.
HMM...
I WANT TO MAKE SURE NOTHING GOES WRONG.
OH MY!
I CAN'T IMAGINE YOU GETTING ANYTHING WRONG, MEYKO-SAN!
OH, YOU! EVEN I MAKE MISTAKES, YOU KNOW!
RIGHT! BUT YOU EARN FROM YOUR MISTAKES!
THAT'S *LEARN* FROM YOUR MISTAKES!
CLENCH

ALMOST

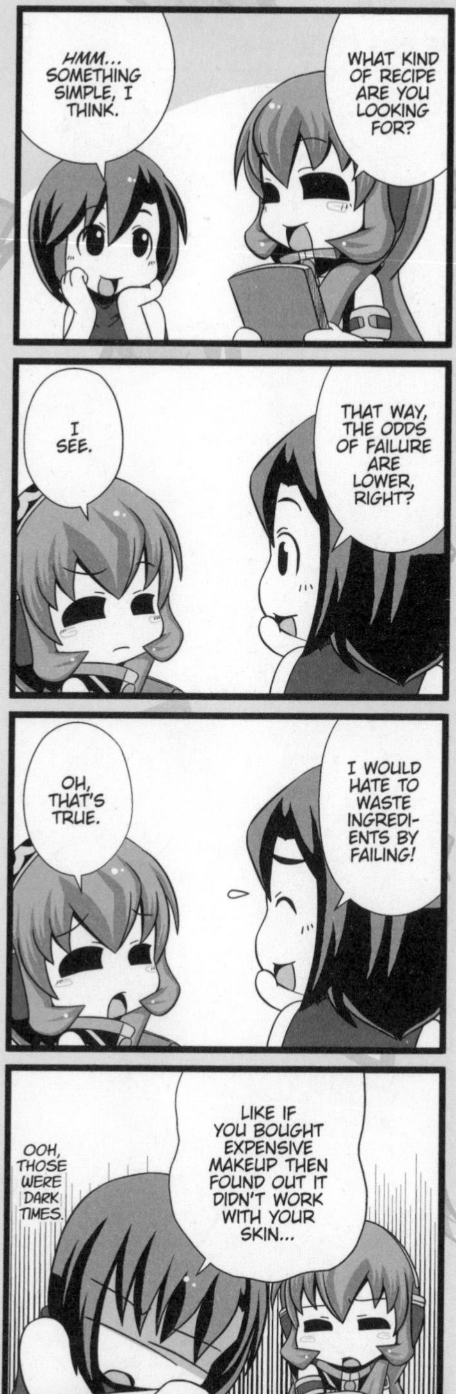
WHAT KIND OF RECIPE ARE YOU LOOKING FOR?
HMM... SOMETHING SIMPLE, I THINK.
THAT WAY, THE ODDS OF FAILURE ARE LOWER, RIGHT?
I SEE.
I WOULD HATE TO WASTE INGREDIENTS BY FAILING!
OH, THAT'S TRUE.
LIKE IF YOU BOUGHT EXPENSIVE MAKEUP THEN FOUND OUT IT DIDN'T WORK WITH YOUR SKIN...
OOH, THOSE WERE DARK TIMES.

I SEE

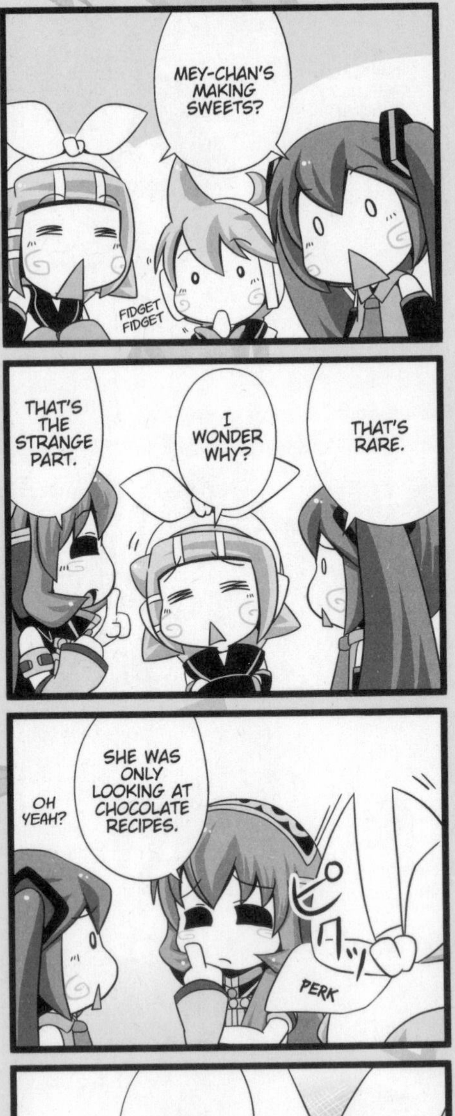
MEY-CHAN'S MAKING SWEETS?
FIDGET FIDGET
THAT'S RARE.
I WONDER WHY?
THAT'S THE STRANGE PART.
SHE WAS ONLY LOOKING AT CHOCOLATE RECIPES.
OH YEAH?
PERK
WELL, WELL. SO *THAT'S* IT.
GLINT

WISE

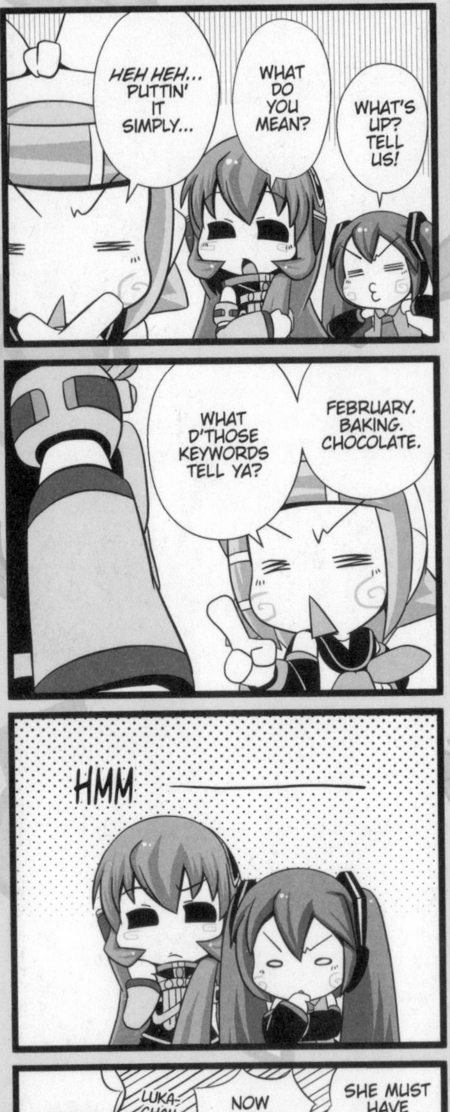
WHAT'S UP? TELL US!
WHAT DO YOU MEAN?
HEH HEH... PUTTIN' IT SIMPLY...
FEBRUARY. BAKING. CHOCOLATE.
WHAT D'THOSE KEYWORDS TELL YA?
HMM
SHE MUST HAVE GAINED WEIGHT OVER THE HOLIDAYS!
NOW SHE'S TRYING TO FINISH THE JOB WITH CHOCOLATE!
LUKA-CHAN, YER SUCH AN AIRHEAD!
WHERE'D YA GET *THAT*?!
SHE'S GIVEN UP...

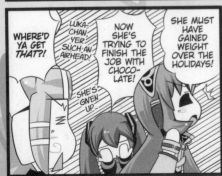

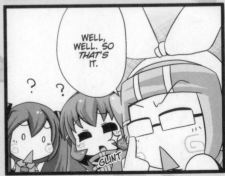

HINT

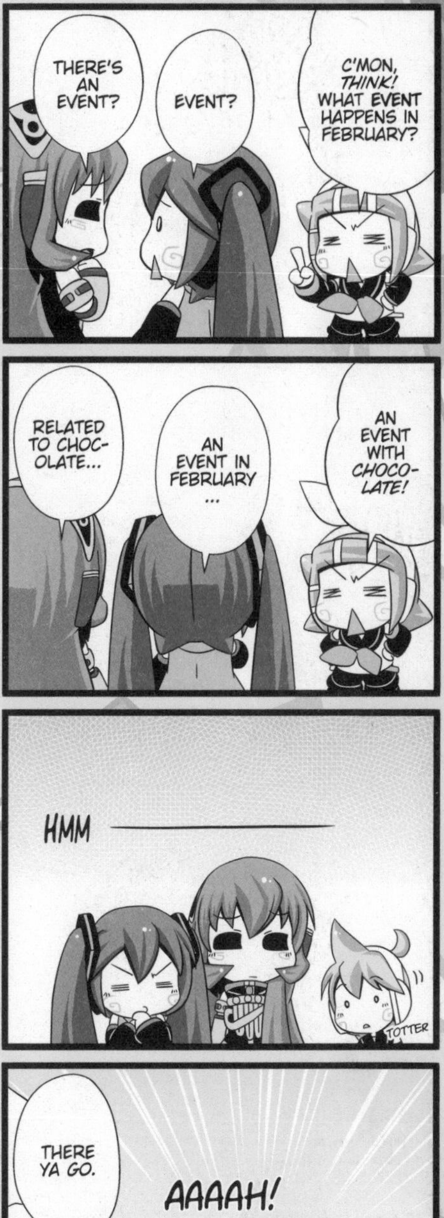
C'MON, THINK! WHAT EVENT HAPPENS IN FEBRUARY?
EVENT?
THERE'S AN EVENT?
AN EVENT WITH CHOCO-LATE!
AN EVENT IN FEBRUARY ...
RELATED TO CHOC-OLATE...
HMM
TOTTER
THERE YA GO.
AAAAH!

CHEER

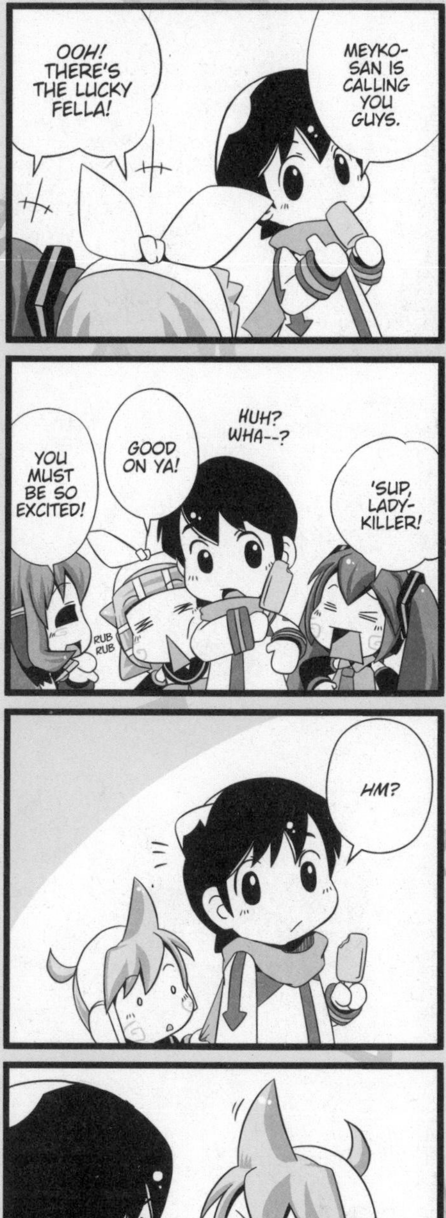
MEYKO-SAN IS CALLING YOU GUYS.
OOH! THERE'S THE LUCKY FELLA!
'SUP, LADY-KILLER!
HUH? WHA--?
GOOD ON YA!
YOU MUST BE SO EXCITED!
RUB RUB
HM?
CLENCH

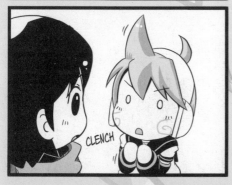

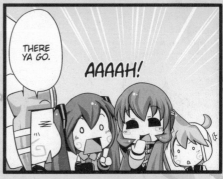

KNEW IT

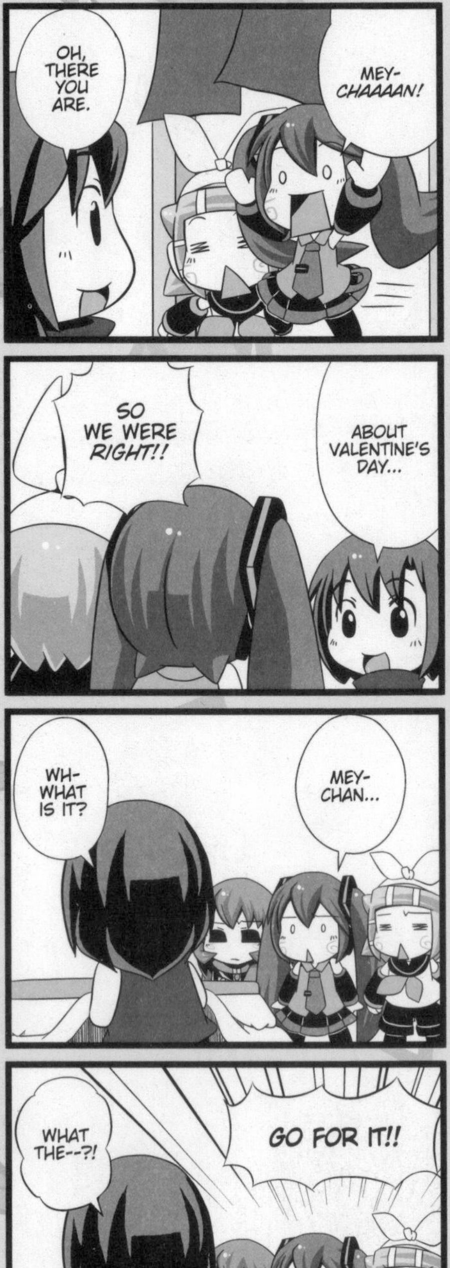
MEY-CHAAAAN!
OH, THERE YOU ARE.
ABOUT VALENTINE'S DAY...
SO WE WERE *RIGHT!!*
MEY-CHAN...
WH-WHAT IS IT?
GO FOR IT!!
WHAT THE--?!

ONE-ACT

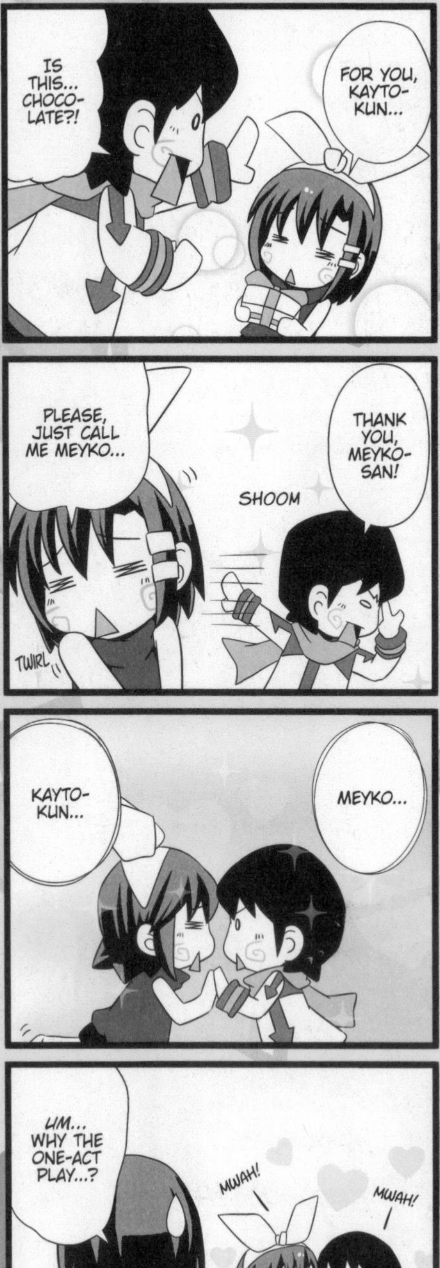
FOR YOU, KAYTO-KUN...
IS THIS... CHOCOLATE?!
THANK YOU, MEYKO-SAN!
SHOOM
PLEASE, JUST CALL ME MEYKO...
TWIRL
MEYKO...
KAYTO-KUN...
MWAH!
MWAH!
UM... WHY THE ONE-ACT PLAY...?

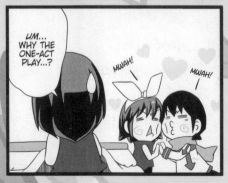

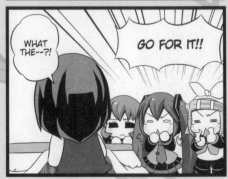

SWING AND A MISS

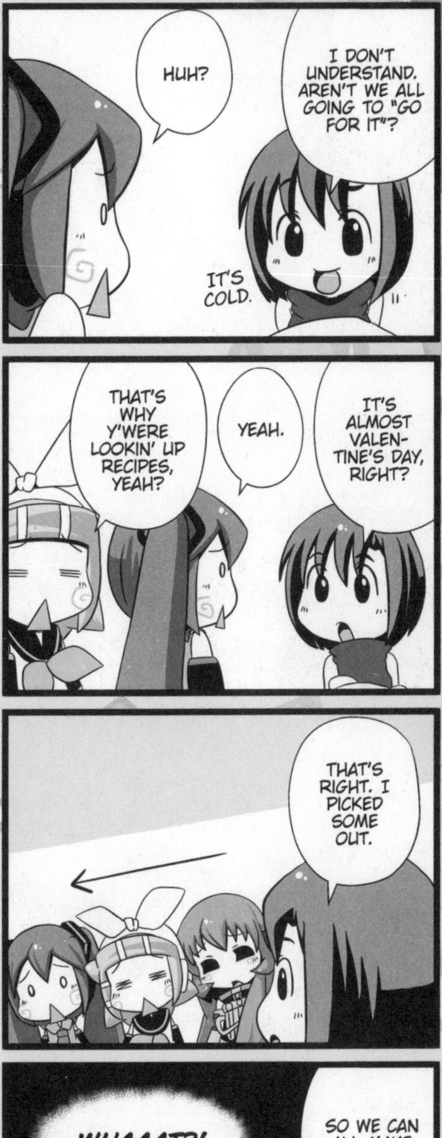
I DON'T UNDERSTAND. AREN'T WE ALL GOING TO "GO FOR IT"?
HUH?
IT'S COLD.
IT'S ALMOST VALEN-TINE'S DAY, RIGHT?
YEAH.
THAT'S WHY Y'WERE LOOKIN' UP RECIPES, YEAH?
THAT'S RIGHT. I PICKED SOME OUT.
SO WE CAN ALL MAKE THEM TOGETHER!
ZWOOSH
WHAAAT?!

MINOR MISHAP

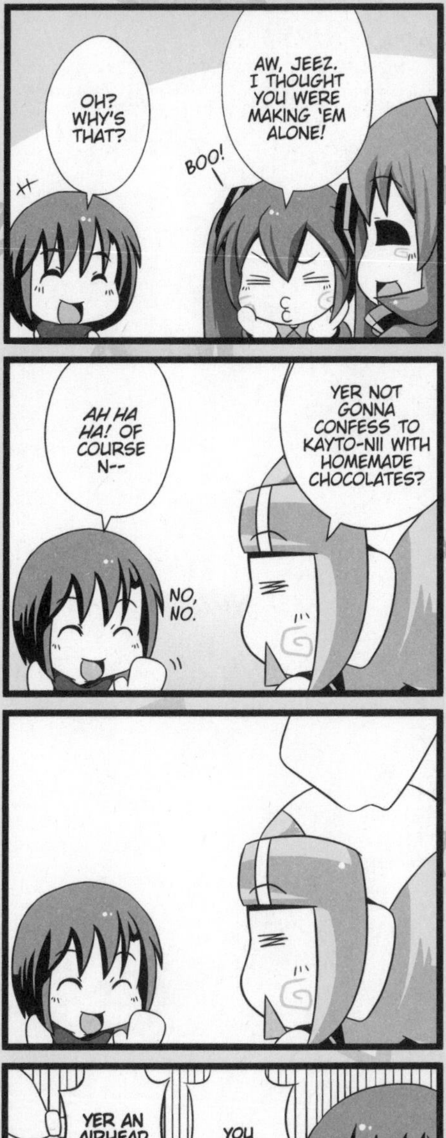
AW, JEEZ. I THOUGHT YOU WERE MAKING 'EM ALONE!
BOO!
OH? WHY'S THAT?
YER NOT GONNA CONFESS TO KAYTO-NII WITH HOMEMADE CHOCOLATES?
NO, NO.
AH HA HA! OF COURSE N--
YOU HADN'T EVEN THOUGHT --?!
YER AN AIRHEAD TOO, MEY-CHAN!!
AH!

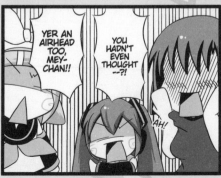

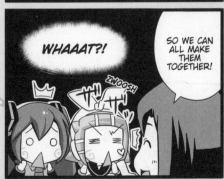

SPRING ONION 32:

HACHUNE MIKU'S CHOCOLATE WAR SIDE B

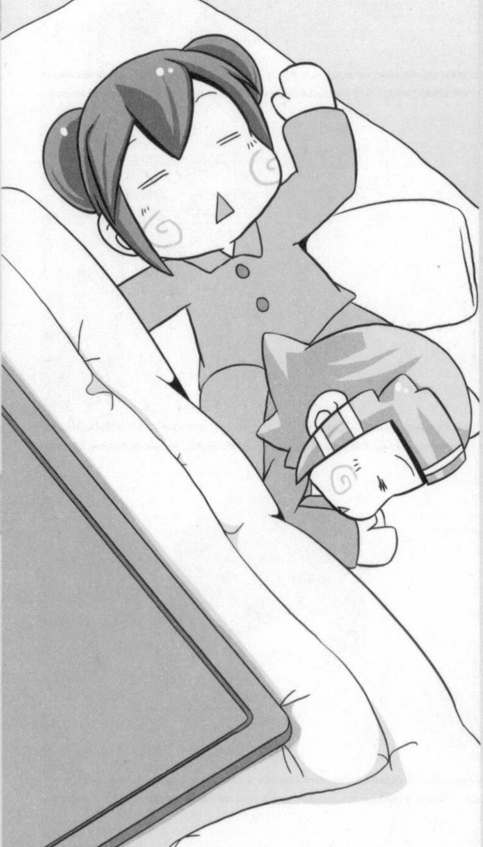

YOU OKAY?

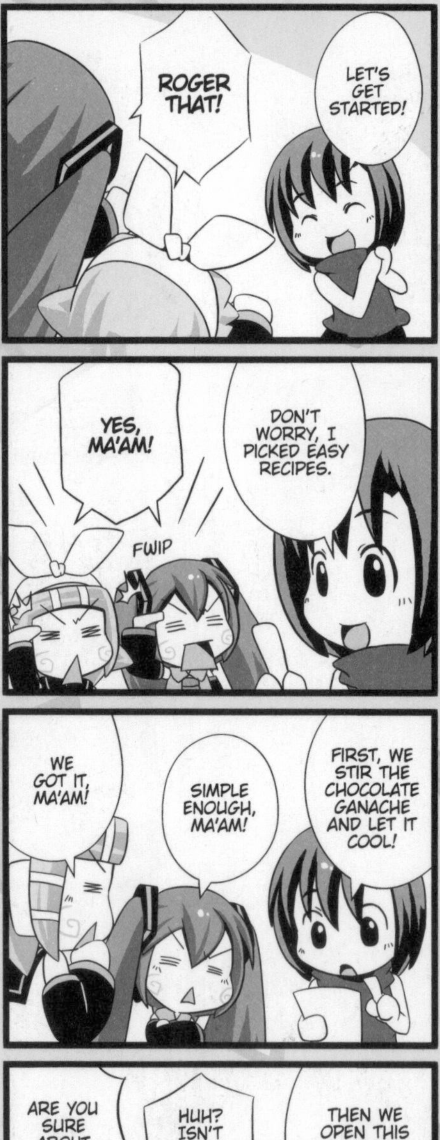
LET'S GET STARTED!
ROGER THAT!
DON'T WORRY, I PICKED EASY RECIPES.
YES, MA'AM!
FWIP
FIRST, WE STIR THE CHOCOLATE GANACHE AND LET IT COOL!
SIMPLE ENOUGH, MA'AM!
WE GOT IT, MA'AM!
THEN WE OPEN THIS CAKE MIX AND HEAT IT UP!
HUH? ISN'T THAT TOO SIMPLE, MA'AM?!
ARE YOU SURE ABOUT THAT, MA'AM?!

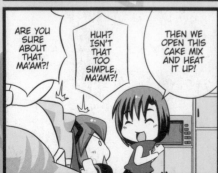

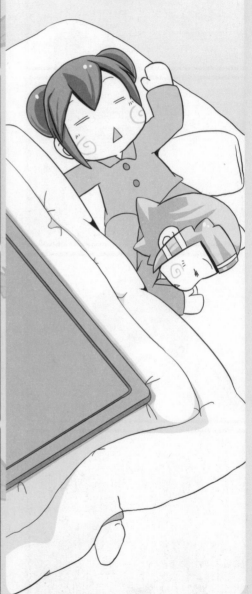

THESE DAYS

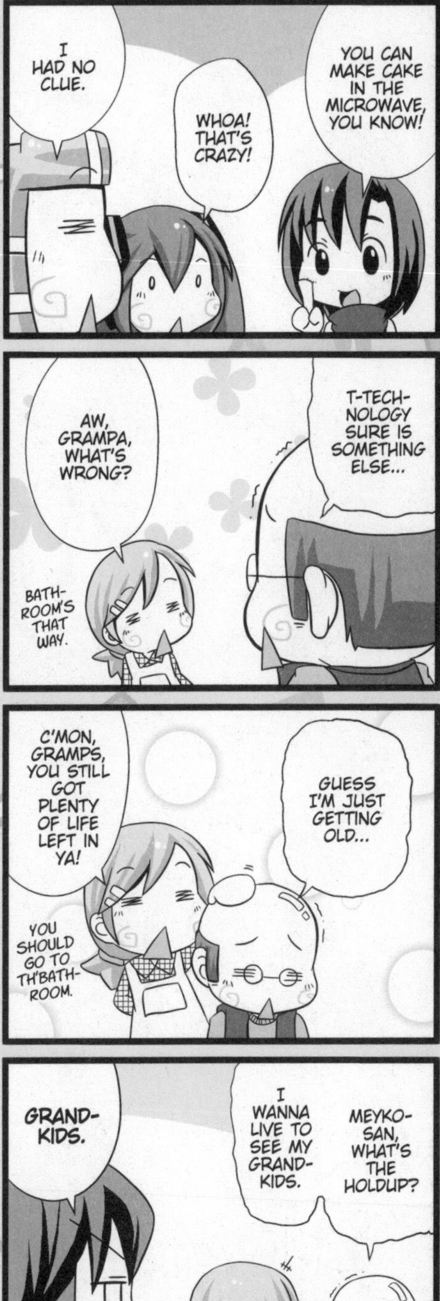
YOU CAN MAKE CAKE IN THE MICROWAVE, YOU KNOW!
WHOA! THAT'S CRAZY!
I HAD NO CLUE.
T-TECHNOLOGY SURE IS SOMETHING ELSE...
AW, GRAMPA, WHAT'S WRONG?
BATHROOM'S THAT WAY.
GUESS I'M JUST GETTING OLD...
C'MON, GRAMPS, YOU STILL GOT PLENTY OF LIFE LEFT IN YA!
YOU SHOULD GO TO TH'BATHROOM.
MEYKO-SAN, WHAT'S THE HOLDUP?
I WANNA LIVE TO SEE MY GRANDKIDS.
GRANDKIDS.
LEAVE HER ALONE, SHE'S SINGLE! HA HA!

ASSIGNMENTS

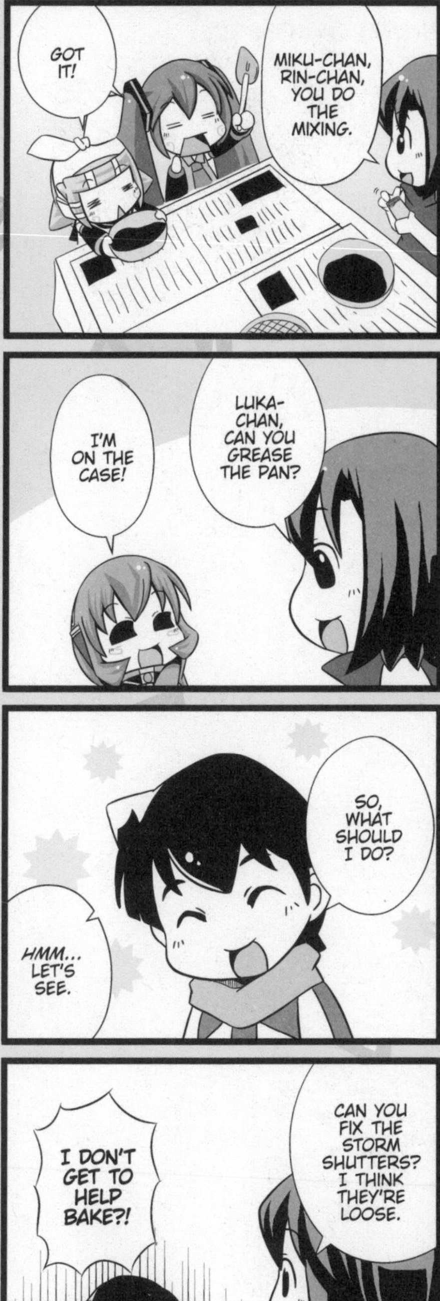
MIKU-CHAN, RIN-CHAN, YOU DO THE MIXING.
GOT IT!
LUKA-CHAN, CAN YOU GREASE THE PAN?
I'M ON THE CASE!
SO, WHAT SHOULD I DO?
HMM... LET'S SEE.
CAN YOU FIX THE STORM SHUTTERS? I THINK THEY'RE LOOSE.
I DON'T GET TO HELP BAKE?!

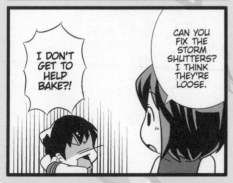

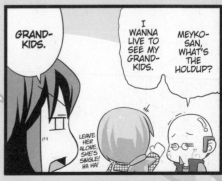

DEAD GIVEAWAY

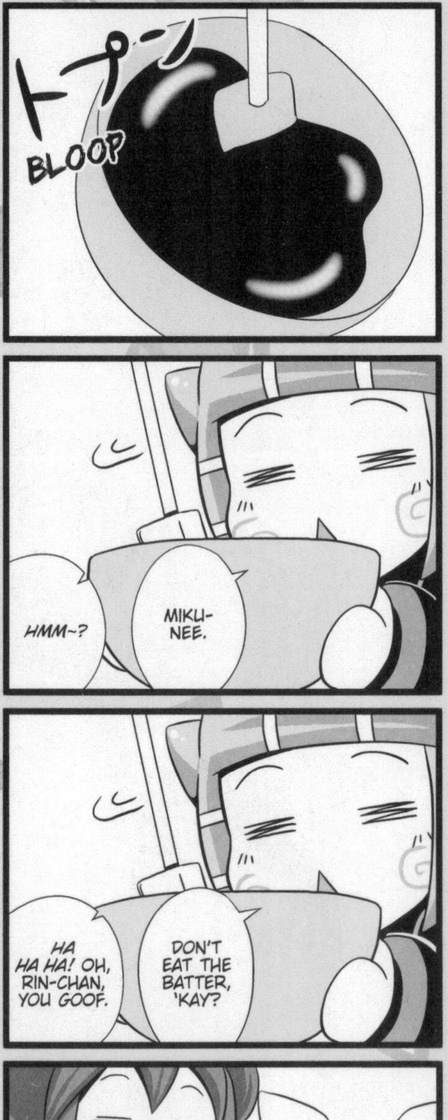

トプーン
BLOOP
MIKU-NEE.
HMM~?
DON'T EAT THE BATTER, 'KAY?
HA HA HA! OH, RIN-CHAN, YOU GOOF.
LIKE I WOULD EVER DO THAT!

ET TU, BRUTE?

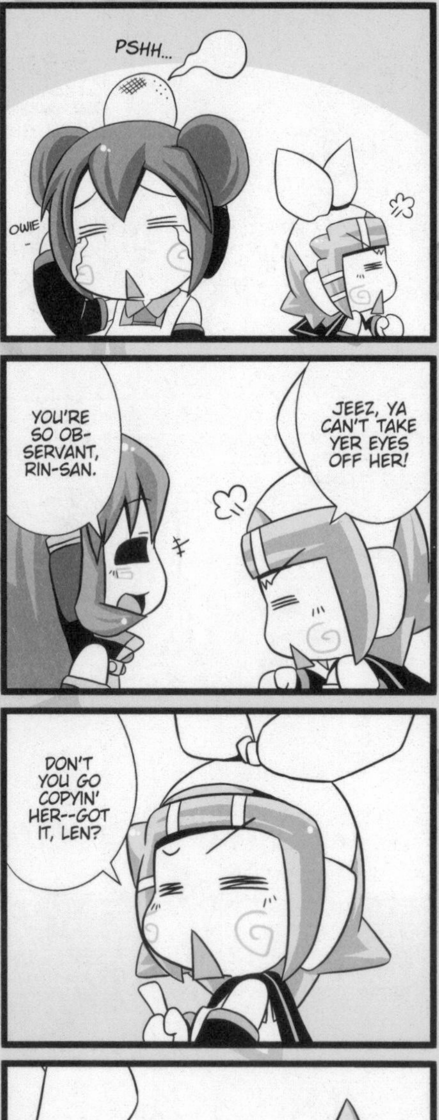

PSHH...
OWIE
JEEZ, YA CAN'T TAKE YER EYES OFF HER!
YOU'RE SO OB-SERVANT, RIN-SAN.
DON'T YOU GO COPYIN' HER--GOT IT, LEN?

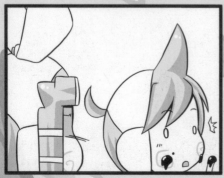

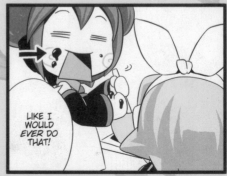

AS ALWAYS

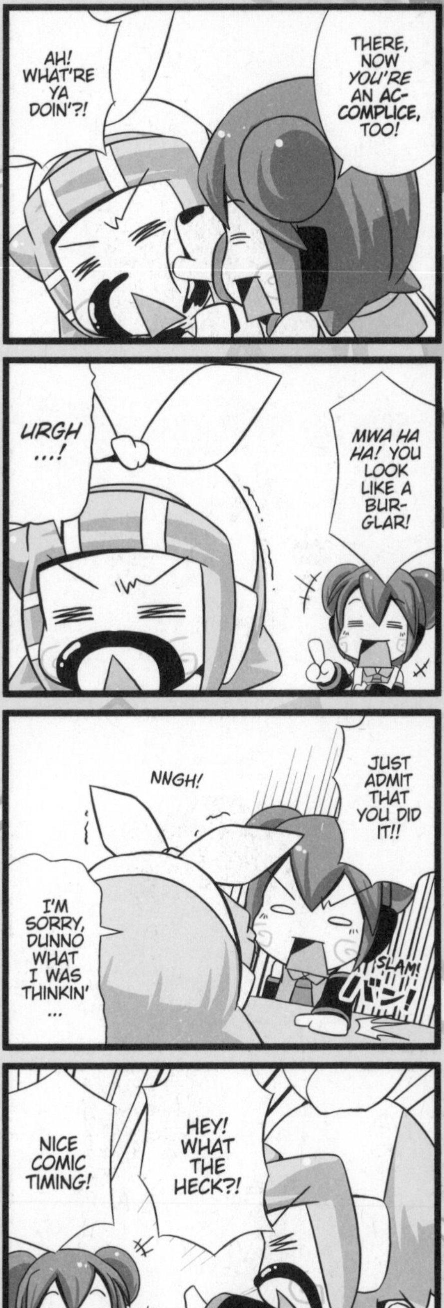
THERE, NOW YOU'RE AN AC-COMPLICE, TOO!
AH! WHAT'RE YA DOIN'?!
MWA HA HA! YOU LOOK LIKE A BUR-GLAR!
URGH ...!
JUST ADMIT THAT YOU DID IT!!
NNGH!
SLAM! バン!
I'M SORRY, DUNNO WHAT I WAS THINKIN' ...
HEY! WHAT THE HECK?!
NICE COMIC TIMING!
BWING

POOF

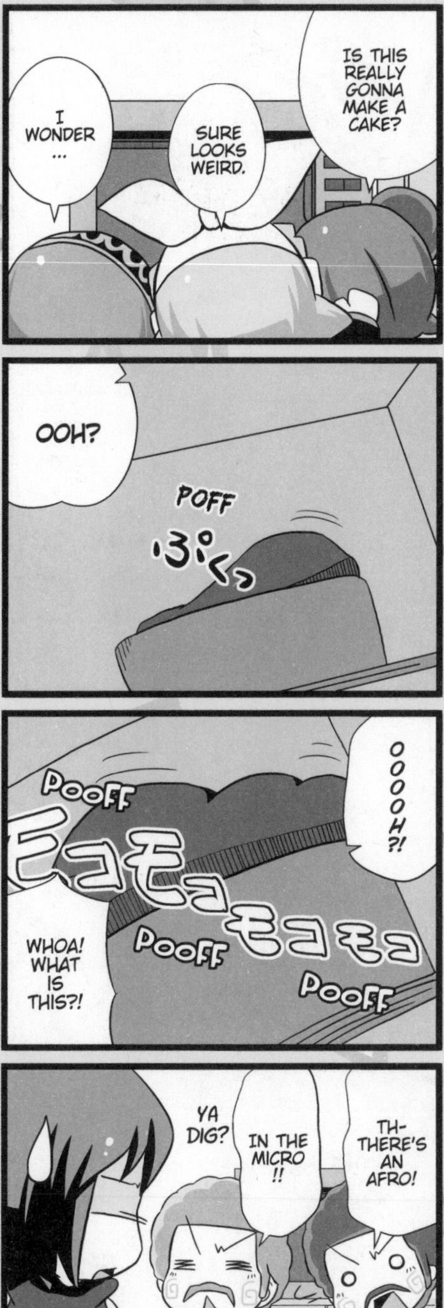
IS THIS REALLY GONNA MAKE A CAKE?
SURE LOOKS WEIRD.
I WONDER ...
OOH?
POFF ぷくっ
OOOOOH?!
POOFF
モコモコ モコモコ
POOFF
POOFF
WHOA! WHAT IS THIS?!
TH-THERE'S AN AFRO!
IN THE MICRO !!
YA DIG?

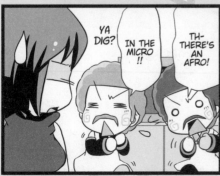

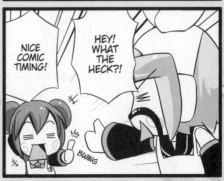

VOILÀ

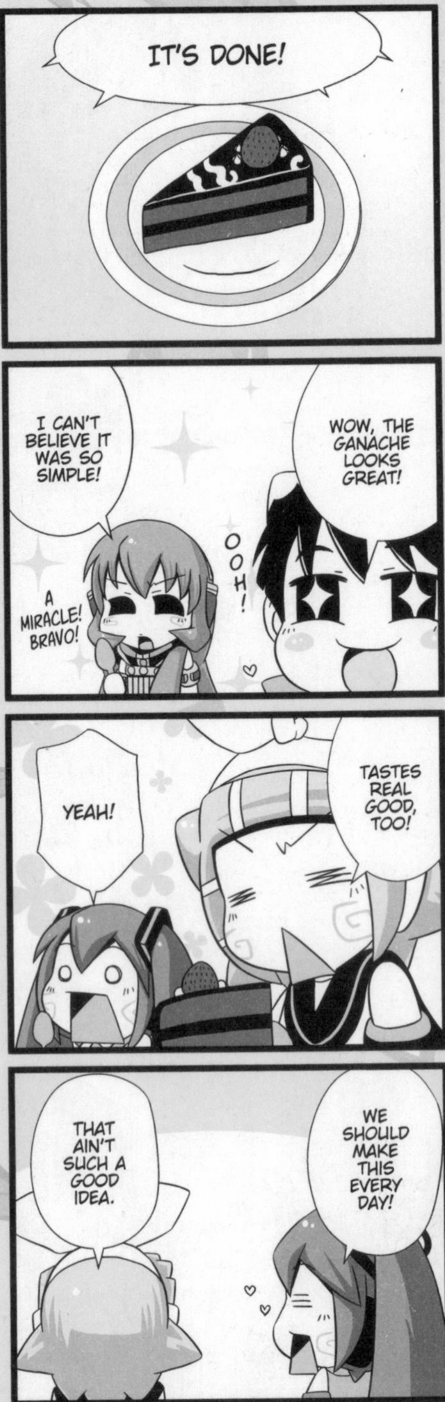
IT'S DONE!
WOW, THE GANACHE LOOKS GREAT!
OOH!
I CAN'T BELIEVE IT WAS SO SIMPLE!
A MIRACLE! BRAVO!
TASTES REAL GOOD, TOO!
YEAH!
WE SHOULD MAKE THIS EVERY DAY!
THAT AIN'T SUCH A GOOD IDEA.

SURPRISE

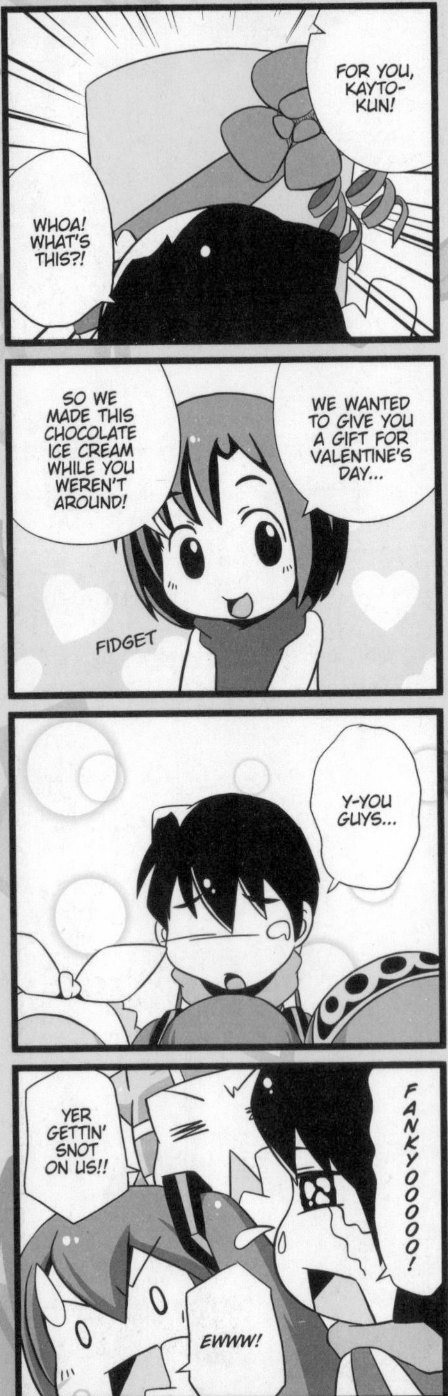
FOR YOU, KAYTO-KUN!
WHOA! WHAT'S THIS?!
WE WANTED TO GIVE YOU A GIFT FOR VALENTINE'S DAY...
SO WE MADE THIS CHOCOLATE ICE CREAM WHILE YOU WEREN'T AROUND!
FIDGET
Y-YOU GUYS...
FANKYOOOOOO!
YER GETTIN' SNOT ON US!!
EWWW!

SKILLED

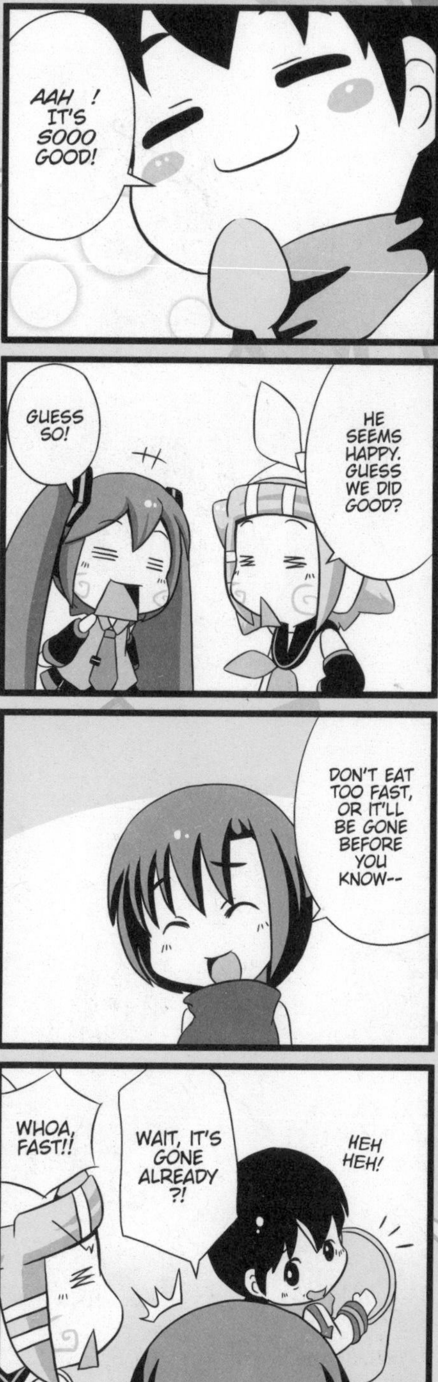
AAH ! IT'S SOOO GOOD!
HE SEEMS HAPPY. GUESS WE DID GOOD?
GUESS SO!
DON'T EAT TOO FAST, OR IT'LL BE GONE BEFORE YOU KNOW--
HEH HEH!
WAIT, IT'S GONE ALREADY ?!
WHOA, FAST!!

MODERATION

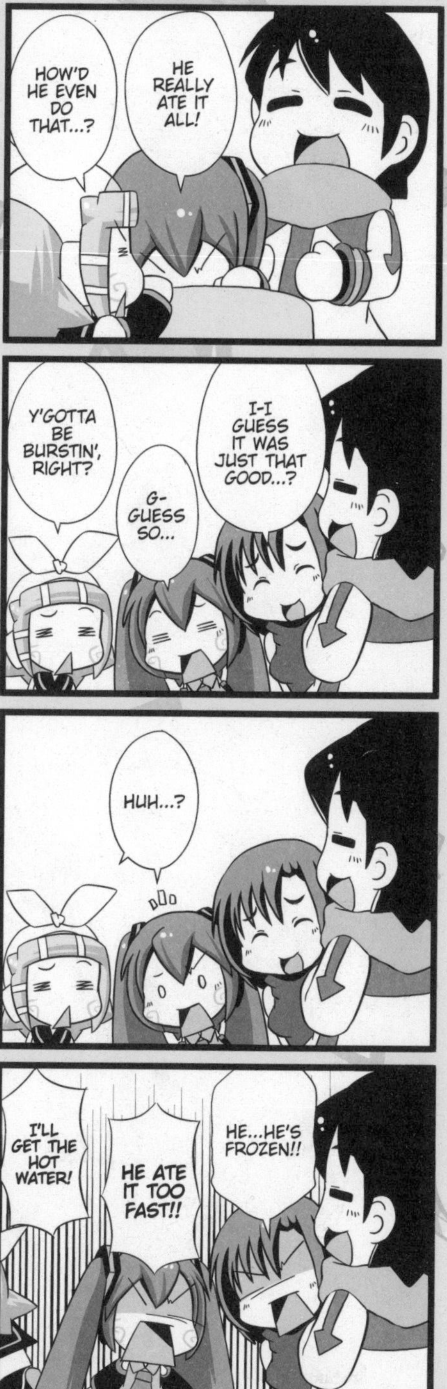
HE REALLY ATE IT ALL!
HOW'D HE EVEN DO THAT...?
I-I GUESS IT WAS JUST THAT GOOD...?
Y'GOTTA BE BURSTIN', RIGHT?
G- GUESS SO...
HUH...?
HE...HE'S FROZEN!!
HE ATE IT TOO FAST!!
I'LL GET THE HOT WATER!

SPRING ONION 33:

HACHUNE MIKU'S COFFEE

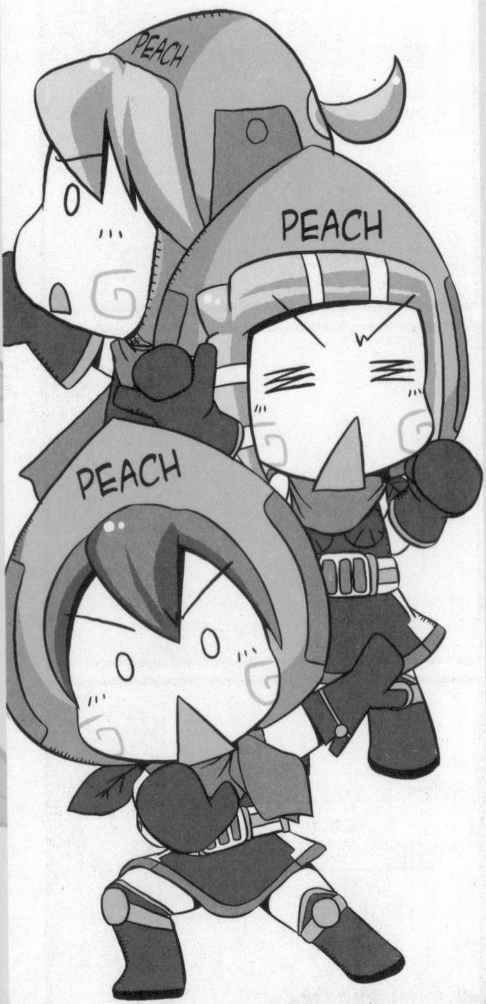
PEACH
PEACH
PEACH

THINKING

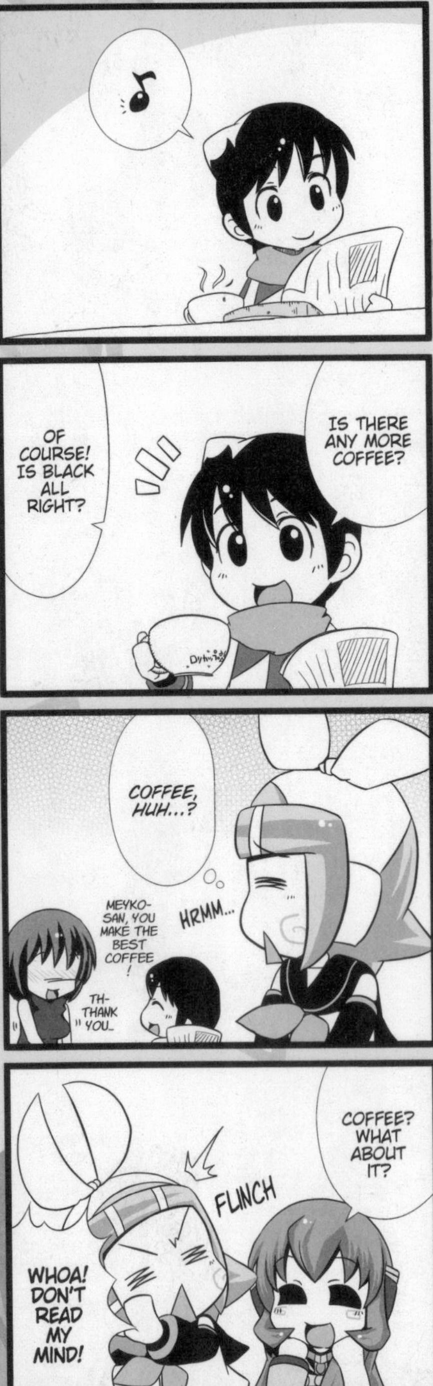
IS THERE ANY MORE COFFEE?
OF COURSE! IS BLACK ALL RIGHT?
COFFEE, HUH...?
HRMM...
MEYKO-SAN, YOU MAKE THE BEST COFFEE!
TH-THANK YOU...
COFFEE? WHAT ABOUT IT?
FLINCH
WHOA! DON'T READ MY MIND!

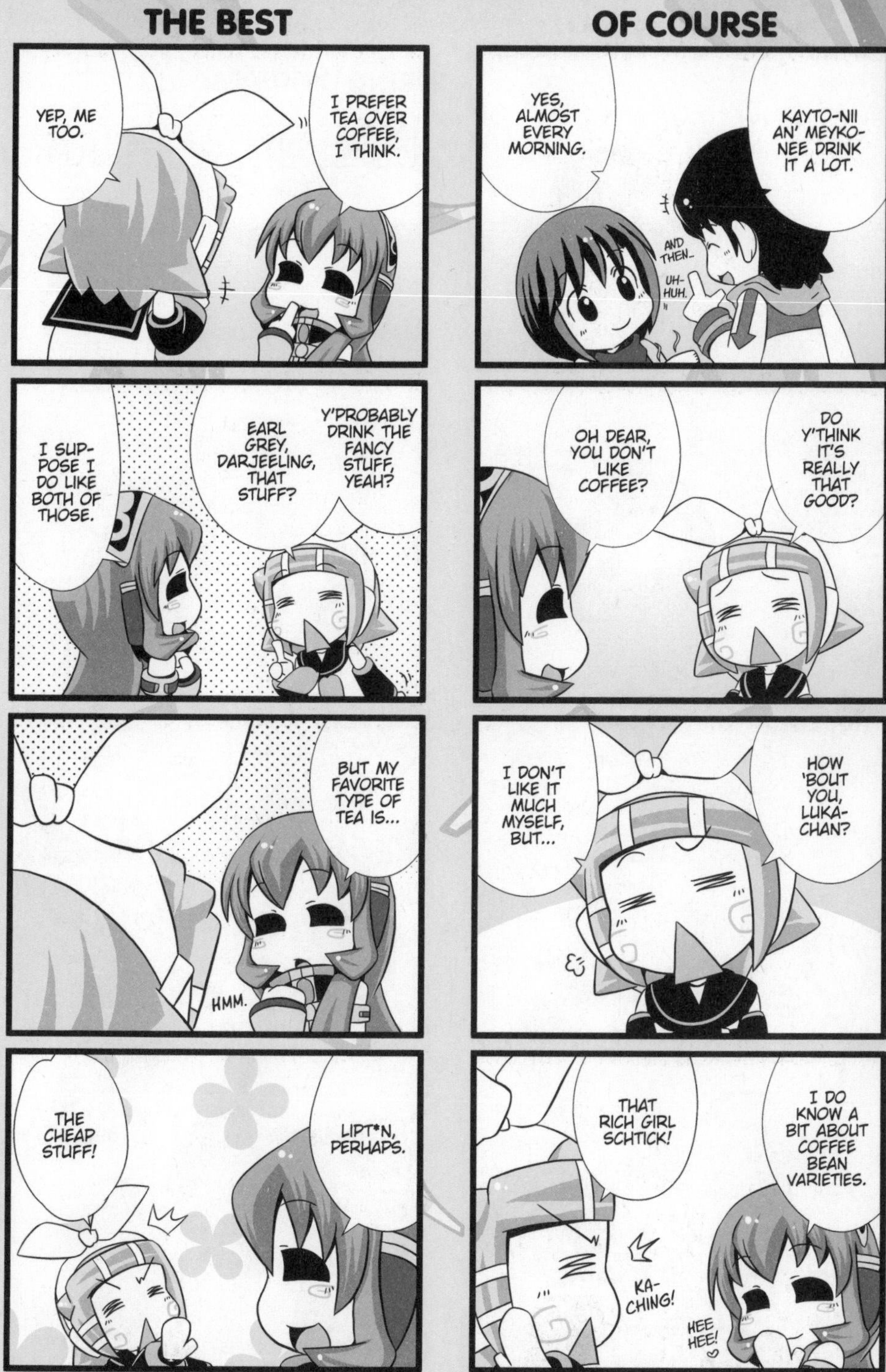
OF COURSE
KAYTO-NII AN' MEYKO-NEE DRINK IT A LOT.
YES, ALMOST EVERY MORNING.
AND THEN...
UH-HUH.
DO Y'THINK IT'S REALLY THAT GOOD?
OH DEAR, YOU DON'T LIKE COFFEE?
HOW 'BOUT YOU, LUKA-CHAN?
I DON'T LIKE IT MUCH MYSELF, BUT...
I DO KNOW A BIT ABOUT COFFEE BEAN VARIETIES.
THAT RICH GIRL SCHTICK!
KA-CHING!
HEE HEE!
THE BEST
I PREFER TEA OVER COFFEE, I THINK.
YEP, ME TOO.
Y'PROBABLY DRINK THE FANCY STUFF, YEAH?
EARL GREY, DARJEELING, THAT STUFF?
I SUPPOSE I DO LIKE BOTH OF THOSE.
BUT MY FAVORITE TYPE OF TEA IS...
HMM.
LIPT*N, PERHAPS.
THE CHEAP STUFF!

WHICH IS IT?

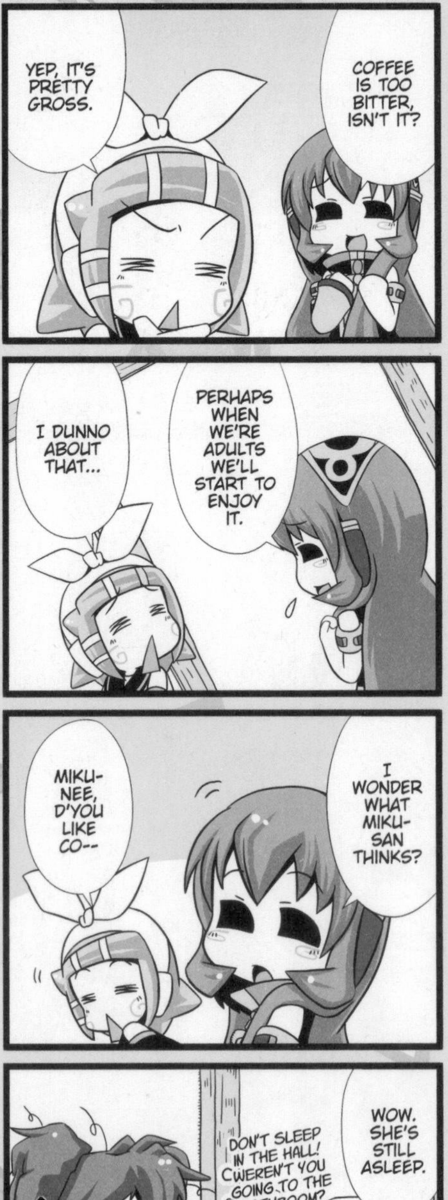

COFFEE IS TOO BITTER, ISN'T IT?
YEP, IT'S PRETTY GROSS.
PERHAPS WHEN WE'RE ADULTS WE'LL START TO ENJOY IT.
I DUNNO ABOUT THAT...
I WONDER WHAT MIKU-SAN THINKS?
MIKU-NEE, D'YOU LIKE CO--
WOW. SHE'S STILL ASLEEP.
DON'T SLEEP IN THE HALL! WEREN'T YOU GOING TO THE BATHROOM?
ZZZ...

SUBSTITUTION

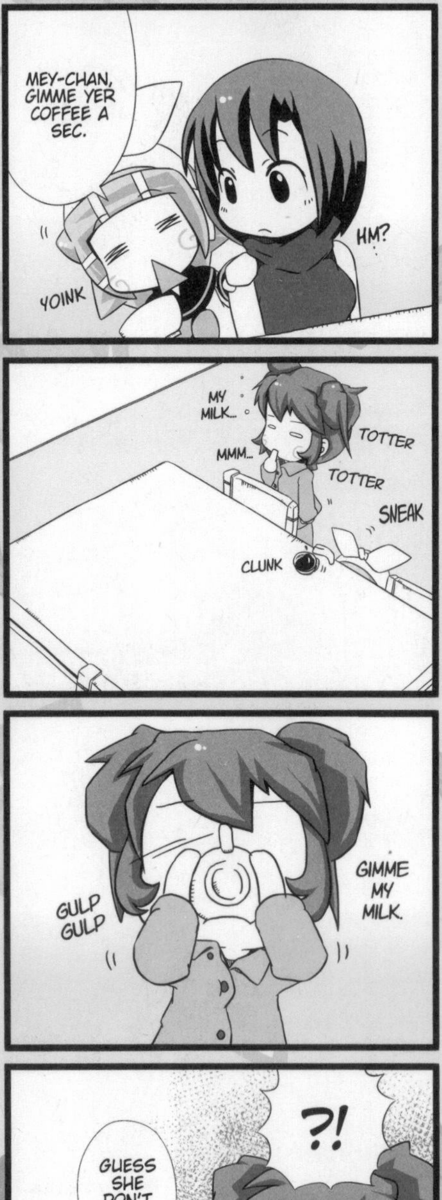

MEY-CHAN, GIMME YER COFFEE A SEC.
HM?
YOINK
MY MILK...
TOTTER
MMM...
TOTTER
SNEAK
CLUNK
GIMME MY MILK.
GULP GULP
?!
GUESS SHE DON'T LIKE IT.
BLEH

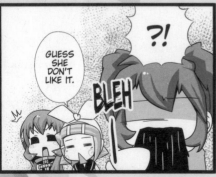

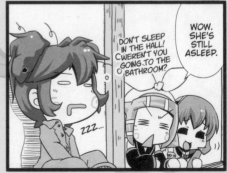

GOOD POINT

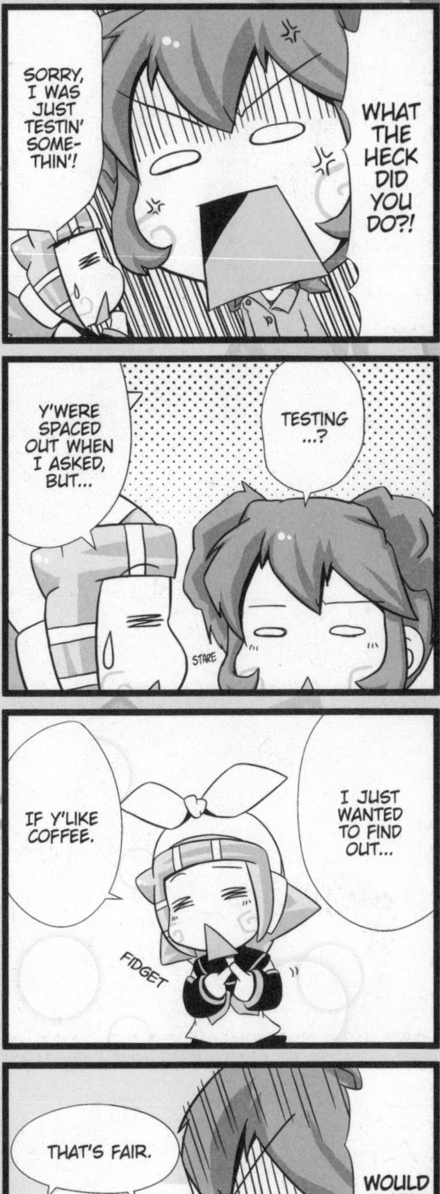
WHAT THE HECK DID YOU DO?!
SORRY, I WAS JUST TESTIN' SOME-THIN'!
TESTING ...?
Y'WERE SPACED OUT WHEN I ASKED, BUT...
STARE
I JUST WANTED TO FIND OUT...
IF Y'LIKE COFFEE.
FIDGET
WOULD I SPIT IT OUT IF I LIKED IT?!
THAT'S FAIR.

THAT REMINDS ME

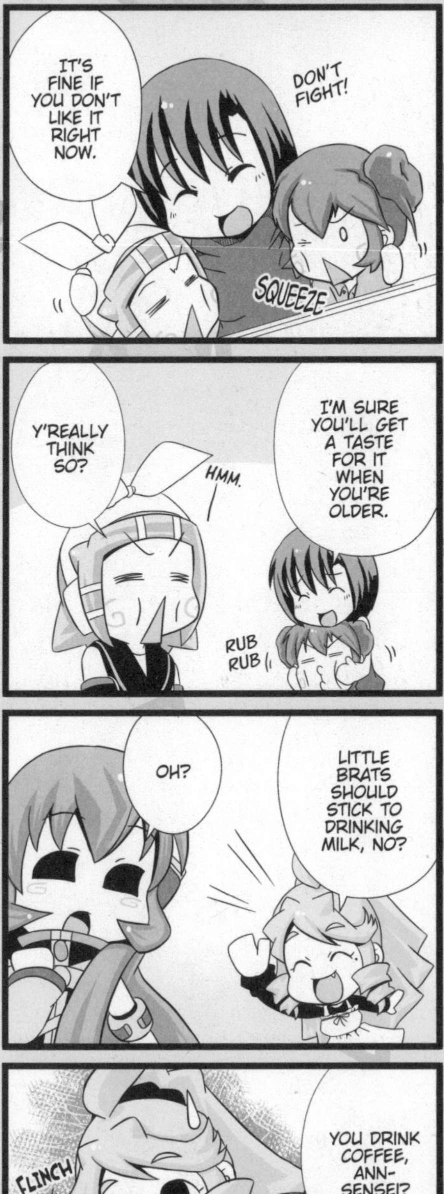
DON'T FIGHT!
IT'S FINE IF YOU DON'T LIKE IT RIGHT NOW.
SQUEEZE
I'M SURE YOU'LL GET A TASTE FOR IT WHEN YOU'RE OLDER.
HMM.
Y'REALLY THINK SO?
RUB RUB
LITTLE BRATS SHOULD STICK TO DRINKING MILK, NO?
OH?
YOU DRINK COFFEE, ANN-SENSEI?
FLINCH
ギクッ

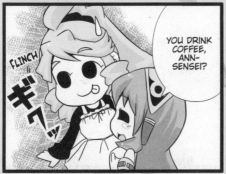

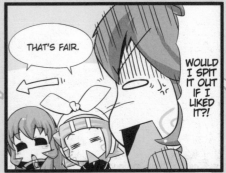

NOPE

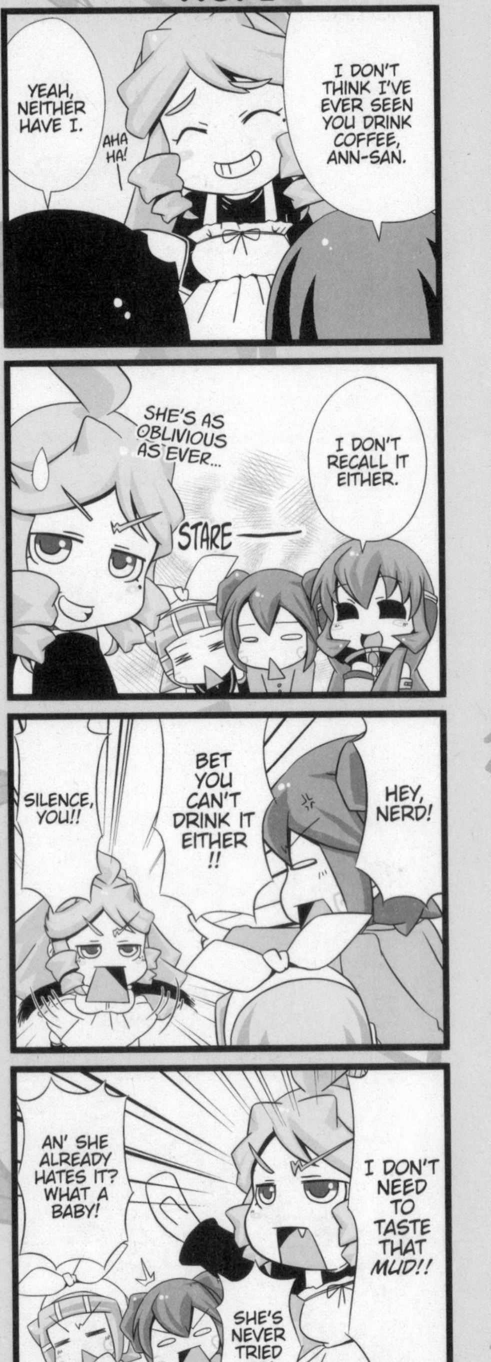
I DON'T THINK I'VE EVER SEEN YOU DRINK COFFEE, ANN-SAN.
AHA HA!
YEAH, NEITHER HAVE I.
I DON'T RECALL IT EITHER.
SHE'S AS OBLIVIOUS AS EVER...
STARE———
HEY, NERD!
BET YOU CAN'T DRINK IT EITHER!!
SILENCE, YOU!!
I DON'T NEED TO TASTE THAT MUD!!
AN' SHE ALREADY HATES IT? WHAT A BABY!
SHE'S NEVER TRIED IT?!

DEFEAT

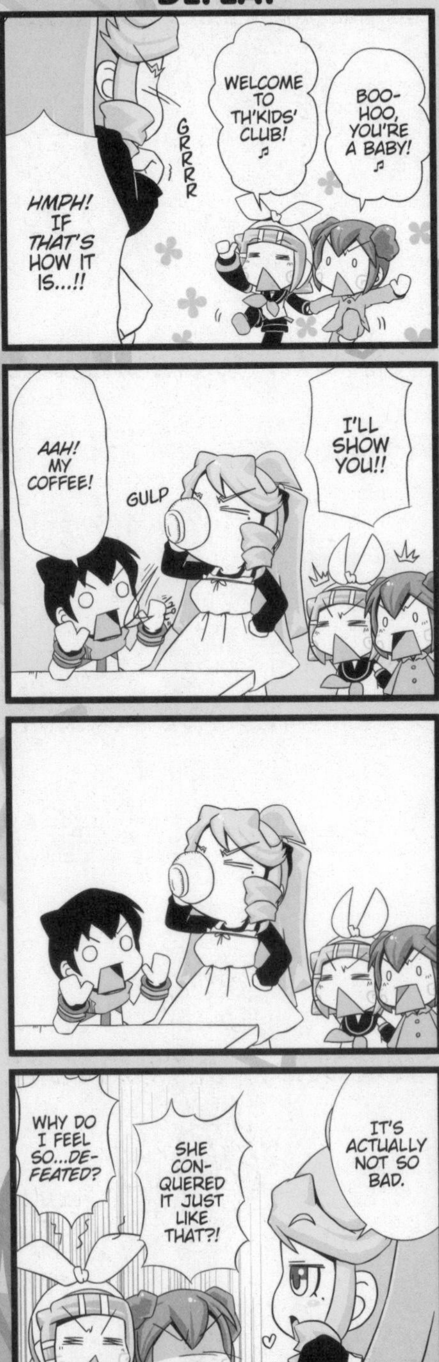
BOO-HOO, YOU'RE A BABY! ♪
WELCOME TO TH'KIDS' CLUB! ♪
GRRRR
HMPH! IF THAT'S HOW IT IS...!!
I'LL SHOW YOU!!
GULP
AAH! MY COFFEE!
IT'S ACTUALLY NOT SO BAD.
SHE CONQUERED IT JUST LIKE THAT?!
WHY DO I FEEL SO...DE-FEATED?

SURPRISE

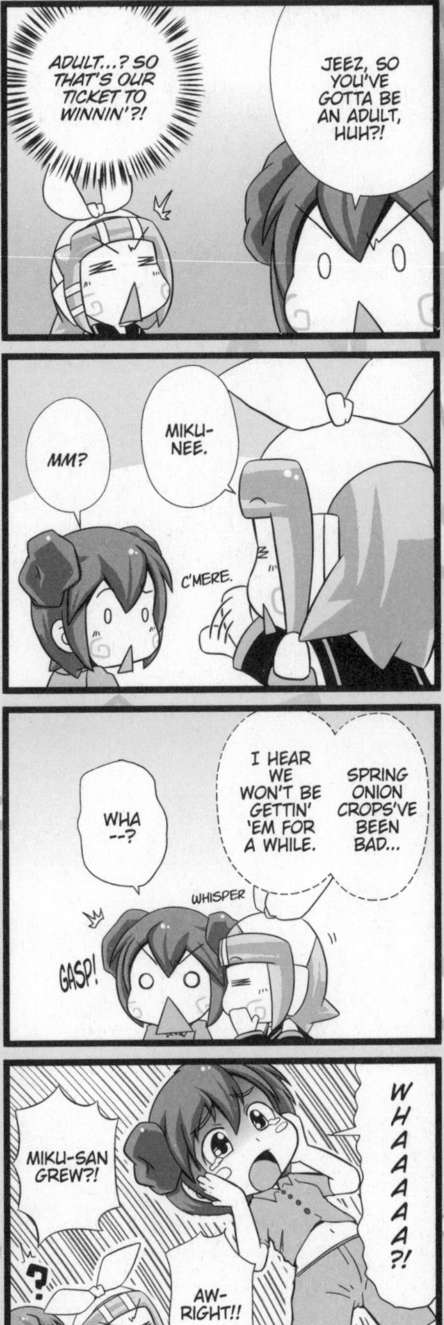
JEEZ, SO YOU'VE GOTTA BE AN ADULT, HUH?!
ADULT...? SO THAT'S OUR TICKET TO WINNIN'?!
MIKU-NEE.
MM?
C'MERE.
SPRING ONION CROPS'VE BEEN BAD...
I HEAR WE WON'T BE GETTIN' 'EM FOR A WHILE.
WHA--?
WHISPER
GASP!
WHAAAAAAA?!
MIKU-SAN GREW?!
AW-RIGHT!!

END RESULT

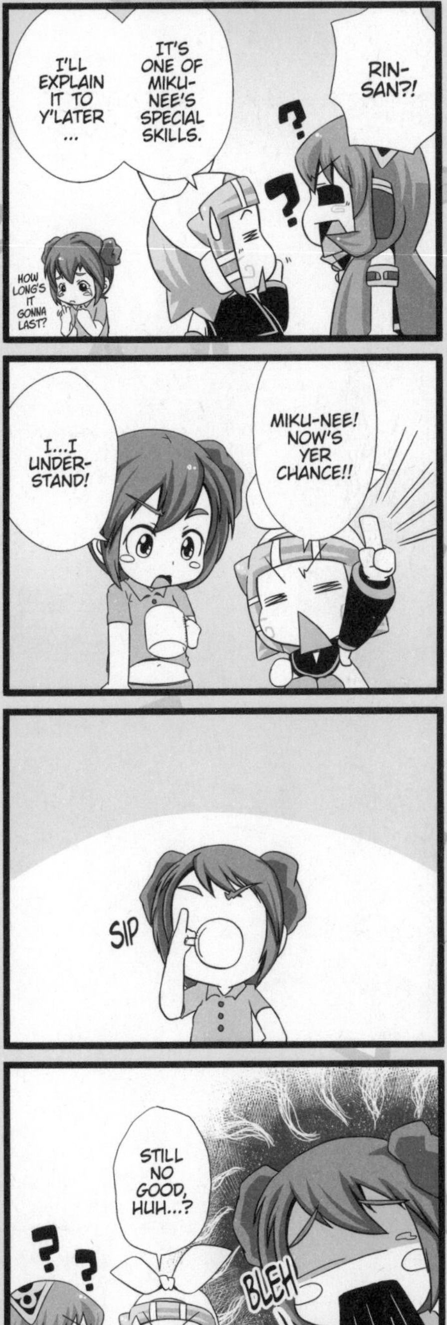
RIN-SAN?!
IT'S ONE OF MIKU-NEE'S SPECIAL SKILLS.
I'LL EXPLAIN IT TO Y'LATER...
HOW LONG'S IT GONNA LAST?
MIKU-NEE! NOW'S YER CHANCE!!
I...I UNDERSTAND!
SIP
BLEH
STILL NO GOOD, HUH...?

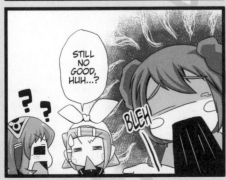

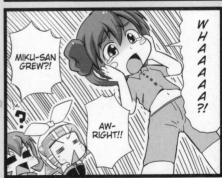

SPRING ONION 34:

HACHUNE MIKU'S BATH

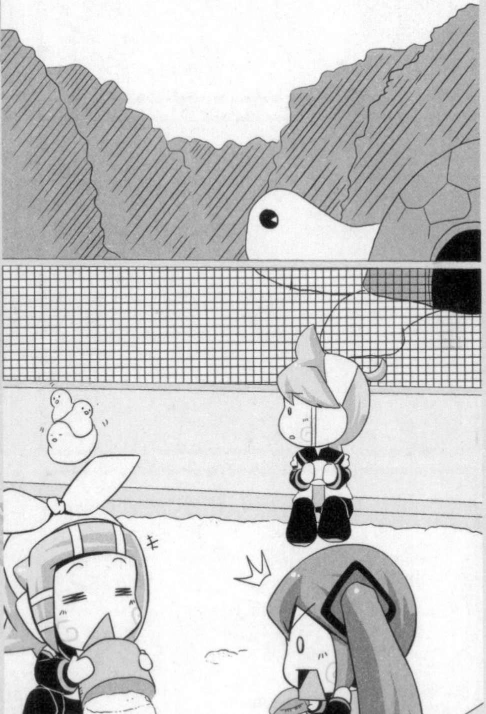

SEEING THINGS

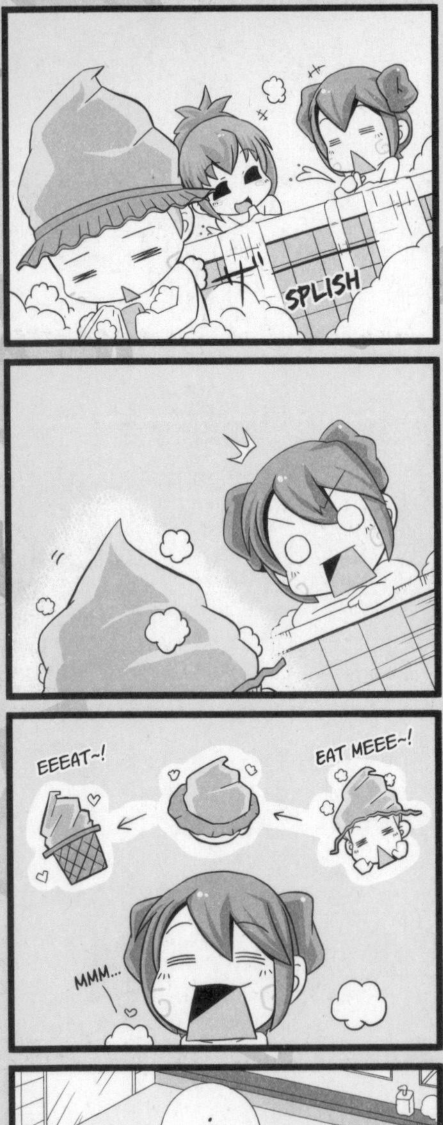
SPLISH
EAT MEEE~!
EEEAT~!
MMM...
......?
HEE HEE...

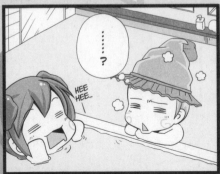

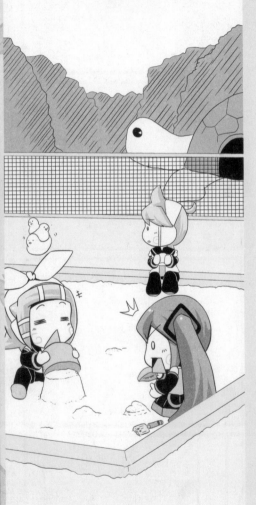

YOU, TOO?

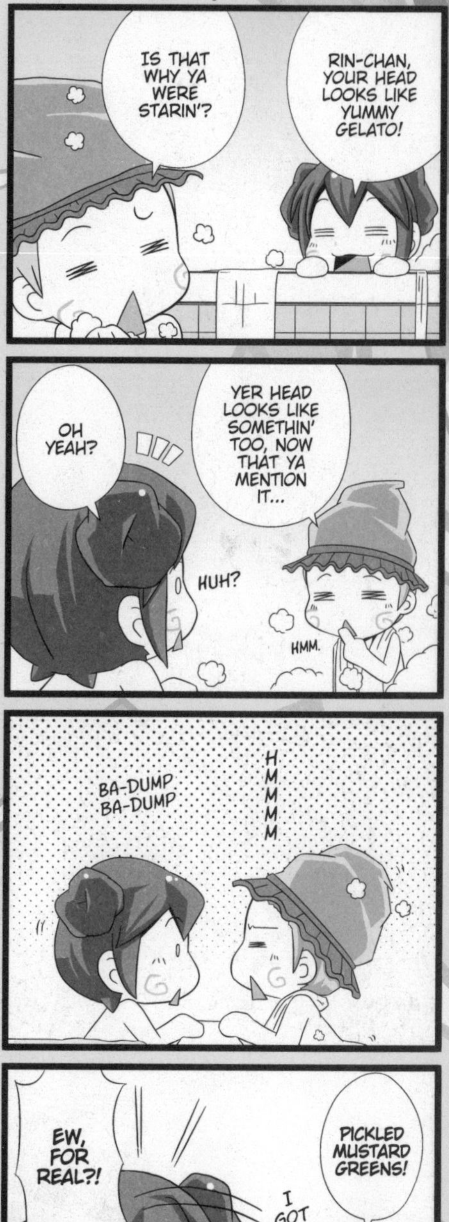
RIN-CHAN, YOUR HEAD LOOKS LIKE YUMMY GELATO!
IS THAT WHY YA WERE STARIN'?
YER HEAD LOOKS LIKE SOMETHIN' TOO, NOW THAT YA MENTION IT...
OH YEAH?
HUH?
HMM.
HMMMMM
BA-DUMP BA-DUMP
PICKLED MUSTARD GREENS!
I GOT IT!
EW, FOR REAL?!
HMPH!
RUDE!

CROSSFIRE

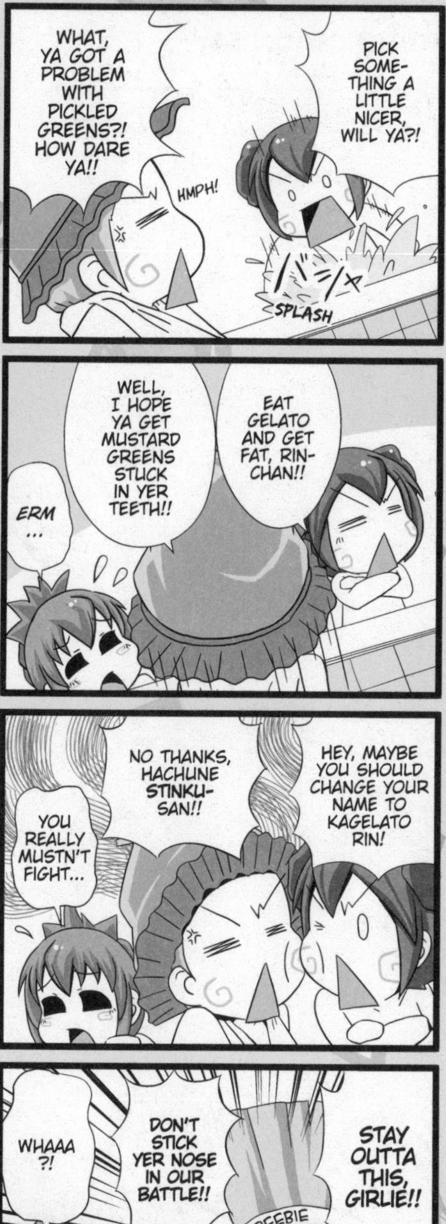
PICK SOME-THING A LITTLE NICER, WILL YA?!
WHAT, YA GOT A PROBLEM WITH PICKLED GREENS?! HOW DARE YA!!
HMPH!
SPLASH
EAT GELATO AND GET FAT, RIN-CHAN!!
WELL, I HOPE YA GET MUSTARD GREENS STUCK IN YER TEETH!!
ERM ...
HEY, MAYBE YOU SHOULD CHANGE YOUR NAME TO KAGELATO RIN!
NO THANKS, HACHUNE STINKU-SAN!!
YOU REALLY MUSTN'T FIGHT...
STAY OUTTA THIS, GIRLIE!!
DON'T STICK YER NOSE IN OUR BATTLE!!
FREEBIE
WHAAA?!
THIS HAT REPELS WATER!

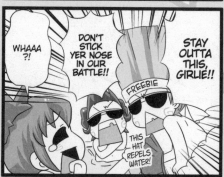

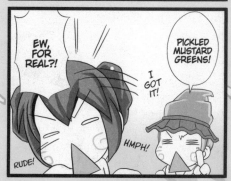

ESCALATION

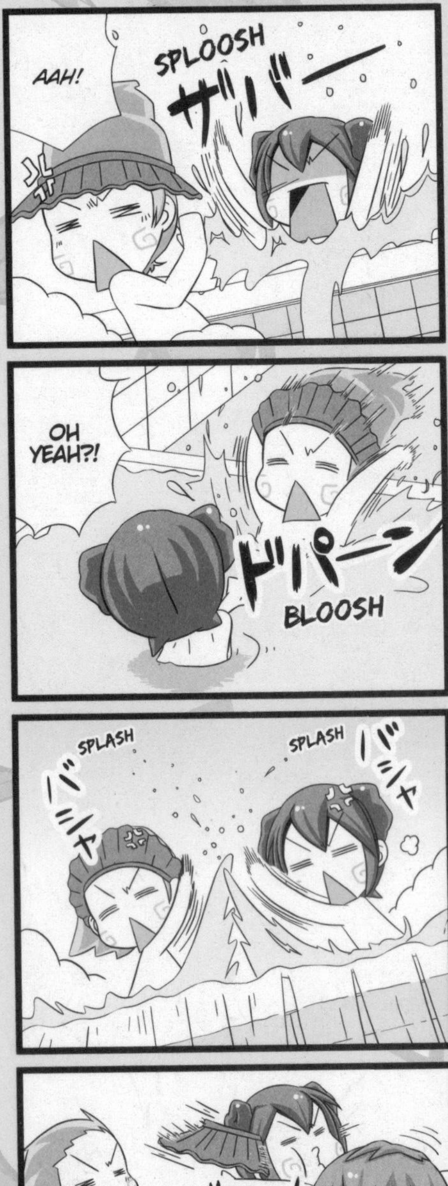

AAH!
SPLOOSH
ザバーー
OH YEAH?!
ドパーーン
BLOOSH
SPLASH
バシャ
SPLASH
バシャ
ベシッ!
THWACK
ブン!
WHIP

CESSATION

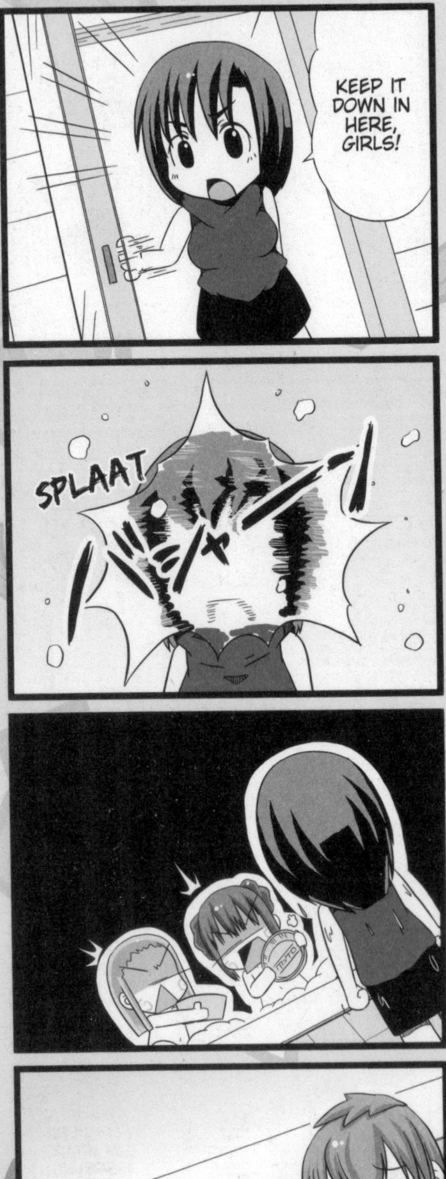

KEEP IT DOWN IN HERE, GIRLS!
SPLAAT
バシャ

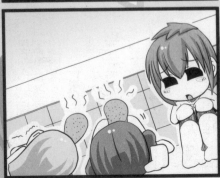

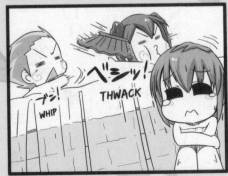

APOLOGY

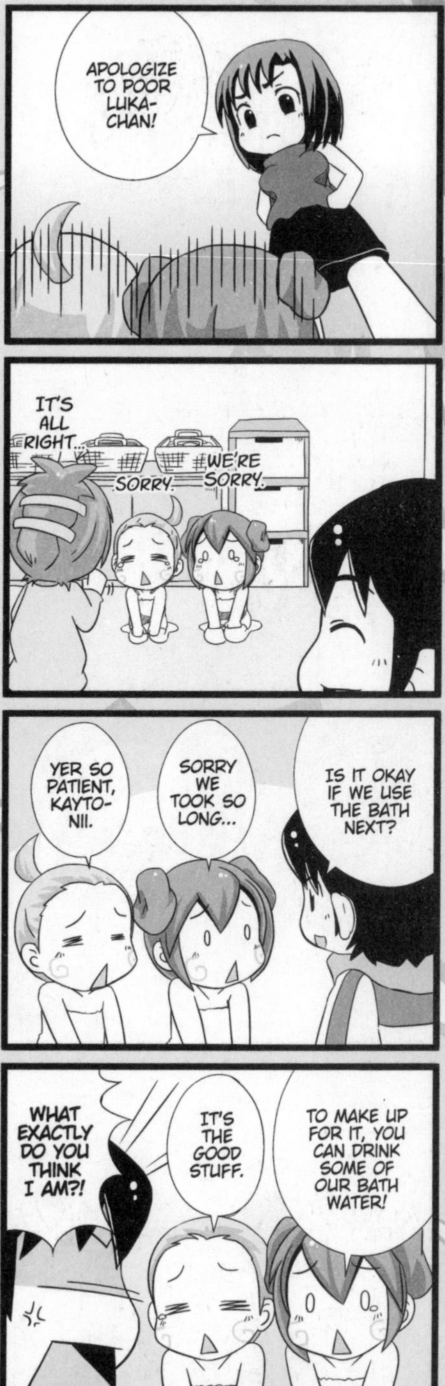
APOLOGIZE TO POOR LUKA-CHAN!
WE'RE SORRY.
SORRY.
IT'S ALL RIGHT...
IS IT OKAY IF WE USE THE BATH NEXT?
SORRY WE TOOK SO LONG...
YER SO PATIENT, KAYTO-NII.
TO MAKE UP FOR IT, YOU CAN DRINK SOME OF OUR BATH WATER!
IT'S THE GOOD STUFF.
WHAT EXACTLY DO YOU THINK I AM?!

SECRET

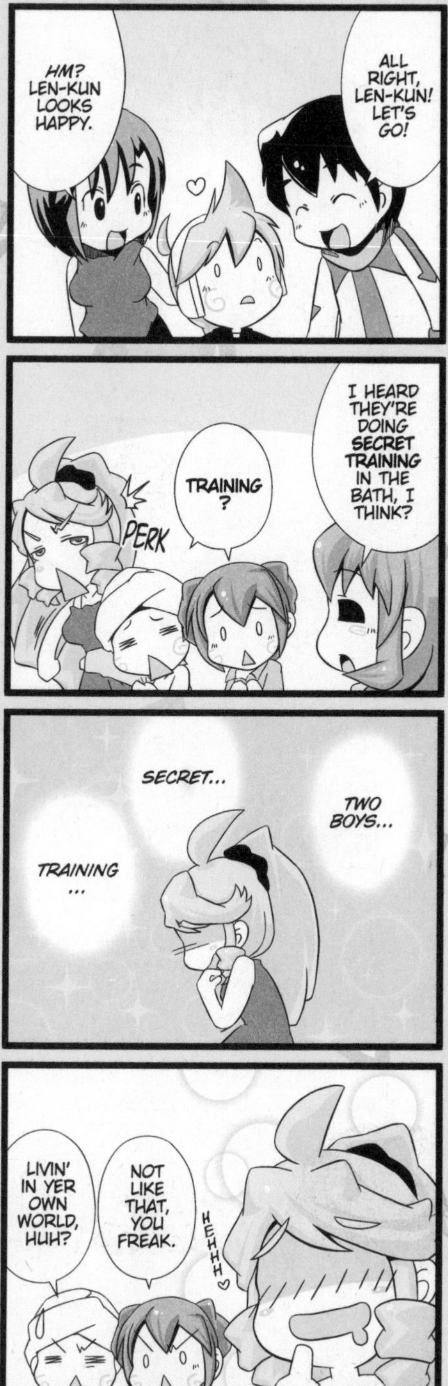
ALL RIGHT, LEN-KUN! LET'S GO!
HM? LEN-KUN LOOKS HAPPY.
I HEARD THEY'RE DOING SECRET TRAINING IN THE BATH, I THINK?
TRAINING?
PERK
TWO BOYS...
SECRET...
TRAINING...
HEHHHH
NOT LIKE THAT, YOU FREAK.
LIVIN' IN YER OWN WORLD, HUH?

TRAINING

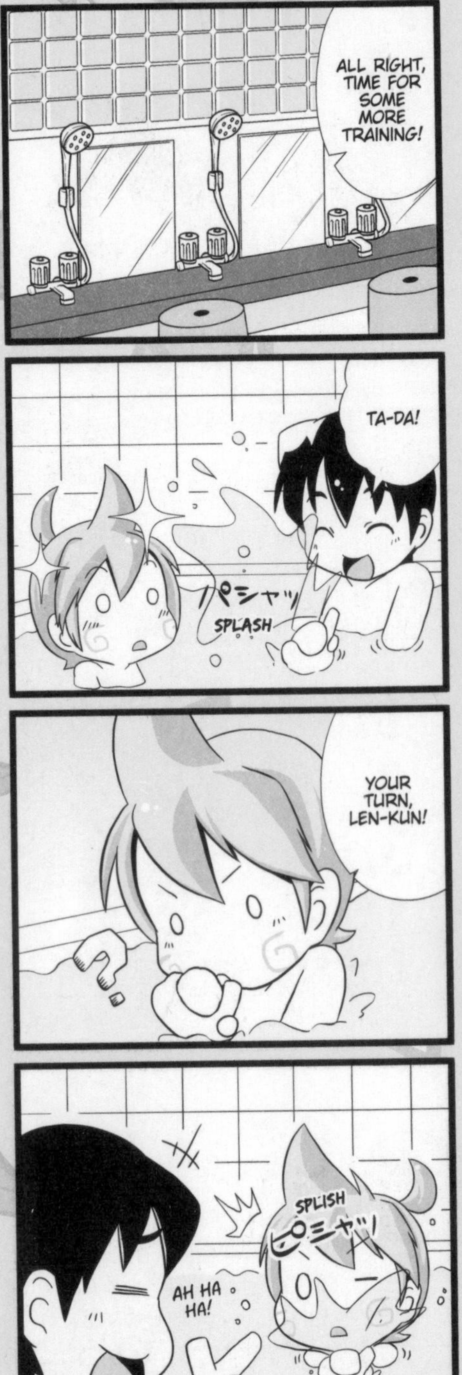
ALL RIGHT, TIME FOR SOME MORE TRAINING!
TA-DA!
パシャッ
SPLASH
YOUR TURN, LEN-KUN!
SPLISH
AH HA HA!

YOU DID IT!

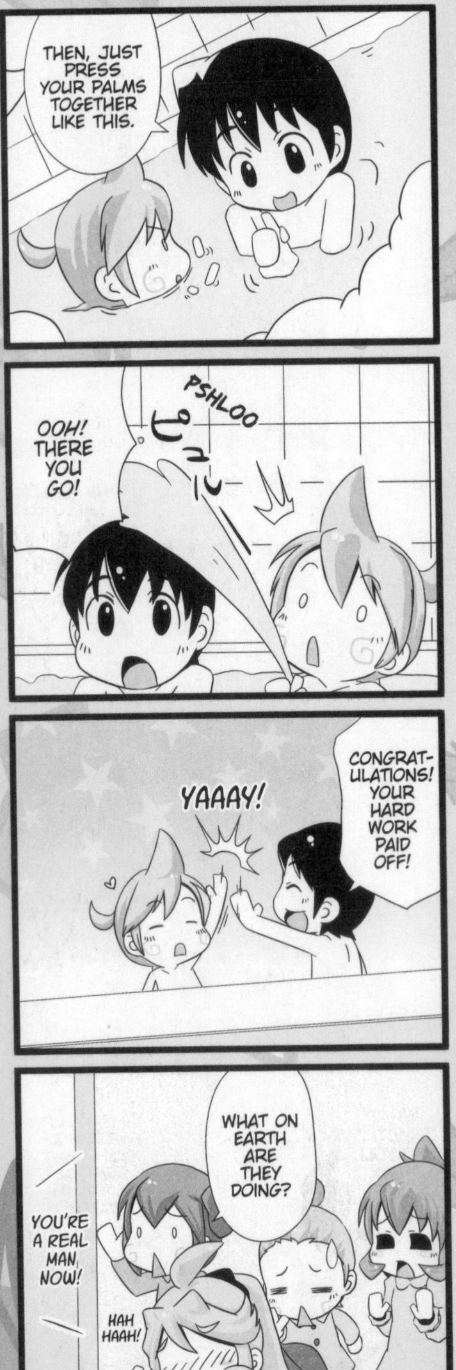
THEN, JUST PRESS YOUR PALMS TOGETHER LIKE THIS.
PSHLOO
OOH! THERE YOU GO!
CONGRAT-ULATIONS! YOUR HARD WORK PAID OFF!
YAAAY!
WHAT ON EARTH ARE THEY DOING?
YOU'RE A REAL MAN, NOW!
HAH HAAH!

WRONG

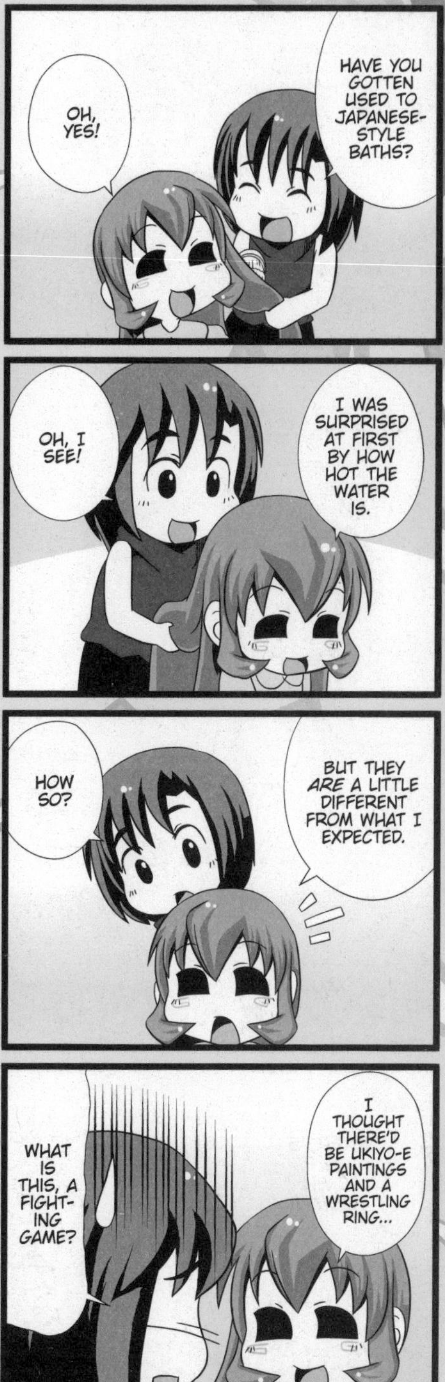
HAVE YOU GOTTEN USED TO JAPANESE-STYLE BATHS?
OH, YES!
I WAS SURPRISED AT FIRST BY HOW HOT THE WATER IS.
OH, I SEE!
BUT THEY *ARE* A LITTLE DIFFERENT FROM WHAT I EXPECTED.
HOW SO?
I THOUGHT THERE'D BE UKIYO-E PAINTINGS AND A WRESTLING RING...
WHAT IS THIS, A FIGHT-ING GAME?

MAYBE SOMEDAY

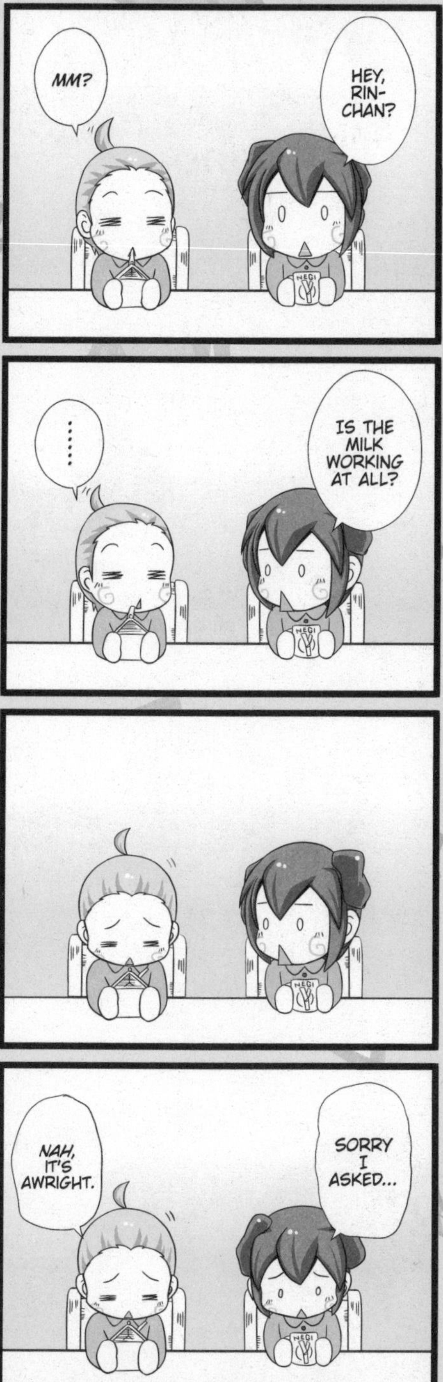
HEY, RIN-CHAN?
MM?
IS THE MILK WORKING AT ALL?
......
SORRY I ASKED...
NAH, IT'S AWRIGHT.

MOBILE VERSION LoiPara! BAND EDITION #3

WHAT INSTRUMENTS IS A BAND SUPPOSED TO HAVE, ANYWAY?
LEMME SEE..
YER BASIC BAND'S GOTTA BE A THREE PIECE, RIGHT?
THREE PIECE?
Y'KNOW, GUITAR, BASS, AND DRUMS.
I SUPPOSE MANY ROCK BANDS ARE LIKE THAT.
RIN-CHAN SHOULD PLAY DRUMS, THEN.
I AGREE!
WHY'RE YA DECIDIN' THAT NOW?!
AAAAH!
SHOCK
BAM
AND IF THIS WAS BASEBALL, SHE'D BE CATCHER.
I AGREE!
WHERE'S THAT COMIN' FROM?!
WHAT'S THAT S'POSED TO MEAN?!

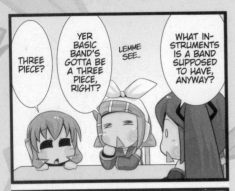

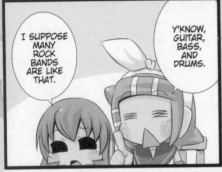

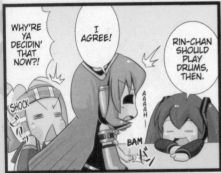

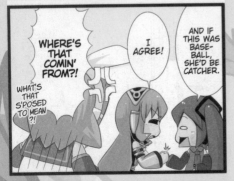

MOBILE VERSION

LoiPara! BAND EDITION #4

SHE'S JUST THE MOST GROUNDED, Y'KNOW?
YES, A PERCUSSIONIST MUST BE RELIABLE!
YA... Y'THINK?
A CATCHER'S THE SAME WAY.
Y-YER MAKIN' ME BLUSH ...
YOU'RE THE CONTROL TOWER, THE PLAYMAKER!
AAAH!
KICK KICK
バタバタ
OKAY, Y'GOT ME! I'LL BE THE DRUMMER!
YAY! NOW OUR RHYTHM'LL BE PERFECT!
WE'RE COUNTING ON YOU!
AND IT'S NOT 'CAUSE YOU'RE FAT OR ANYTHING!
SO DON'T WORRY ABOUT THAT.
DAMMIT!!
SHUT YER TRAPS ALREADY!!

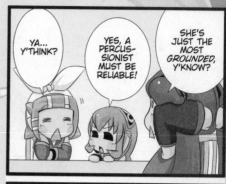

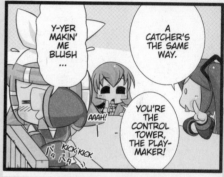

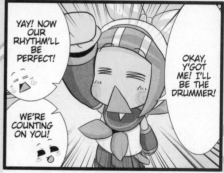

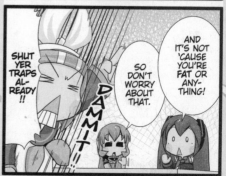

SPRING ONION 35

HACHUNE MIKU'S MOBILE SIDE A

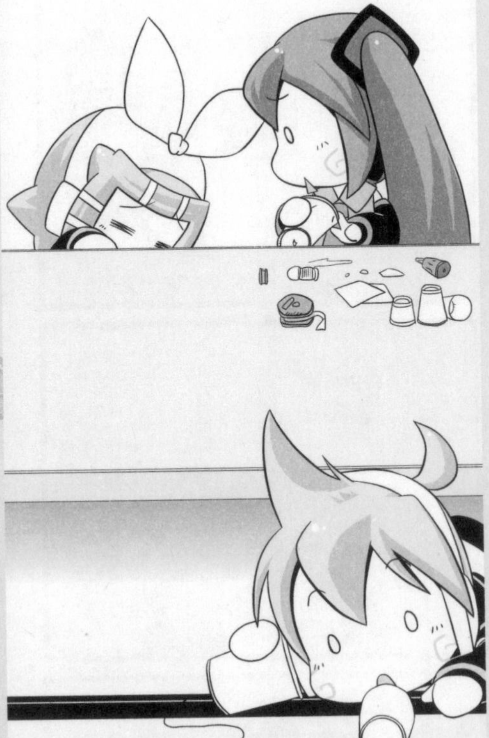

NO THANK YOU

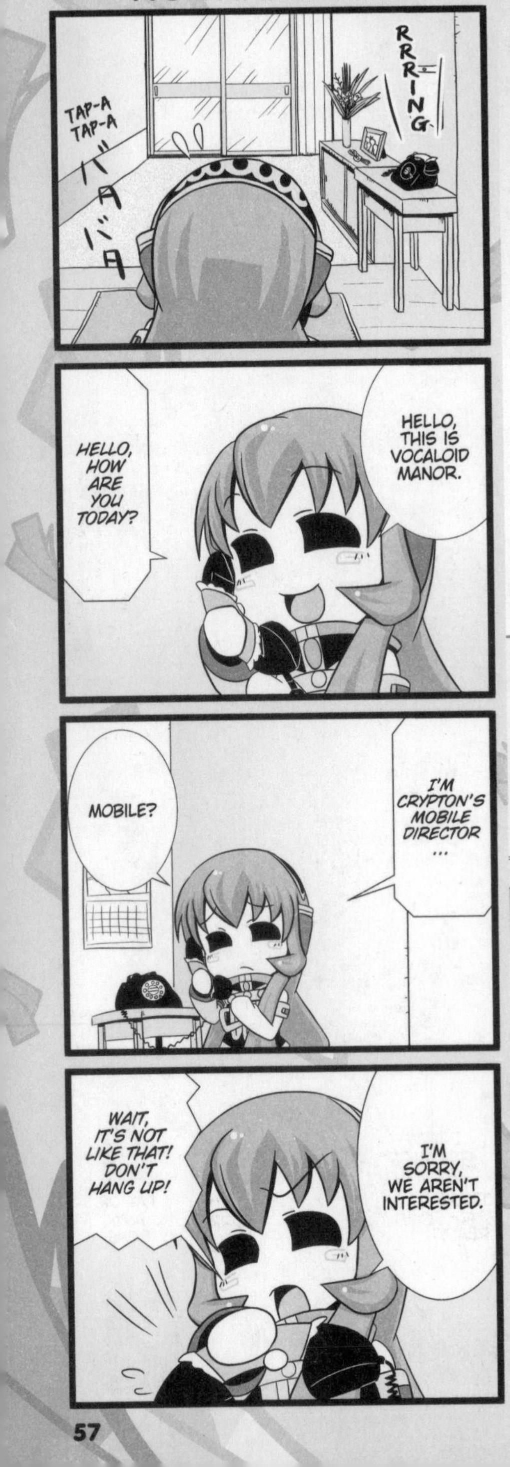
RRRING
TAP-A TAP-A
HELLO, THIS IS VOCALOID MANOR.
HELLO, HOW ARE YOU TODAY?
I'M CRYPTON'S MOBILE DIRECTOR ...
MOBILE?
I'M SORRY, WE AREN'T INTERESTED.
WAIT, IT'S NOT LIKE THAT! DON'T HANG UP!

WASSHOI

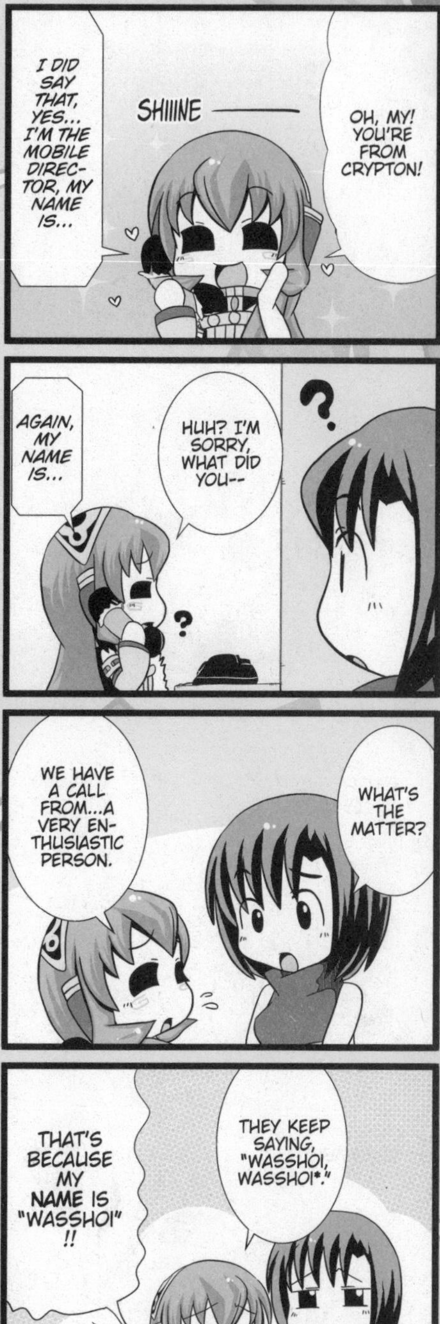
OH, MY! YOU'RE FROM CRYPTON!
SHIIINE ——
I DID SAY THAT, YES... I'M THE MOBILE DIREC-TOR, MY NAME IS...
HUH? I'M SORRY, WHAT DID YOU--
AGAIN, MY NAME IS...
WHAT'S THE MATTER?
WE HAVE A CALL FROM...A VERY EN-THUSIASTIC PERSON.
THEY KEEP SAYING, "WASSHOI, WASSHOI*."
THAT'S BECAUSE MY NAME IS "WASSHOI" !!
HUH?

FILTERING

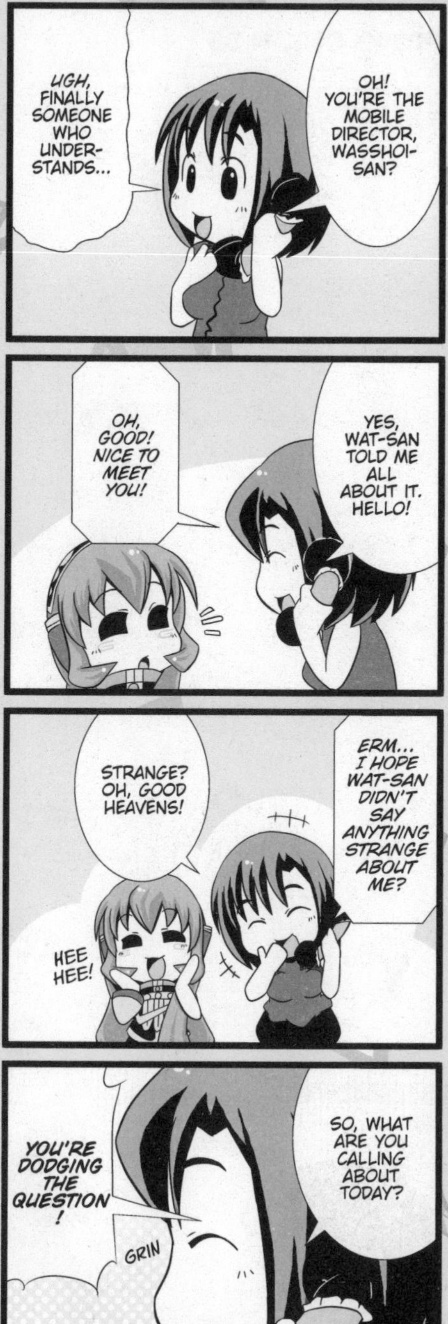
OH! YOU'RE THE MOBILE DIRECTOR, WASSHOI-SAN?
UGH, FINALLY SOMEONE WHO UNDER-STANDS...
YES, WAT-SAN TOLD ME ALL ABOUT IT. HELLO!
OH, GOOD! NICE TO MEET YOU!
ERM... I HOPE WAT-SAN DIDN'T SAY ANYTHING STRANGE ABOUT ME?
STRANGE? OH, GOOD HEAVENS!
HEE HEE!
SO, WHAT ARE YOU CALLING ABOUT TODAY?
YOU'RE DODGING THE QUESTION!
GRIN

*A cheer or chant used at festivals in Japan.

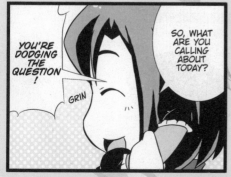

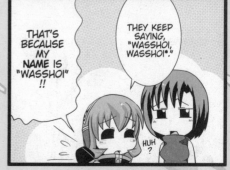

DISPARITY

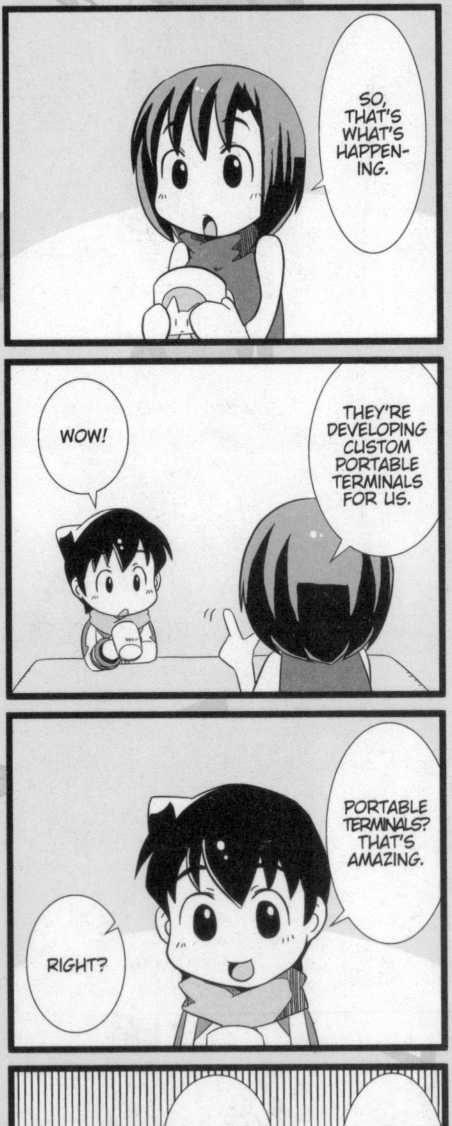

SO, THAT'S WHAT'S HAPPEN-ING.
THEY'RE DEVELOPING CUSTOM PORTABLE TERMINALS FOR US.
WOW!
PORTABLE TERMINALS? THAT'S AMAZING.
RIGHT?
I MEAN, WE'RE STILL USING A ROTARY PHONE!
RIGHT?
JEEZ.

INTELLIGENCE AGENT

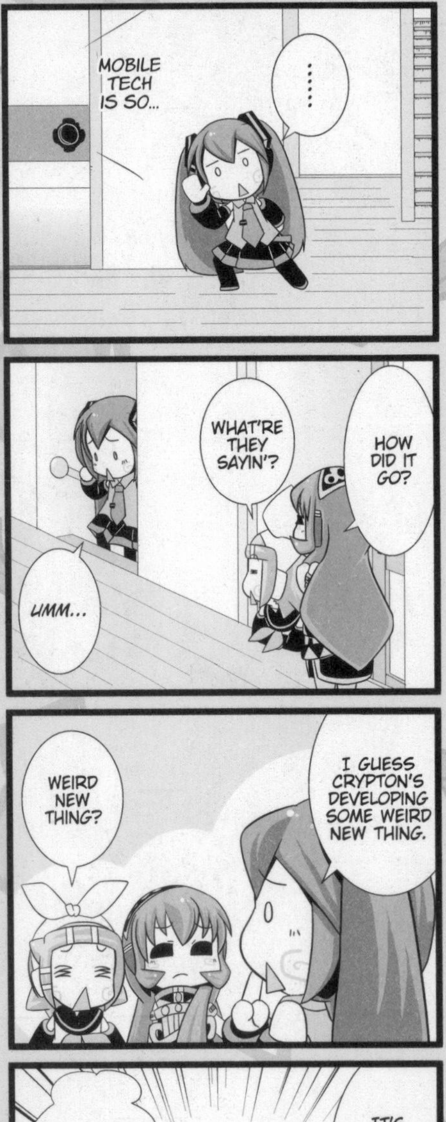

......
MOBILE TECH IS SO...
HOW DID IT GO?
WHAT'RE THEY SAYIN'?
UMM...
I GUESS CRYPTON'S DEVELOPING SOME WEIRD NEW THING.
WEIRD NEW THING?
IT'S CALLED A "POR-TABLE TORCH-ABLE."
TORCHABLE ?!

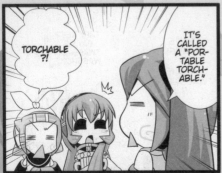

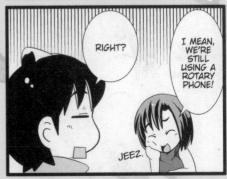

IMAGINATION

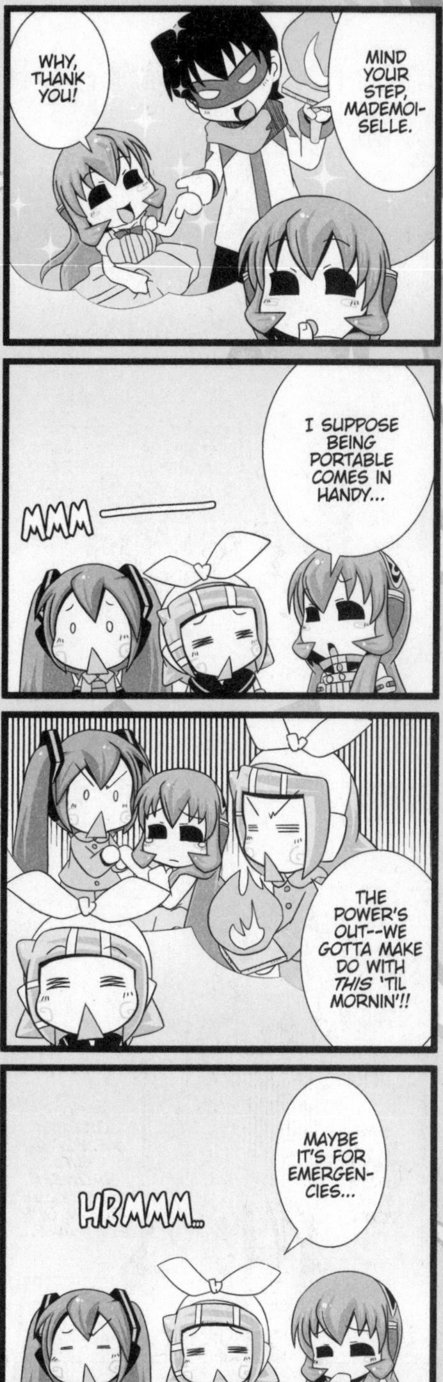
MIND YOUR STEP, MADEMOI-SELLE.
WHY, THANK YOU!
I SUPPOSE BEING PORTABLE COMES IN HANDY...
MMM
THE POWER'S OUT--WE GOTTA MAKE DO WITH *THIS* 'TIL MORNIN'!!
MAYBE IT'S FOR EMERGEN-CIES...
HRMMM...

CRISIS

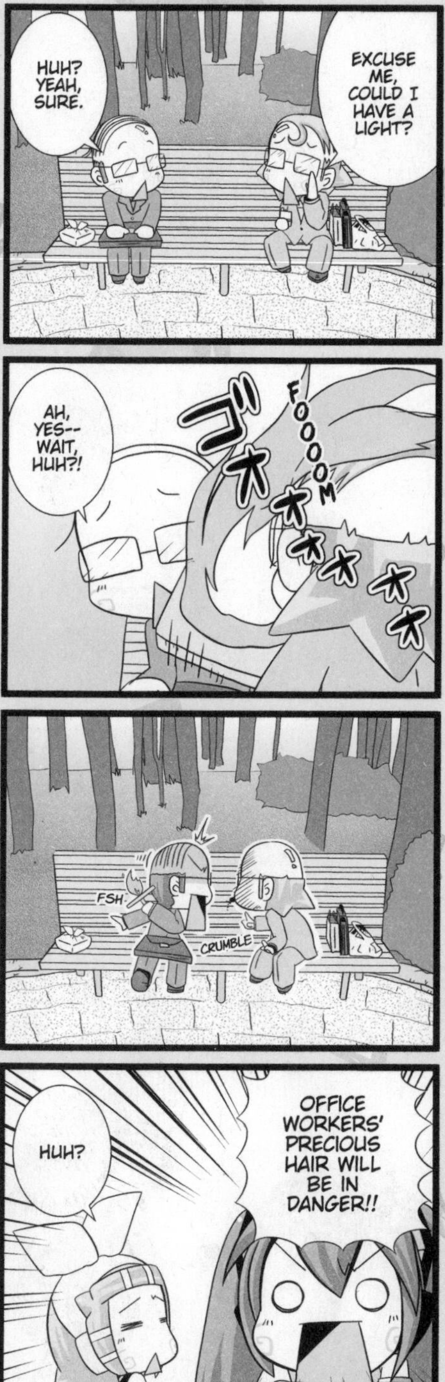
EXCUSE ME, COULD I HAVE A LIGHT?
HUH? YEAH, SURE.
FOOOOOM
ゴオォォォォォ
AH, YES--WAIT, HUH?!
FSH
CRUMBLE
OFFICE WORKERS' PRECIOUS HAIR WILL BE IN DANGER!!
HUH?

KEY POINT

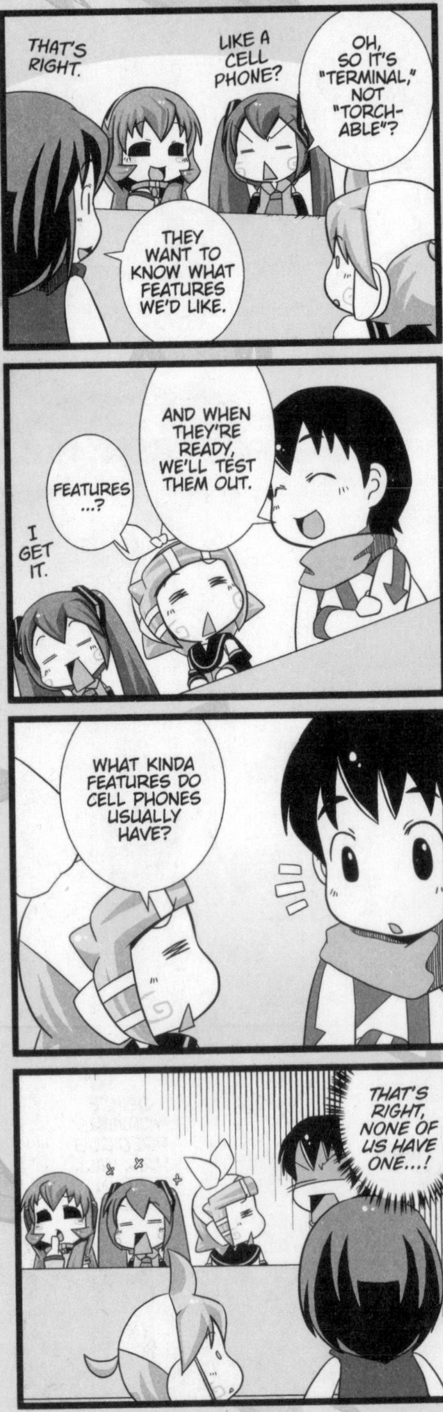
OH, SO IT'S "TERMINAL," NOT "TORCH-ABLE"?
LIKE A CELL PHONE?
THAT'S RIGHT.
THEY WANT TO KNOW WHAT FEATURES WE'D LIKE.
AND WHEN THEY'RE READY, WE'LL TEST THEM OUT.
FEATURES ...?
I GET IT.
WHAT KINDA FEATURES DO CELL PHONES USUALLY HAVE?
THAT'S RIGHT, NONE OF US HAVE ONE...!

SPEAKING IN TONGUES?

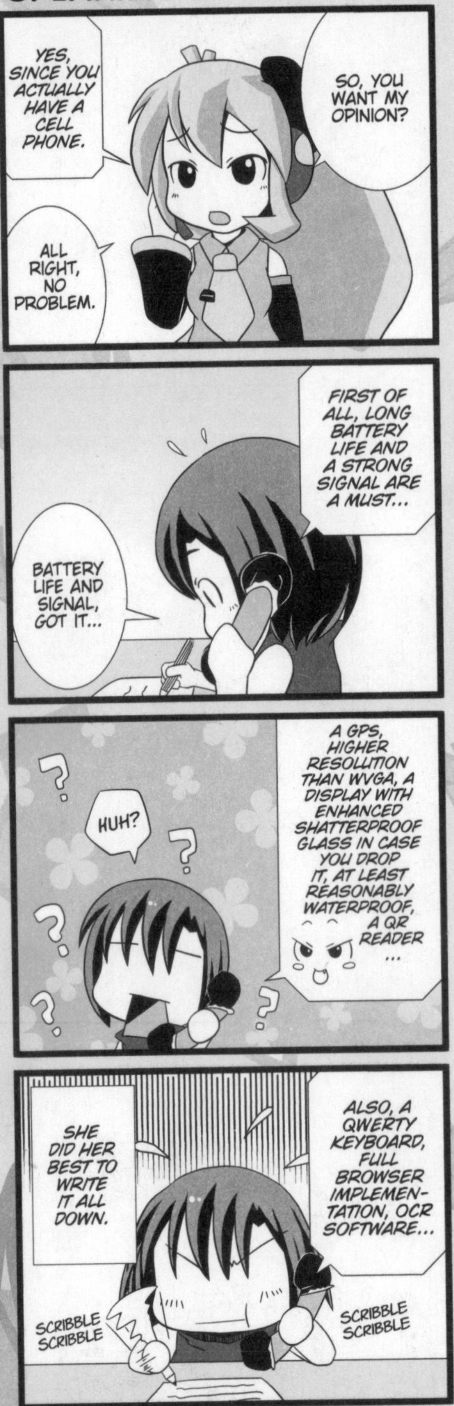
SO, YOU WANT MY OPINION?
YES, SINCE YOU ACTUALLY HAVE A CELL PHONE.
ALL RIGHT, NO PROBLEM.
FIRST OF ALL, LONG BATTERY LIFE AND A STRONG SIGNAL ARE A MUST...
BATTERY LIFE AND SIGNAL, GOT IT...
A GPS, HIGHER RESOLUTION THAN WVGA, A DISPLAY WITH ENHANCED SHATTERPROOF GLASS IN CASE YOU DROP IT, AT LEAST REASONABLY WATERPROOF, A QR READER ...
HUH?
ALSO, A QWERTY KEYBOARD, FULL BROWSER IMPLEMENTATION, OCR SOFTWARE...
SCRIBBLE SCRIBBLE
SHE DID HER BEST TO WRITE IT ALL DOWN.
SCRIBBLE SCRIBBLE

LEAK

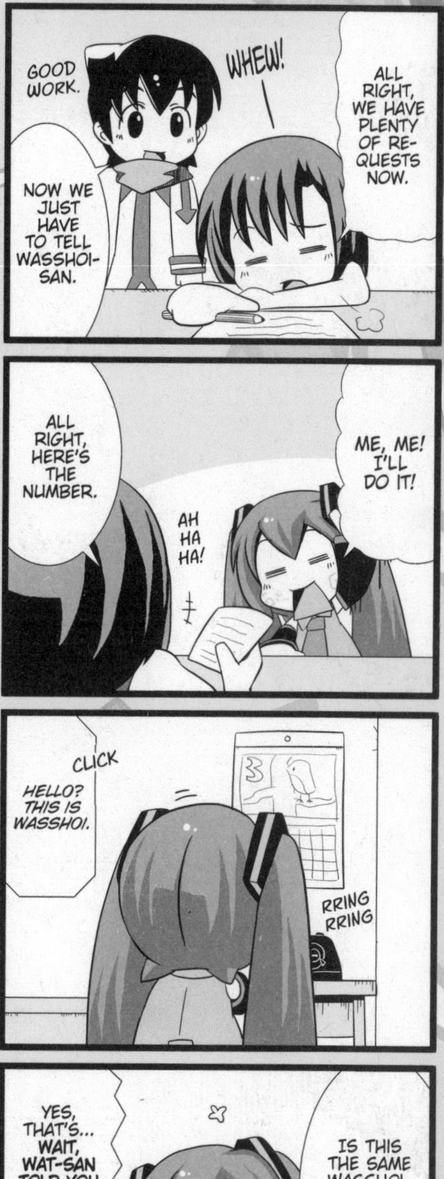
ALL RIGHT, WE HAVE PLENTY OF RE-QUESTS NOW.
WHEW!
GOOD WORK.
NOW WE JUST HAVE TO TELL WASSHOI-SAN.
ME, ME! I'LL DO IT!
AH HA HA!
ALL RIGHT, HERE'S THE NUMBER.
RRING RRING
CLICK
HELLO? THIS IS WASSHOI.
IS THIS THE SAME WASSHOI-SAN WHO LOVES FATTENING FOOD?
YES, THAT'S... WAIT, WAT-SAN TOLD YOU THAT, DIDN'T HE?!

GRIN

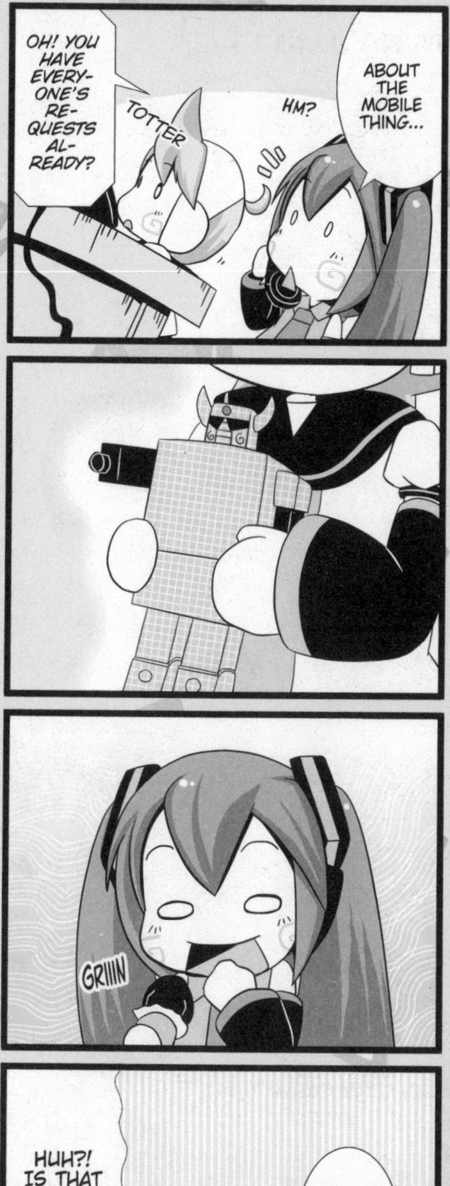
ABOUT THE MOBILE THING...
HM?
TOTTER
OH! YOU HAVE EVERY-ONE'S RE-QUESTS AL-READY?
GRIIIN
HERE'S THE DEAL...
MUMBLE MUMBLE...
HUH?! IS THAT REALLY WHAT YOU ALL WANT...?

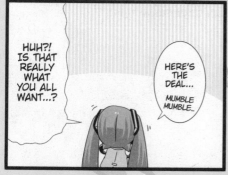

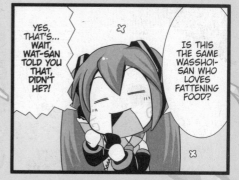

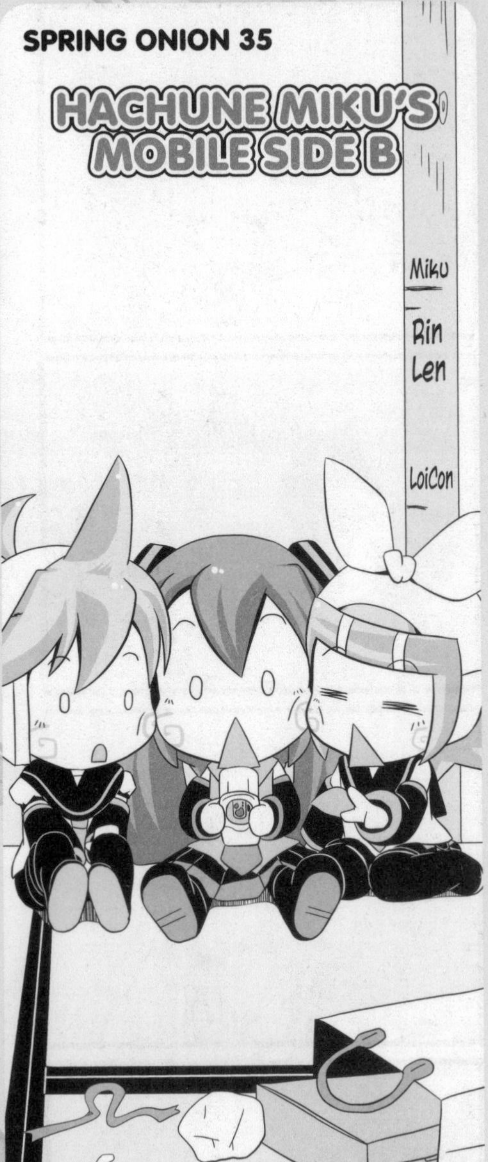
SPRING ONION 35
HACHUNE MIKU'S MOBILE SIDE B
Miku
Rin
Len
LoiCon

COMPLETE

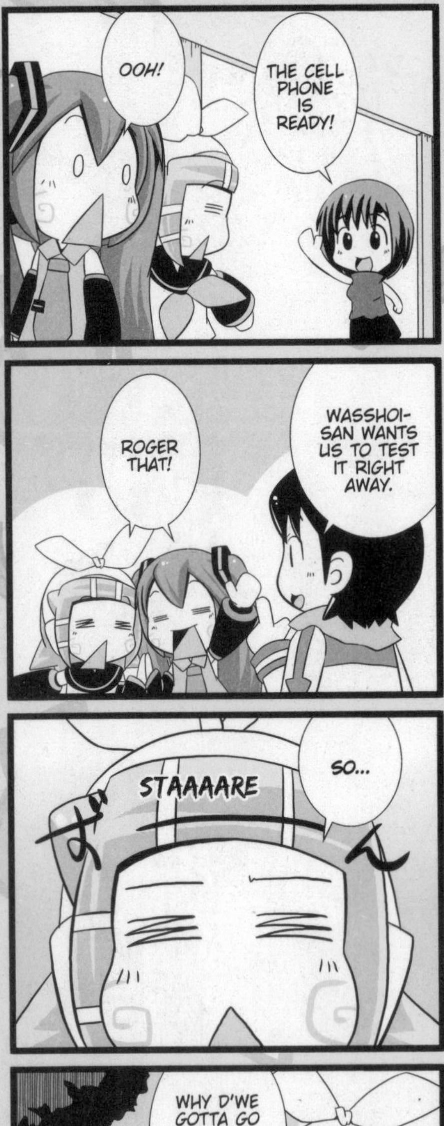
THE CELL PHONE IS READY!
OOH!
WASSHOI-SAN WANTS US TO TEST IT RIGHT AWAY.
ROGER THAT!
SO...
STAAAARE
WHY D'WE GOTTA GO ALL THE WAY TO THE PARK?
I'M NOT SURE ...
YAY!

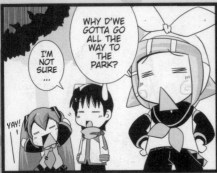

MYSTERY

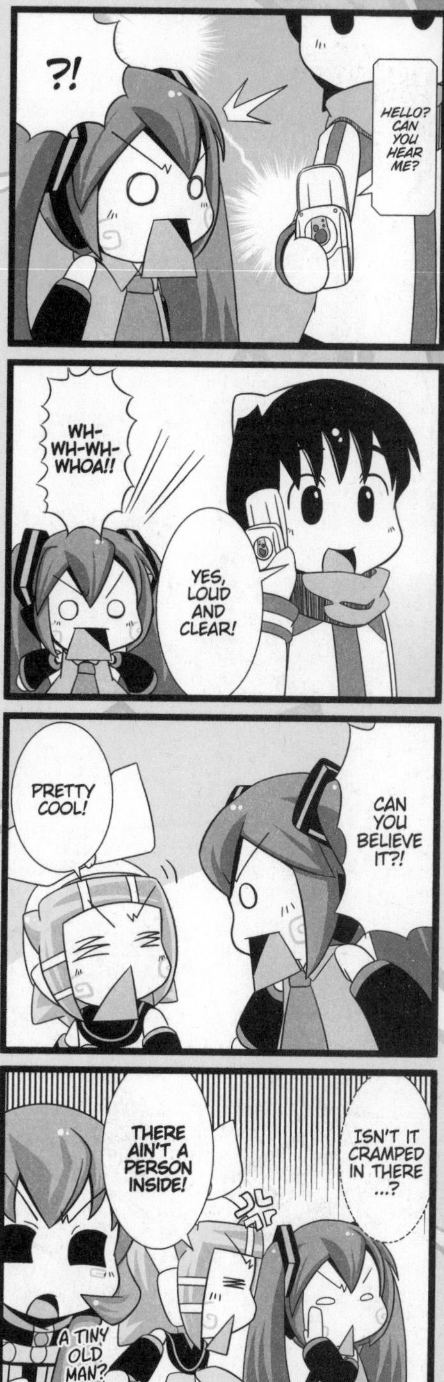
?!
HELLO? CAN YOU HEAR ME?
WH-WH-WH-WHOA!!
YES, LOUD AND CLEAR!
CAN YOU BELIEVE IT?!
PRETTY COOL!
ISN'T IT CRAMPED IN THERE ...?
THERE AIN'T A PERSON INSIDE!
A TINY OLD MAN?

FIRST TIME

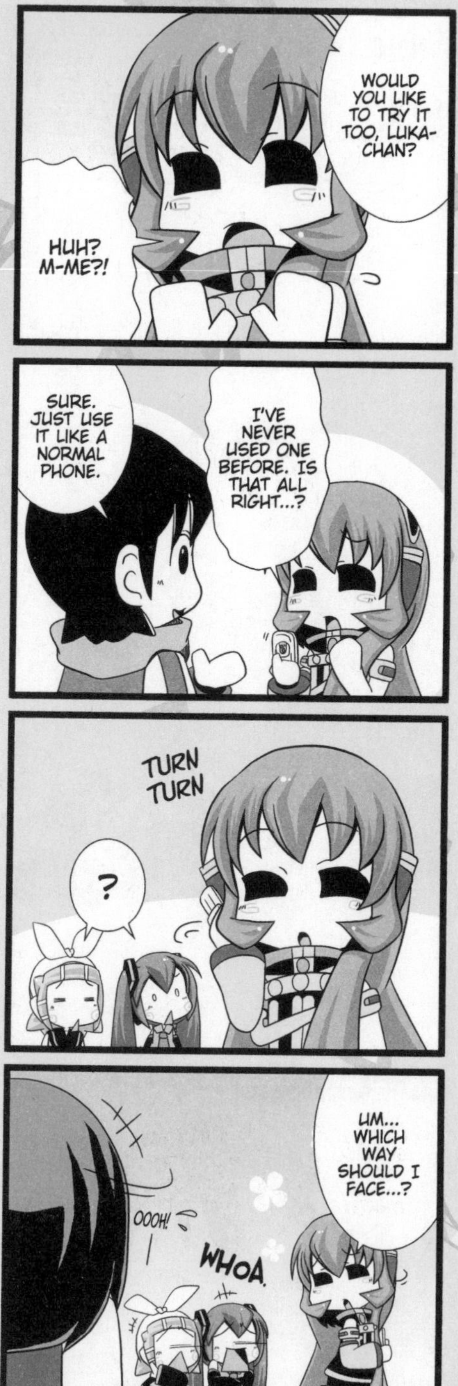
WOULD YOU LIKE TO TRY IT TOO, LUKA-CHAN?
HUH? M-ME?!
I'VE NEVER USED ONE BEFORE. IS THAT ALL RIGHT...?
SURE. JUST USE IT LIKE A NORMAL PHONE.
TURN TURN
?
UM... WHICH WAY SHOULD I FACE...?
WHOA
OOOH!

FLYING

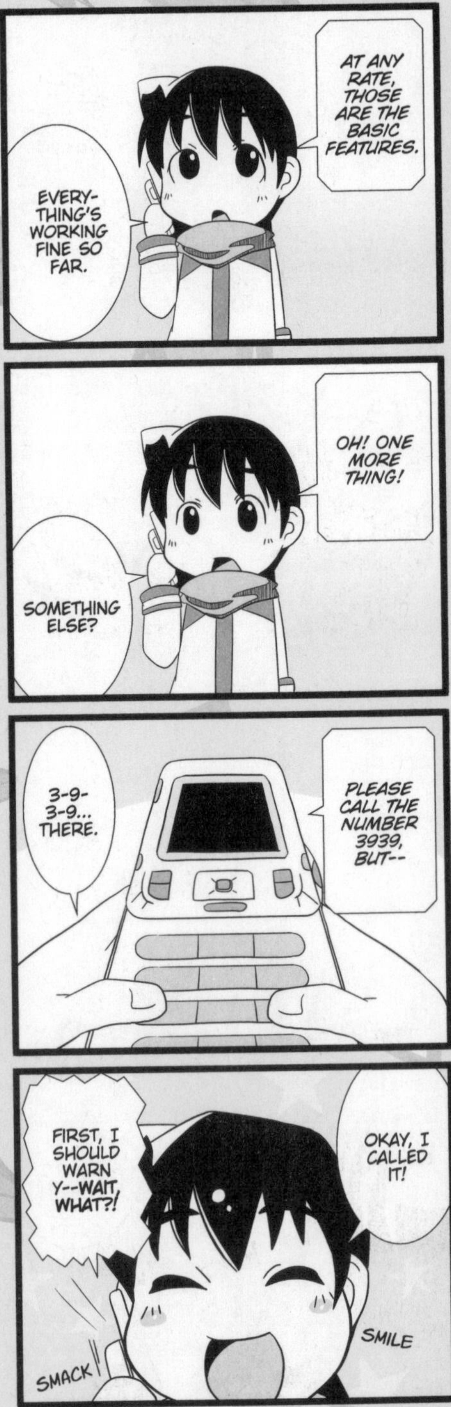
AT ANY RATE, THOSE ARE THE BASIC FEATURES.
EVERY-THING'S WORKING FINE SO FAR.
OH! ONE MORE THING!
SOMETHING ELSE?
PLEASE CALL THE NUMBER 3939, BUT--
3-9-3-9... THERE.
OKAY, I CALLED IT!
FIRST, I SHOULD WARN Y--WAIT, WHAT?!
SMILE
SMACK

SPLASHDOWN

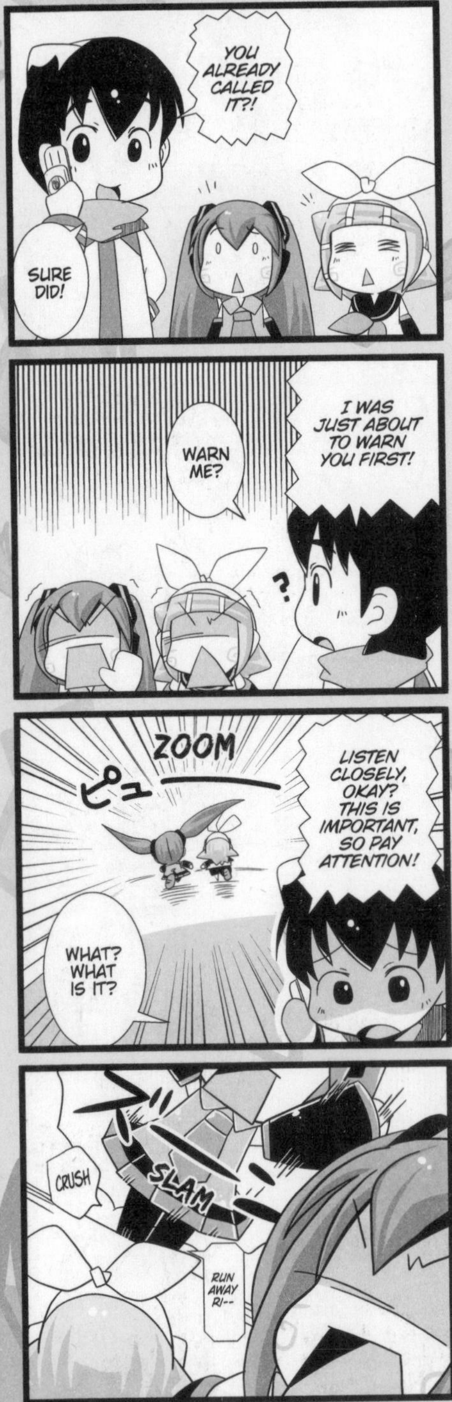
YOU ALREADY CALLED IT?!
SURE DID!
I WAS JUST ABOUT TO WARN YOU FIRST!
WARN ME?
?
LISTEN CLOSELY, OKAY? THIS IS IMPORTANT, SO PAY ATTENTION!
ZOOM
ピュ
WHAT? WHAT IS IT?
SLAM
CRUSH
RUN AWAY RI--

REQUESTS

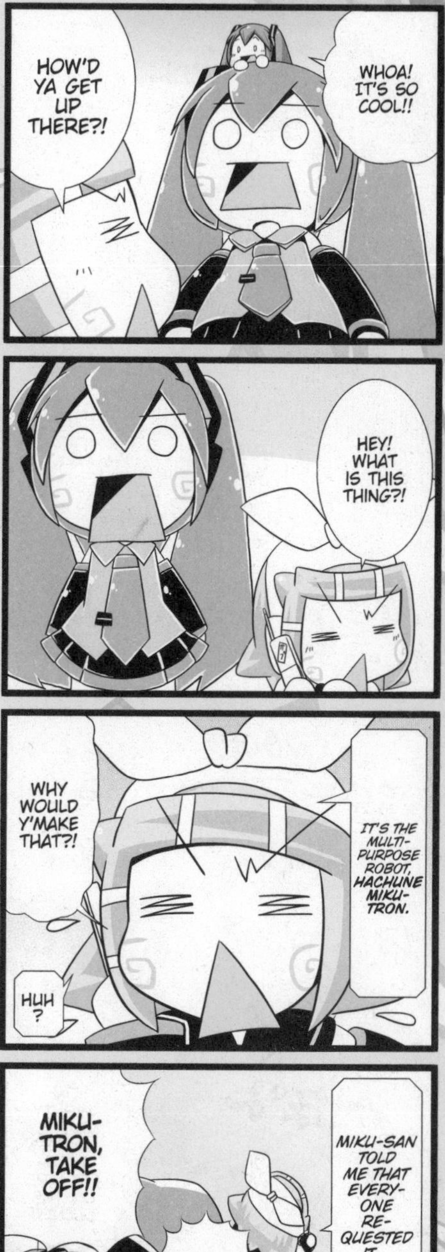
WHOA! IT'S SO COOL!!
HOW'D YA GET UP THERE?!
HEY! WHAT IS THIS THING?!
IT'S THE MULTI-PURPOSE ROBOT, HACHUNE MIKU-TRON.
WHY WOULD Y'MAKE THAT?!
HUH ?
MIKU-SAN TOLD ME THAT EVERY-ONE RE-QUESTED IT...
MIKU-TRON, TAKE OFF!!
SHE FOOLED YA BIG TIME!!

BEAST MODE

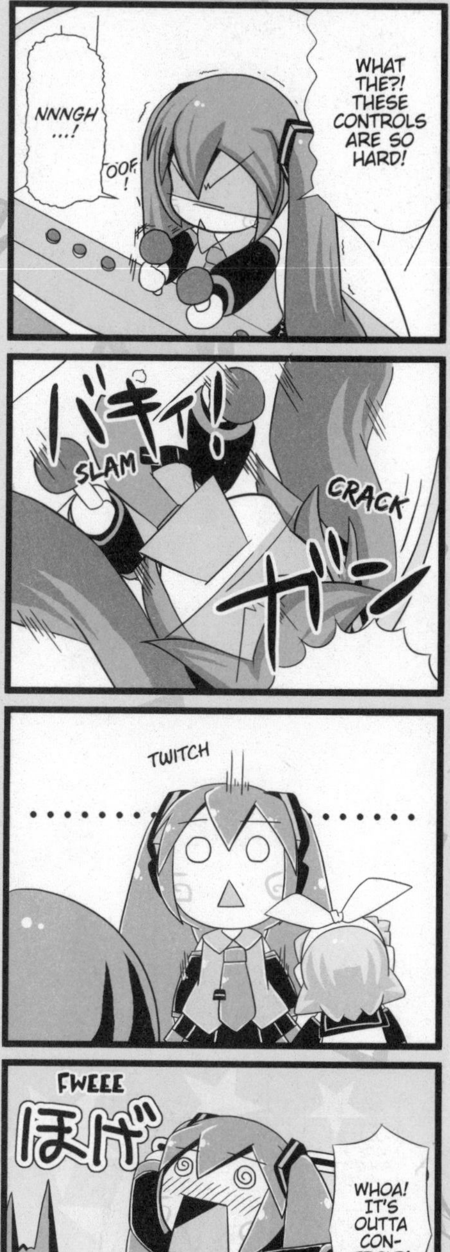
WHAT THE?! THESE CONTROLS ARE SO HARD!
NNNGH ...!
OOF !
バキィ!!
SLAM
CRACK
ガー
TWITCH
WHOA! IT'S OUTTA CON-TROL?!
FWEEE
ほげ

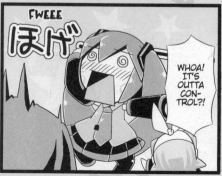

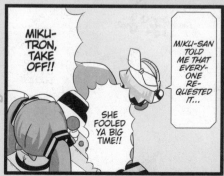

CHAOS

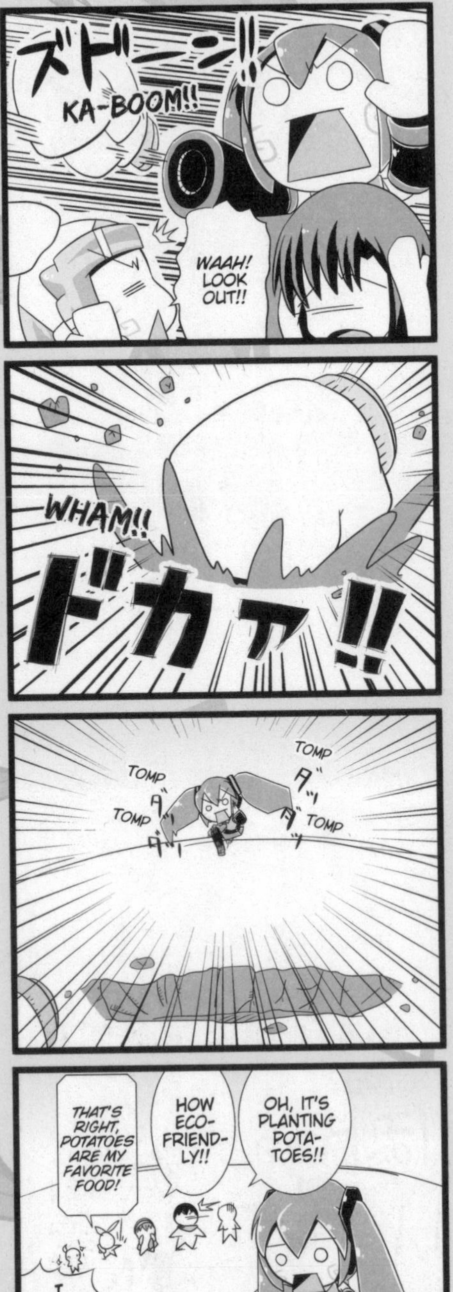
ズドーーン!!
KA-BOOM!!
WAAH! LOOK OUT!!
WHAM!!
ドカァ!!
TOMP ダッ
TOMP ダッ
TOMP ダッ
TOMP ダッ
OH, IT'S PLANTING POTA-TOES!!
HOW ECO-FRIEND-LY!!
THAT'S RIGHT, POTATOES ARE MY FAVORITE FOOD!
I DUNNO WHAT T'MAKE FUN OF FIRST!

PROMPT ARRIVAL

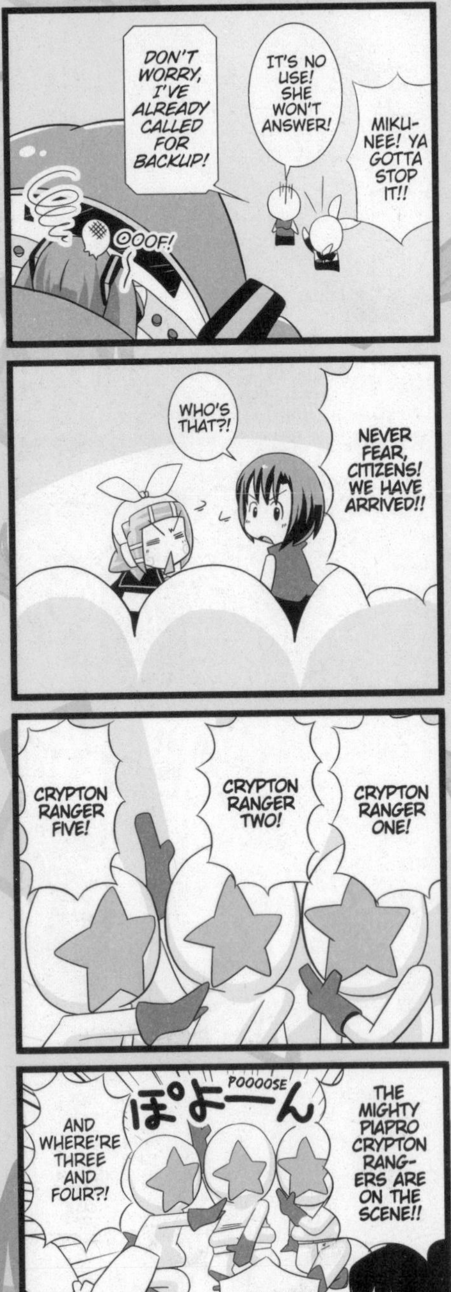
MIKU-NEE! YA GOTTA STOP IT!!
IT'S NO USE! SHE WON'T ANSWER!
DON'T WORRY, I'VE ALREADY CALLED FOR BACKUP!
OOOF!
NEVER FEAR, CITIZENS! WE HAVE ARRIVED!!
WHO'S THAT?!
CRYPTON RANGER ONE!
CRYPTON RANGER TWO!
CRYPTON RANGER FIVE!
THE MIGHTY PIAPRO CRYPTON RANG-ERS ARE ON THE SCENE!!
ぽよーん
POOOOSE
AND WHERE'RE THREE AND FOUR?!
WHY ARE YOU IN SUCH BAD SHAPE?!

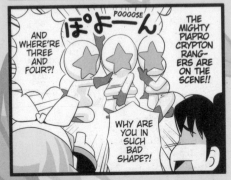

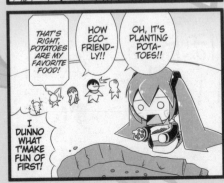

JUSTICE PREVAILS

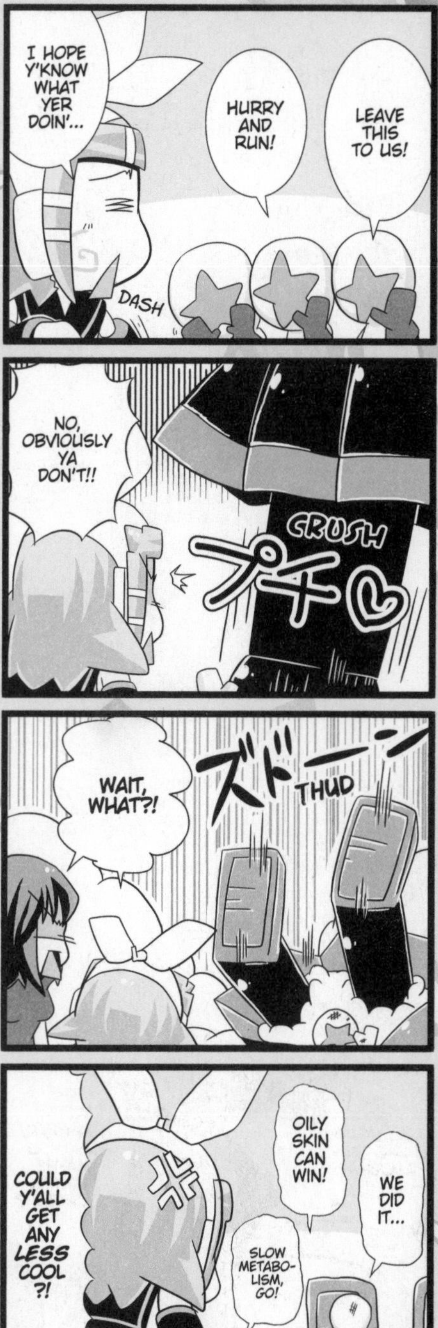
LEAVE THIS TO US!
HURRY AND RUN!
I HOPE Y'KNOW WHAT YER DOIN'...
DASH
NO, OBVIOUSLY YA DON'T!!
CRUSH
プチ♡
ズドーーン
THUD
WAIT, WHAT?!
WE DID IT...
OILY SKIN CAN WIN!
SLOW METABO-LISM, GO!
COULD Y'ALL GET ANY LESS COOL ?!

KA-BOOM

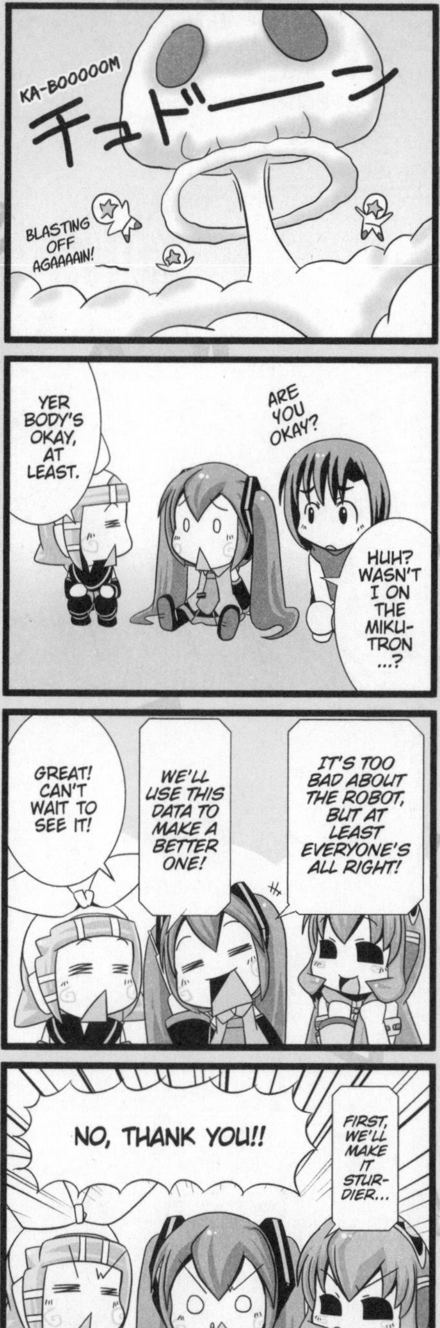
KA-BOOOOOM
チュドーーン
BLASTING OFF AGAAAAIN!
ARE YOU OKAY?
YER BODY'S OKAY, AT LEAST.
HUH? WASN'T I ON THE MIKU-TRON ...?
IT'S TOO BAD ABOUT THE ROBOT, BUT AT LEAST EVERYONE'S ALL RIGHT!
WE'LL USE THIS DATA TO MAKE A BETTER ONE!
GREAT! CAN'T WAIT TO SEE IT!
FIRST, WE'LL MAKE IT STUR-DIER...
NO, THANK YOU!!
FWIP

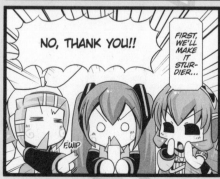

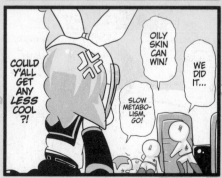

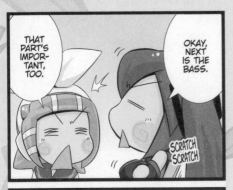

MOBILE VERSION LoiPara! BAND EDITION #5

OKAY, NEXT IS THE BASS.
THAT PART'S IMPORTANT, TOO.
SCRATCH SCRATCH
IT AIN'T FLASHY, BUT IT SETS THE RHYTHM ...
BASS IS THE PULSE OF THE SONG!
SO, THE UNSUNG HERO OF THE BAND?
PRETTY IMPORTANT FOR SOMETHING SO LAME!
SO, WHO'S GONNA PLAY BASS?
URK!
RIN-CHAN, CAN YOU MAYBE MULTIPLY YOURSELF?
DO I LOOK LIKE AN AMOEBA?

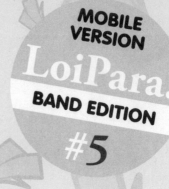

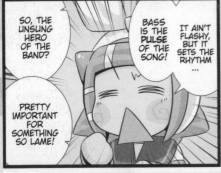

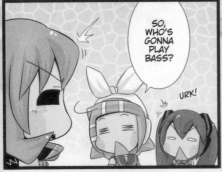

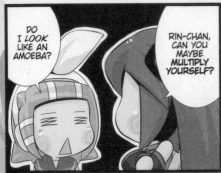

MOBILE VERSION

LoiPara! BAND EDITION

#6

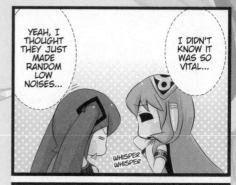

I DIDN'T KNOW IT WAS SO VITAL...
YEAH, I THOUGHT THEY JUST MADE RANDOM LOW NOISES...
WHISPER WHISPER
SO? WHO'S GONNA PLAY BASS?
ずい
LOOM
OH NO...
I... I CAN'T DO IT!
IT SHOULD BE SOMEONE MORE RELIABLE THAN US...
TAP TAP
HMM?
LEN-KUN, WHEN'D YOU GET HERE?!
GLINT

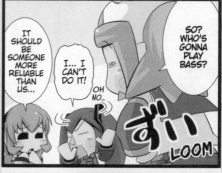

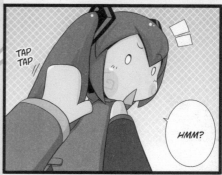

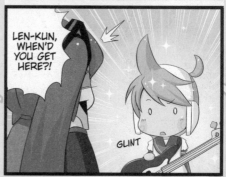

SPRING ONION 36

HACHUNE MIKU'S FLOWER-VIEWING WITH EVERYONE! SIDE A

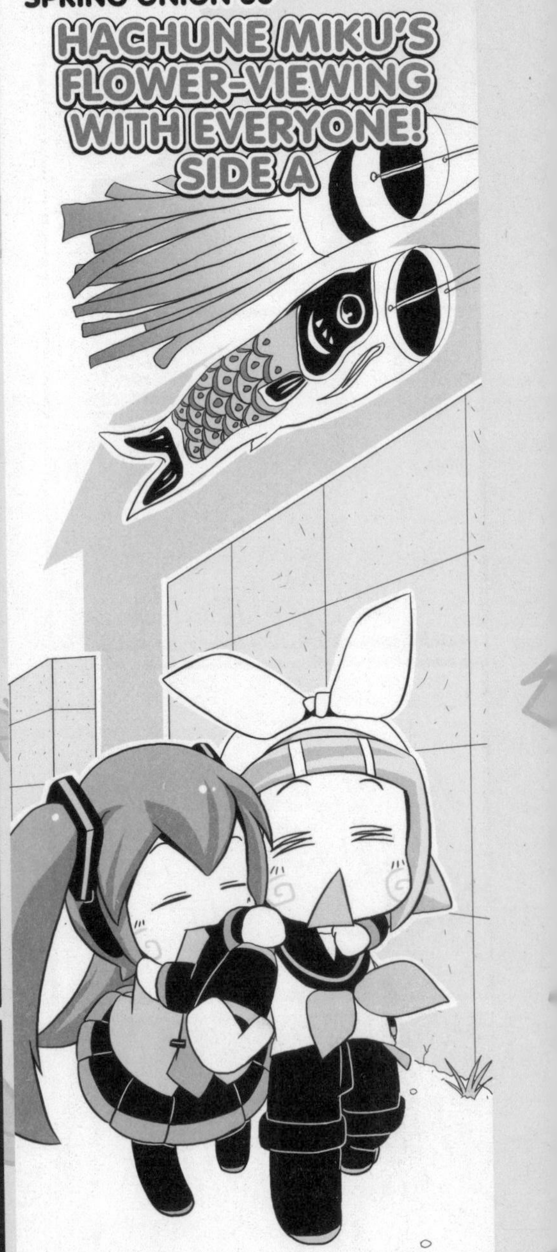

LOTSA GRUB

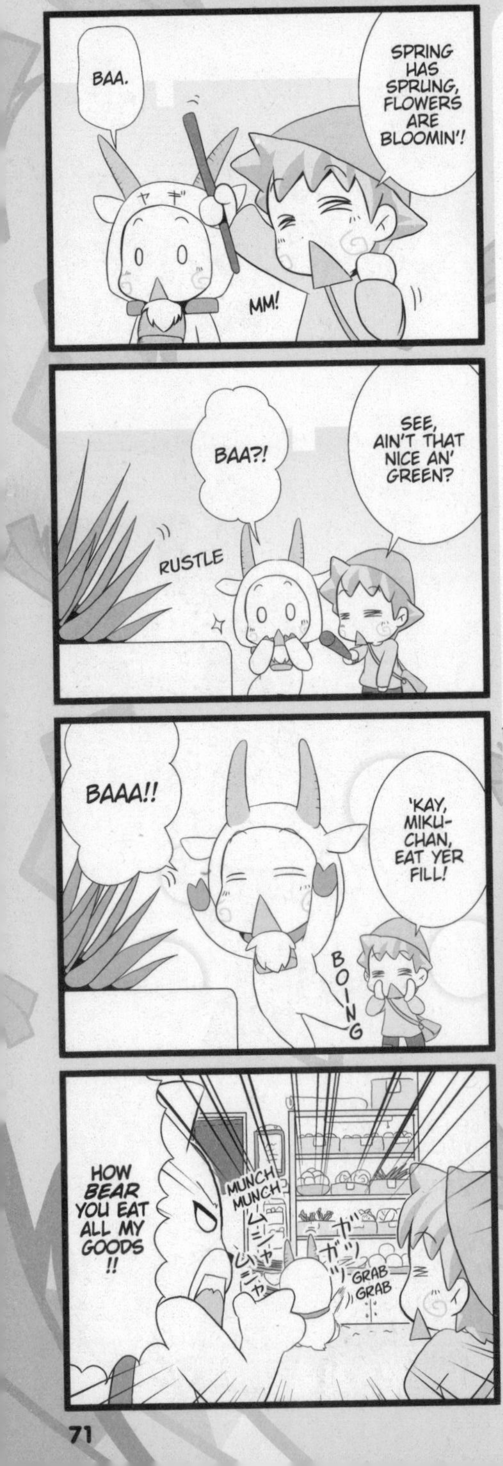
SPRING HAS SPRUNG, FLOWERS ARE BLOOMIN'!
BAA.
ヤギ
MM!
SEE, AIN'T THAT NICE AN' GREEN?
BAA?!
RUSTLE
'KAY, MIKU-CHAN, EAT YER FILL!
BAAA!!
BOING
GRAB GRAB
MUNCH MUNCH
HOW BEAR YOU EAT ALL MY GOODS!!

REBELLIOUS AGE

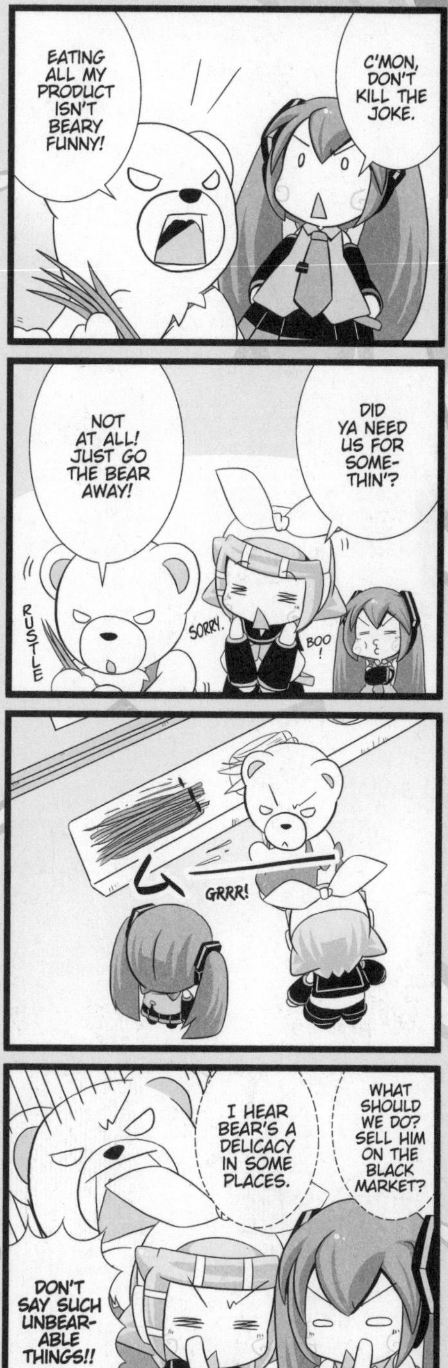
C'MON, DON'T KILL THE JOKE.
EATING ALL MY PRODUCT ISN'T BEARY FUNNY!
DID YA NEED US FOR SOME-THIN'?
NOT AT ALL! JUST GO THE BEAR AWAY!
BOO!
SORRY.
RUSTLE
GRRR!
WHAT SHOULD WE DO? SELL HIM ON THE BLACK MARKET?
I HEAR BEAR'S A DELICACY IN SOME PLACES.
DON'T SAY SUCH UNBEAR-ABLE THINGS!!

GLARE

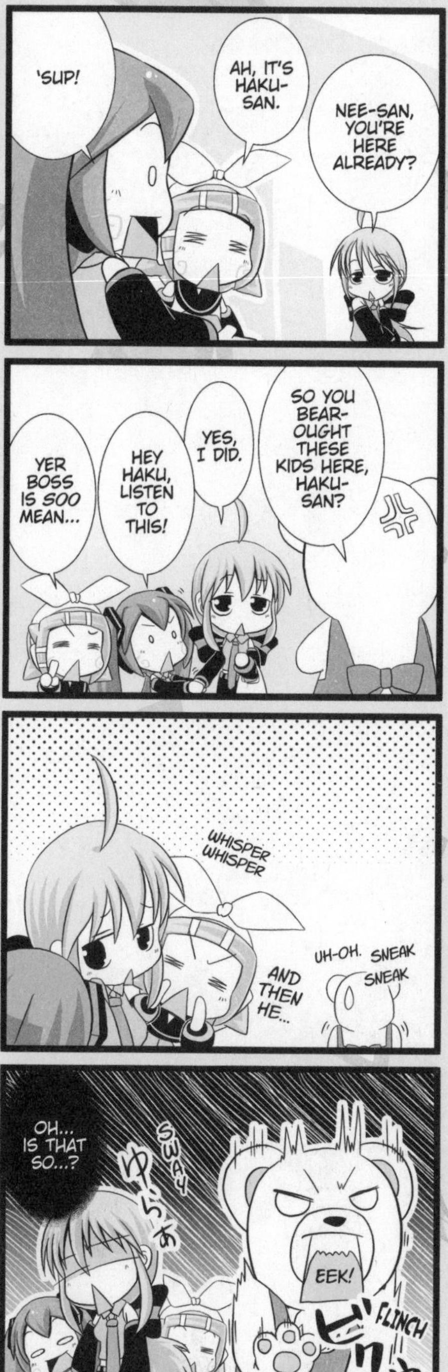
NEE-SAN, YOU'RE HERE ALREADY?
AH, IT'S HAKU-SAN.
'SUP!
SO YOU BEAR-OUGHT THESE KIDS HERE, HAKU-SAN?
YES, I DID.
HEY HAKU, LISTEN TO THIS!
YER BOSS IS SOO MEAN...
SNEAK SNEAK
UH-OH.
WHISPER WHISPER
AND THEN HE...
FLINCH
EEK!
SWAY
OH... IS THAT SO...?

ONE-HIT KO

YOU JUST BOUGHT A NEW TV, DIDN'T YOU, BOSS?
AN HD, HIGH-POWER, STATE-OF-THE-ART ONE...
WHEN YOU WERE OUT ON DELIVERY A FEW DAYS AGO...
IT STARTED DOING SOMETHING REALLY WEIRD.
IT WAS PLAYING THIS WEIRD VIDEO...DID YOU SET THAT UP?
ダラー
SWEAT
I THOUGHT MAYBE IT WAS BROKEN, SO I CHECKED THE SETTINGS, AND...
THE OWNER'S NAME WAS SET TO DEVIL...
?
GRAAAAAAAH!!
ダダダ
DAAASH

STRATEGY MEETING

I'LL BEAR ANYTHING, JUST PLEASE STOP WITH THE SCARY STUFF!
FLAIL FLAIL
あたふたあたふ
OH HO...
HE SAYS HE'LL DO WHATEVER WE WANT TO MAKE UP FOR IT.
WAAAH!
WHAT-EVER WE WANT?
OH HO HO! HOW ABOUT THAT...
AIN'T THAT A DREAM COME TRUE.
GRIN
GRIN
A-ALL AT ONCE?!
IF I HAVE TO PICK...
WHISPER WHISPER
ALL AT ONCE...
STAB IT IN...
MUMBLE

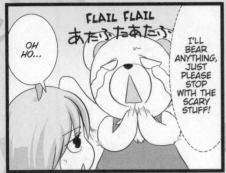

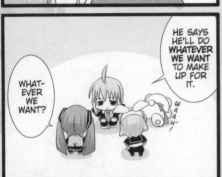

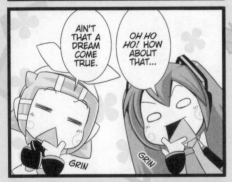

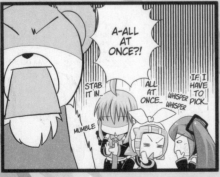

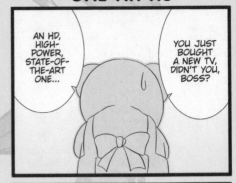

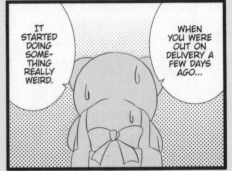

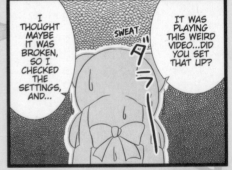

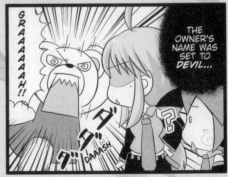

FAMOUS SAYING

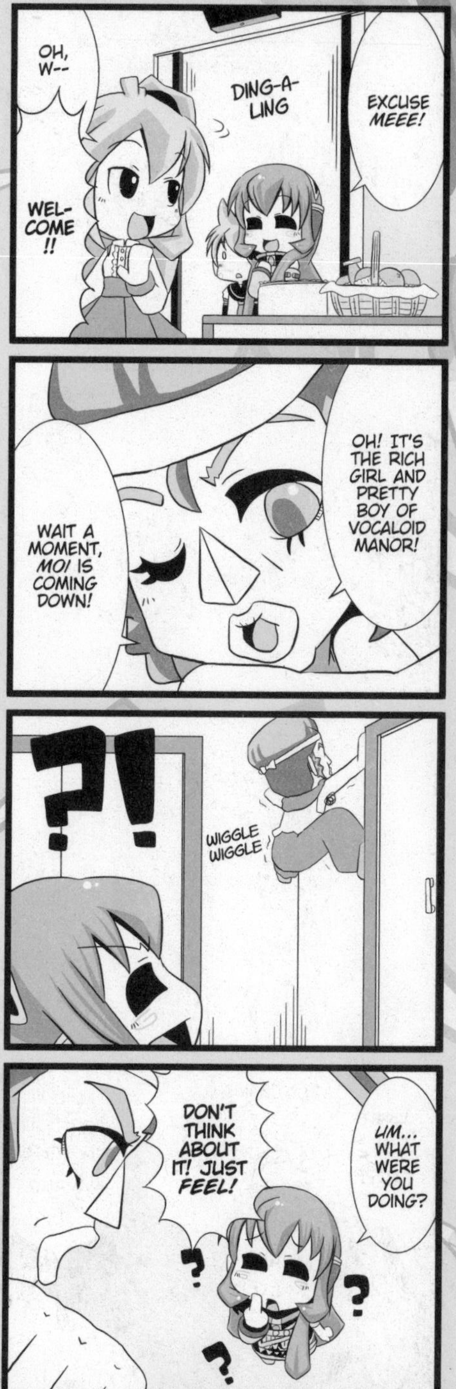
EXCUSE MEEE!
DING-A-LING
OH, W--
WEL-COME!!
OH! IT'S THE RICH GIRL AND PRETTY BOY OF VOCALOID MANOR!
WAIT A MOMENT, *MOI* IS COMING DOWN!
?!
WIGGLE WIGGLE
UM... WHAT WERE YOU DOING?
DON'T THINK ABOUT IT! JUST *FEEL*!

WRONG

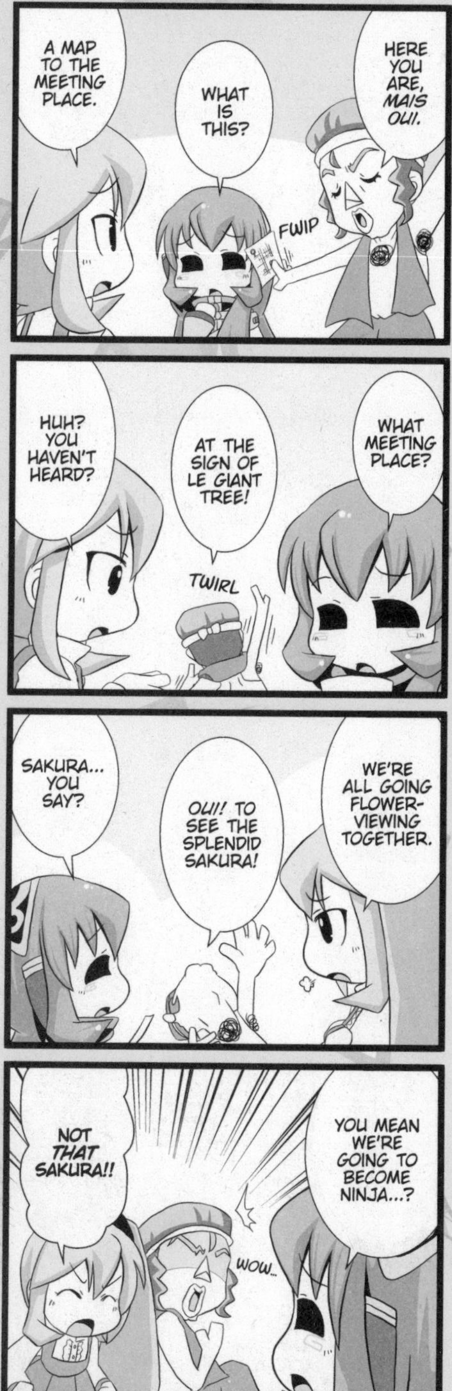
HERE YOU ARE, *MAIS OUI*.
WHAT IS THIS?
A MAP TO THE MEETING PLACE.
FWIP
WHAT MEETING PLACE?
AT THE SIGN OF LE GIANT TREE!
HUH? YOU HAVEN'T HEARD?
TWIRL
WE'RE ALL GOING FLOWER-VIEWING TOGETHER.
OUI! TO SEE THE SPLENDID SAKURA!
SAKURA... YOU SAY?
YOU MEAN WE'RE GOING TO BECOME NINJA...?
NOT *THAT* SAKURA!!
WOW..

LEAVE IT TO MEYKO-SAN

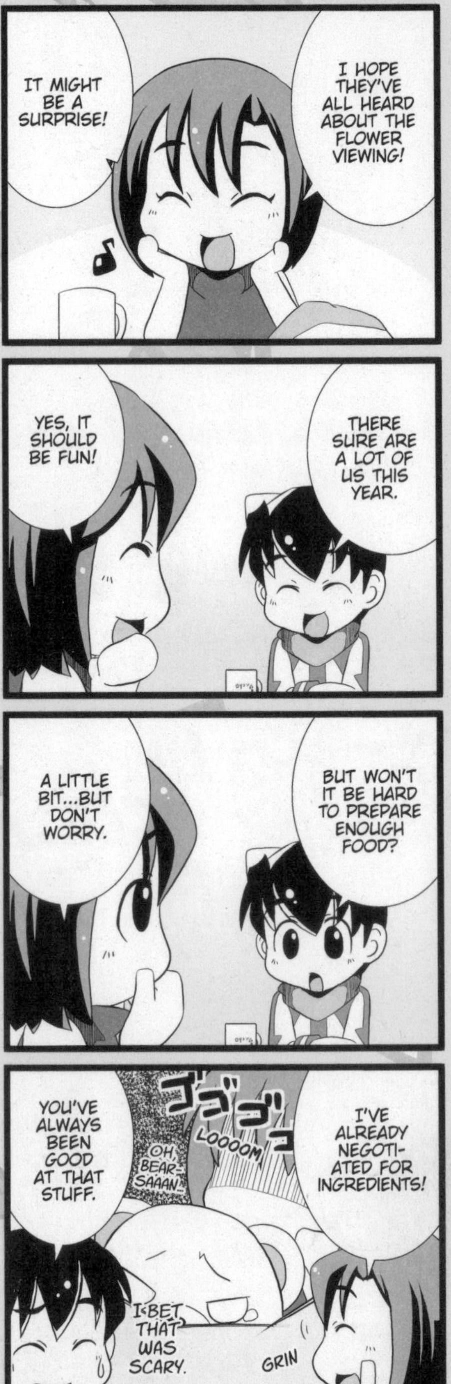
I HOPE THEY'VE ALL HEARD ABOUT THE FLOWER VIEWING!
IT MIGHT BE A SURPRISE!
THERE SURE ARE A LOT OF US THIS YEAR.
YES, IT SHOULD BE FUN!
BUT WON'T IT BE HARD TO PREPARE ENOUGH FOOD?
A LITTLE BIT...BUT DON'T WORRY.
I'VE ALREADY NEGOTIATED FOR INGREDIENTS!
LOOOOM
OH, BEAR-SAAAN...
YOU'VE ALWAYS BEEN GOOD AT THAT STUFF.
GRIN
I BET THAT WAS SCARY.

TIME FLIES

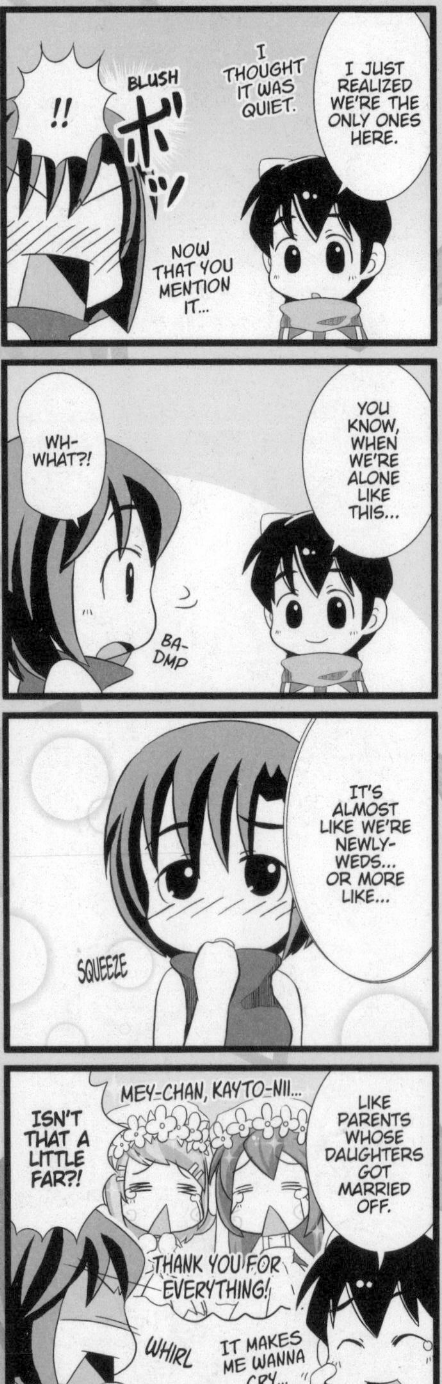
I JUST REALIZED WE'RE THE ONLY ONES HERE.
I THOUGHT IT WAS QUIET.
BLUSH
!!
NOW THAT YOU MENTION IT...
YOU KNOW, WHEN WE'RE ALONE LIKE THIS...
WH-WHAT?!
BA-DMP
IT'S ALMOST LIKE WE'RE NEWLY-WEDS... OR MORE LIKE...
SQUEEZE
LIKE PARENTS WHOSE DAUGHTERS GOT MARRIED OFF.
MEY-CHAN, KAYTO-NII...
ISN'T THAT A LITTLE FAR?!
THANK YOU FOR EVERYTHING!
IT MAKES ME WANNA CRY...
WHIRL

CULPRIT

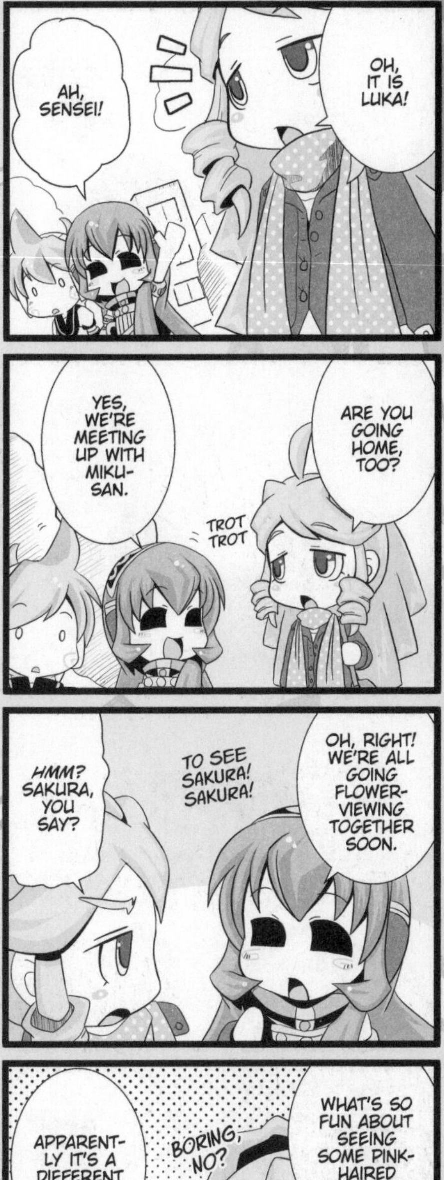

OH, IT IS LUKA!
AH, SENSEI!
ARE YOU GOING HOME, TOO?
YES, WE'RE MEETING UP WITH MIKU-SAN.
TROT TROT
OH, RIGHT! WE'RE ALL GOING FLOWER-VIEWING TOGETHER SOON.
TO SEE SAKURA! SAKURA!
HMM? SAKURA, YOU SAY?
WHAT'S SO FUN ABOUT SEEING SOME PINK-HAIRED NOBODY?
BORING, NO?
APPARENTLY IT'S A DIFFERENT SAKURA.

UNTIMELY END

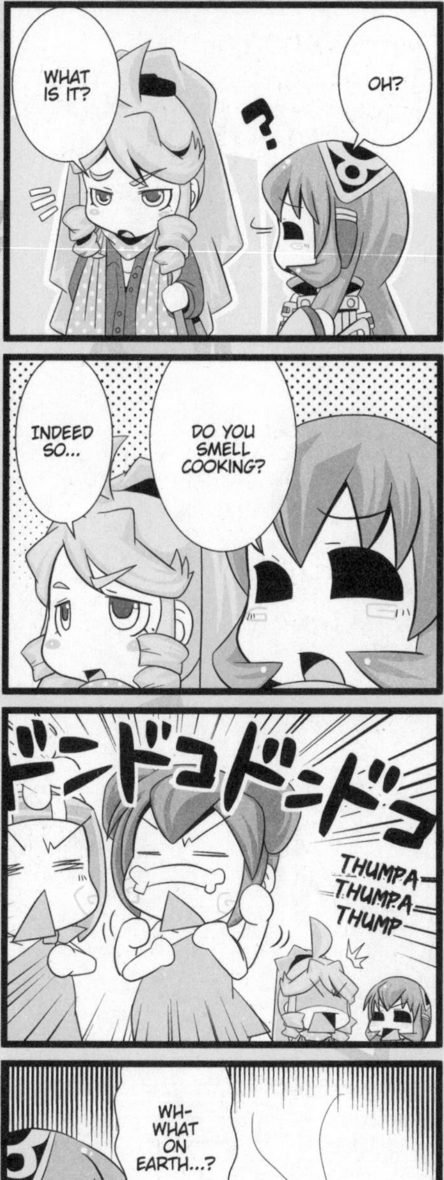

OH?
WHAT IS IT?
DO YOU SMELL COOKING?
INDEED SO...
THUMPA-THUMPA-THUMP
WH-WHAT ON EARTH...?
OOOGA!
BURN BURN
SIZZLE SIZZLE
OOKA!

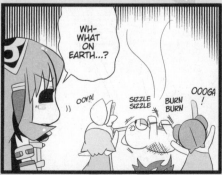

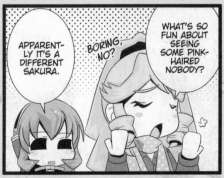

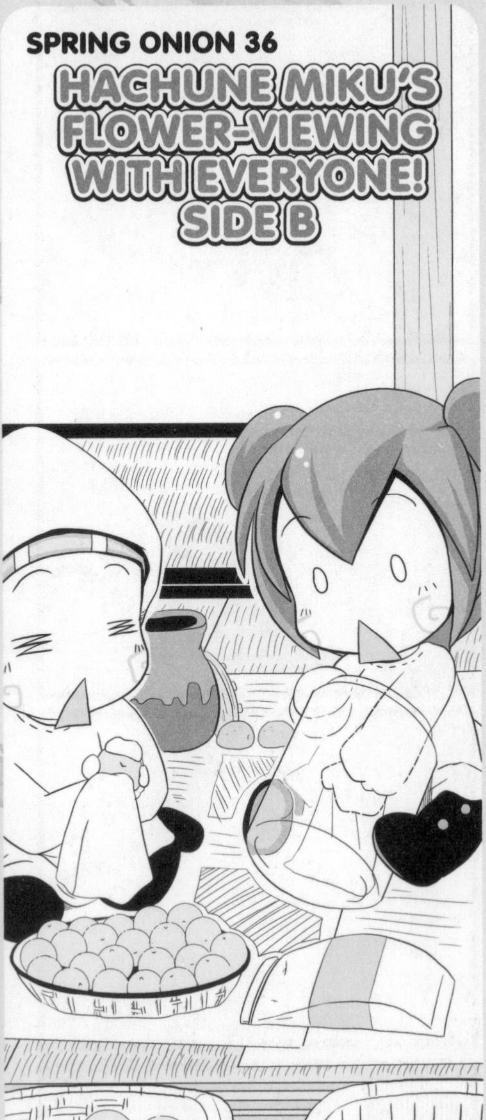
SPRING ONION 36
HACHUNE MIKU'S FLOWER-VIEWING WITH EVERYONE! SIDE B

BLACK

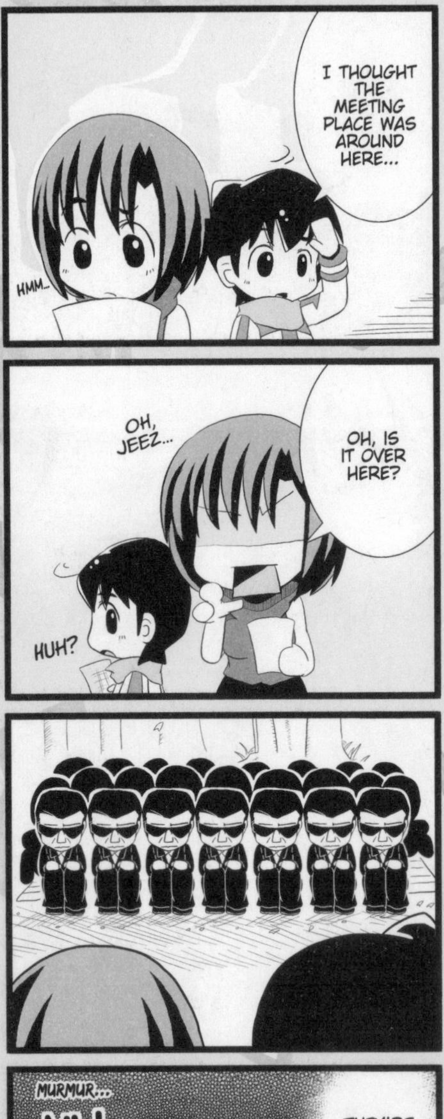
I THOUGHT THE MEETING PLACE WAS AROUND HERE...
HMM...
OH, IS IT OVER HERE?
OH, JEEZ...
HUH?
THEY'RE SO OUT OF PLACE...!
ざわ…
MURMUR...
ざわ…
MURMUR...

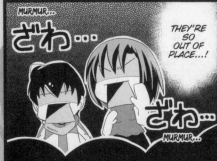

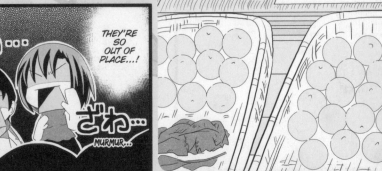

PARTING GIFT

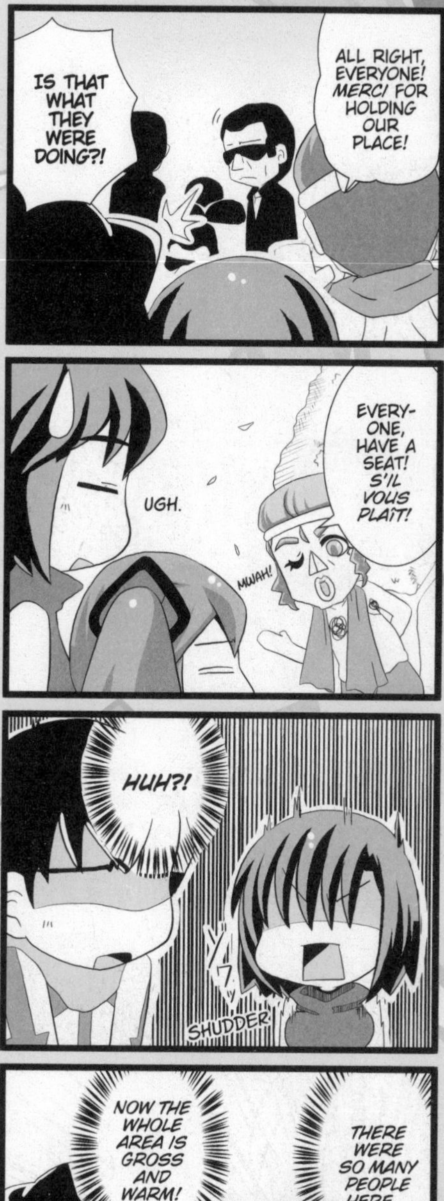
ALL RIGHT, EVERYONE! *MERCI* FOR HOLDING OUR PLACE!
IS THAT WHAT THEY WERE DOING?!
EVERY-ONE, HAVE A SEAT! S'IL VOUS PLAÎT!
MWAH!
UGH.
HUH?!
SHUDDER
THERE WERE SO MANY PEOPLE HERE...
NOW THE WHOLE AREA IS GROSS AND WARM!
PUFF PUFF

SCALE

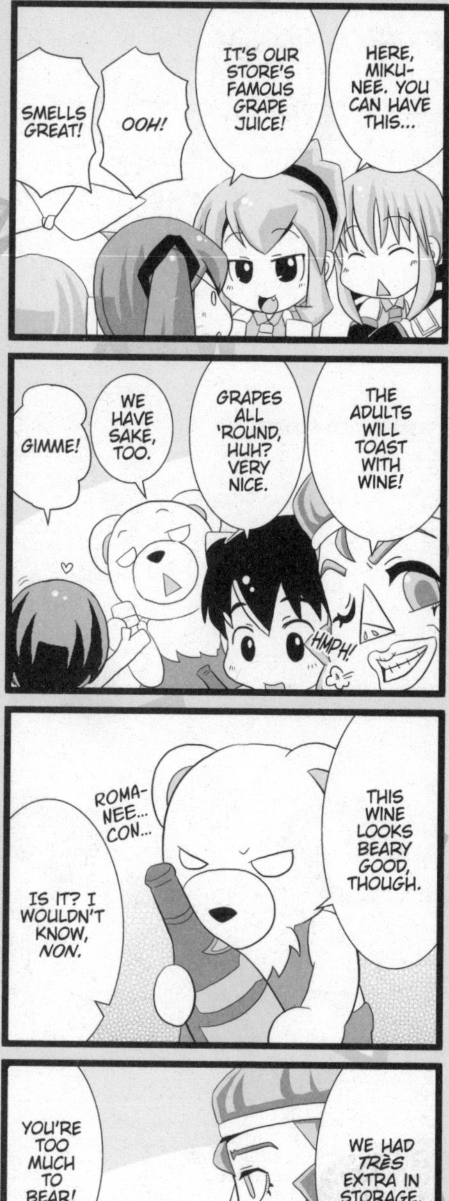
HERE, MIKU-NEE. YOU CAN HAVE THIS...
IT'S OUR STORE'S FAMOUS GRAPE JUICE!
OOH!
SMELLS GREAT!
THE ADULTS WILL TOAST WITH WINE!
GRAPES ALL 'ROUND, HUH? VERY NICE.
WE HAVE SAKE, TOO.
GIMME!
HMPH!
THIS WINE LOOKS BEARY GOOD, THOUGH.
ROMA-NEE... CON...
IS IT? I WOULDN'T KNOW, *NON.*
WE HAD *TRÈS* EXTRA IN STORAGE, SO...
YOU'RE TOO MUCH TO BEAR!

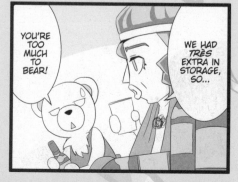

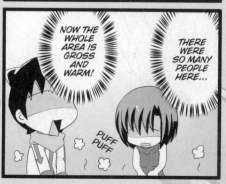

REAL THING

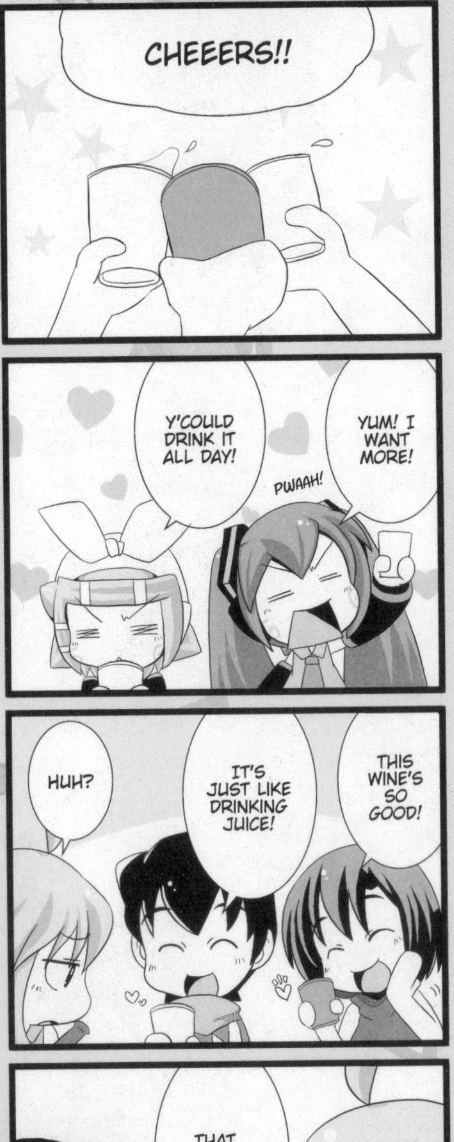
CHEEERS!!
YUM! I WANT MORE!
PWAAH!
Y'COULD DRINK IT ALL DAY!
THIS WINE'S SO GOOD!
IT'S JUST LIKE DRINKING JUICE!
HUH?
THAT... REALLY IS JUICE...
YOU COULDN'T TELL?
PBBT!

OUT

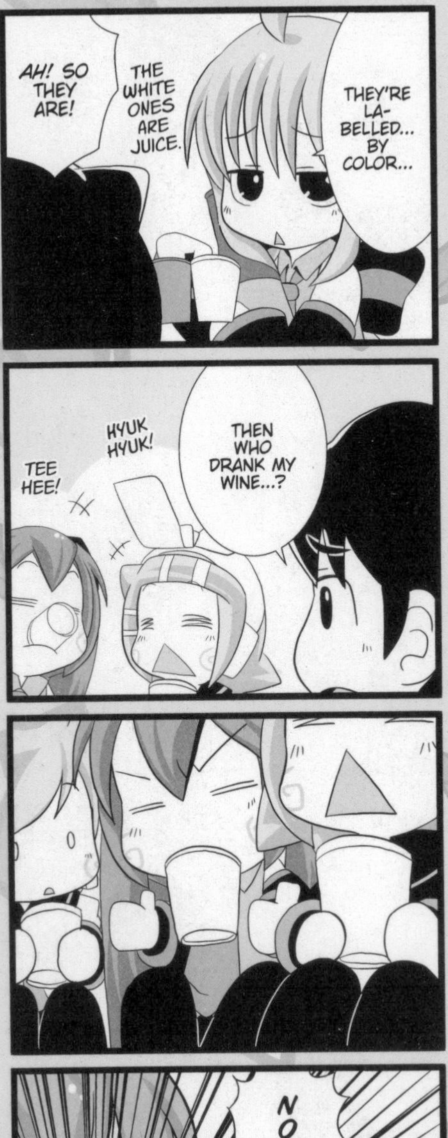
THEY'RE LA-BELLED... BY COLOR...
THE WHITE ONES ARE JUICE.
AH! SO THEY ARE!
THEN WHO DRANK MY WINE...?
HYUK HYUK!
TEE HEE!
NOOOOO!!

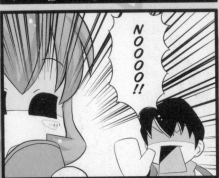

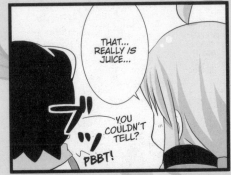

AWAKENING

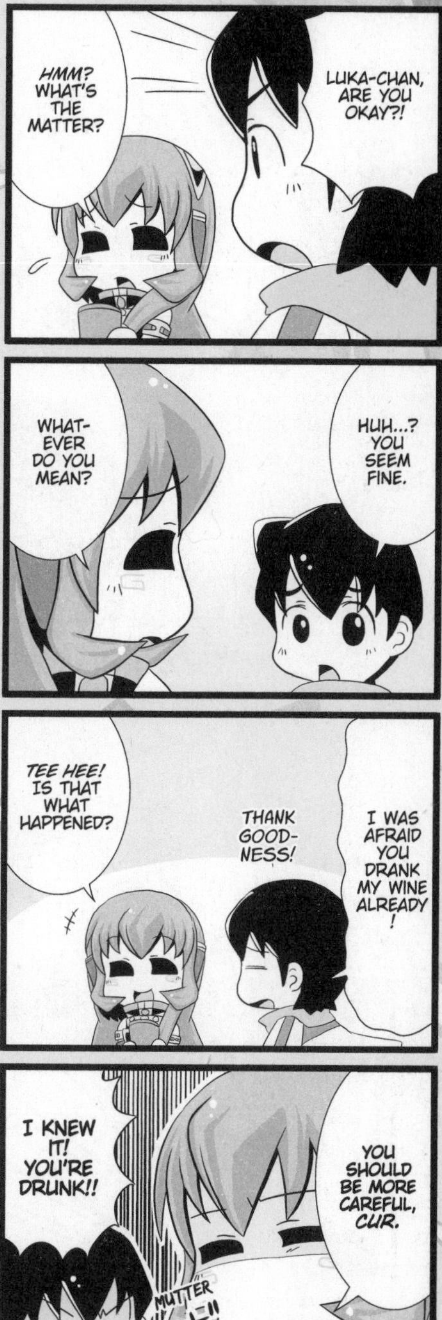
LUKA-CHAN, ARE YOU OKAY?!
HMM? WHAT'S THE MATTER?
HUH...? YOU SEEM FINE.
WHATEVER DO YOU MEAN?
I WAS AFRAID YOU DRANK MY WINE ALREADY!
THANK GOODNESS!
TEE HEE! IS THAT WHAT HAPPENED?
YOU SHOULD BE MORE CAREFUL, CUR.
MUTTER
I KNEW IT! YOU'RE DRUNK!!

THIS ONE TOO

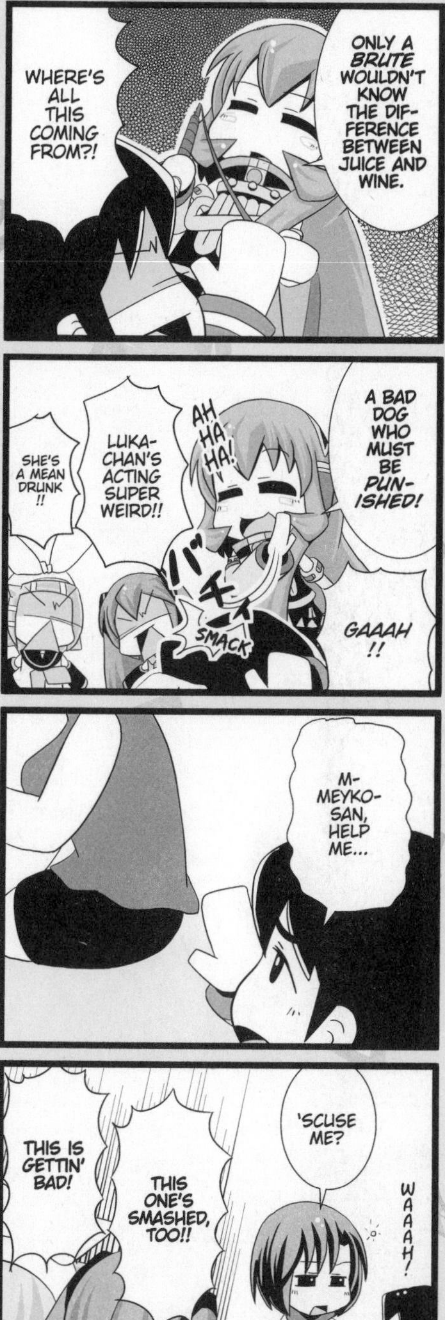
ONLY A BRUTE WOULDN'T KNOW THE DIFFERENCE BETWEEN JUICE AND WINE.
WHERE'S ALL THIS COMING FROM?!
A BAD DOG WHO MUST BE PUNISHED!
AH HA HA!
GAAAH!!
SMACK
LUKA-CHAN'S ACTING SUPER WEIRD!!
SHE'S A MEAN DRUNK!!
M-MEYKO-SAN, HELP ME...
'SCUSE ME?
WAAAAH!
THIS ONE'S SMASHED, TOO!!
THIS IS GETTIN' BAD!

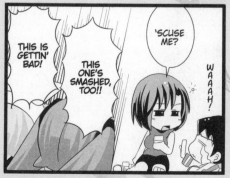

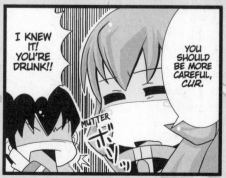

THOROUGHBRED

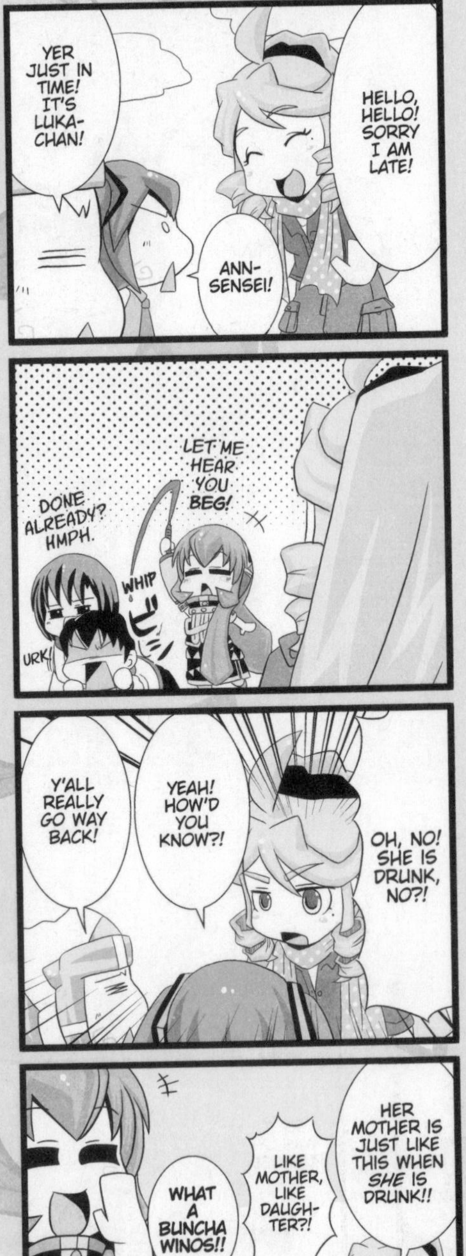
HELLO, HELLO! SORRY I AM LATE!
ANN-SENSEI!
YER JUST IN TIME! IT'S LUKA-CHAN!
LET ME HEAR YOU BEG!
WHIP
DONE ALREADY? HMPH.
URK!
OH, NO! SHE IS DRUNK, NO?!
YEAH! HOW'D YOU KNOW?!
Y'ALL REALLY GO WAY BACK!
HER MOTHER IS JUST LIKE THIS WHEN *SHE* IS DRUNK!!
LIKE MOTHER, LIKE DAUGHTER?!
WHAT A BUNCHA WINOS!!

PROFESSIONAL

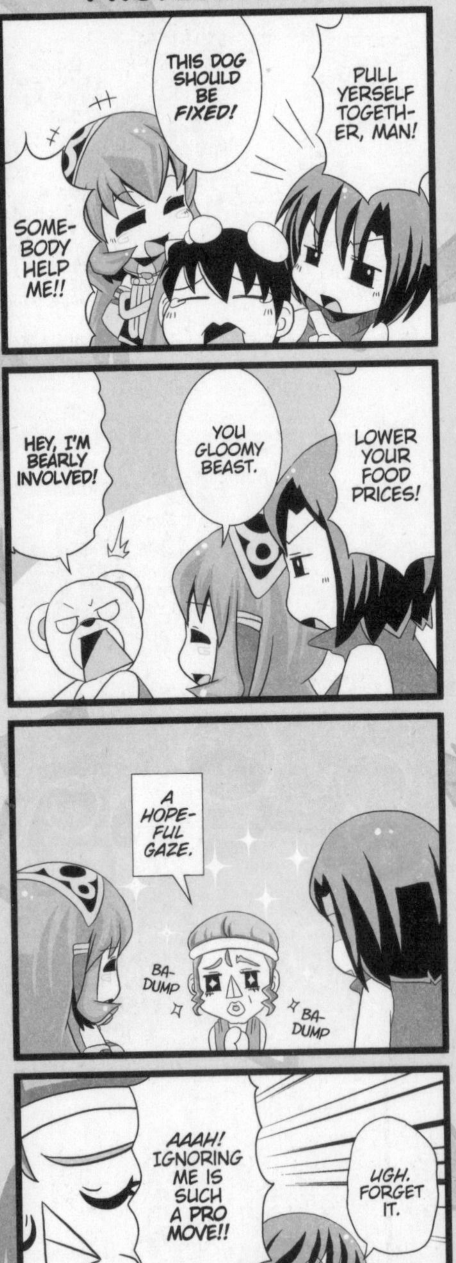
PULL YERSELF TOGETHER, MAN!
THIS DOG SHOULD BE *FIXED*!
SOMEBODY HELP ME!!
LOWER YOUR FOOD PRICES!
YOU GLOOMY BEAST.
HEY, I'M BEARLY INVOLVED!
A HOPEFUL GAZE.
BA-DUMP
BA-DUMP
UGH. FORGET IT.
AAAH! IGNORING ME IS SUCH A PRO MOVE!!

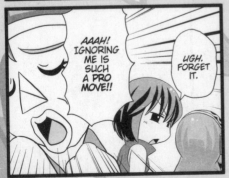

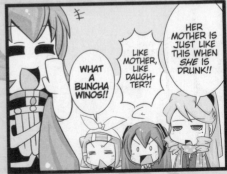

PAIR

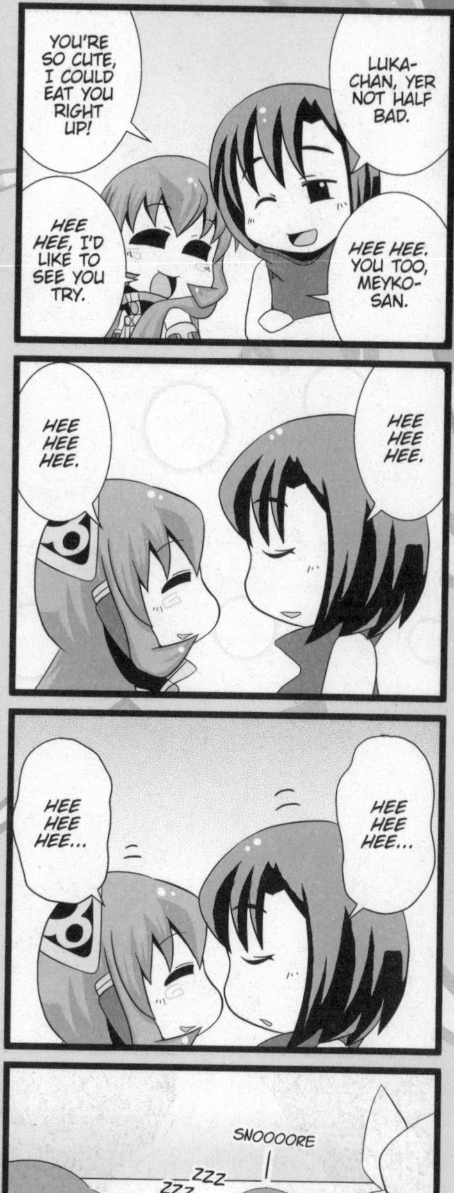
LUKA-CHAN, YER NOT HALF BAD.
YOU'RE SO CUTE, I COULD EAT YOU RIGHT UP!
HEE HEE. YOU TOO, MEYKO-SAN.
HEE HEE, I'D LIKE TO SEE YOU TRY.
HEE HEE HEE.
HEE HEE HEE.
HEE HEE HEE...
HEE HEE HEE...
SNOOOORE
ZZZ ZZZ...
FLOP

AFTERMATH

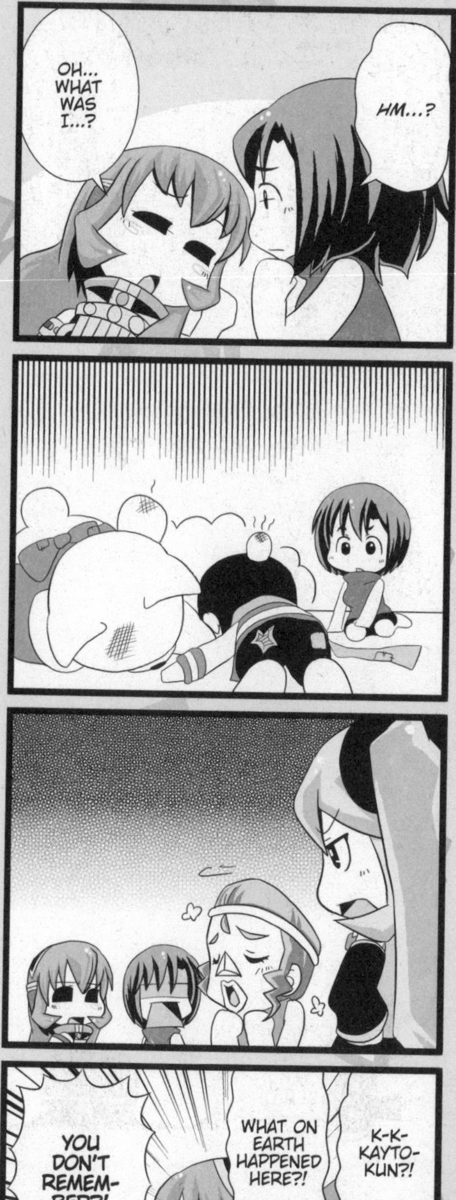
HM...?
OH... WHAT WAS I...?
K-K-KAYTO-KUN?!
WHAT ON EARTH HAPPENED HERE?!
YOU DON'T REMEM-BER?!

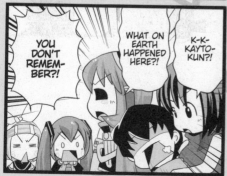

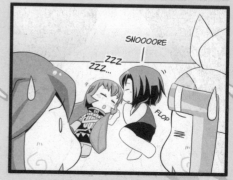

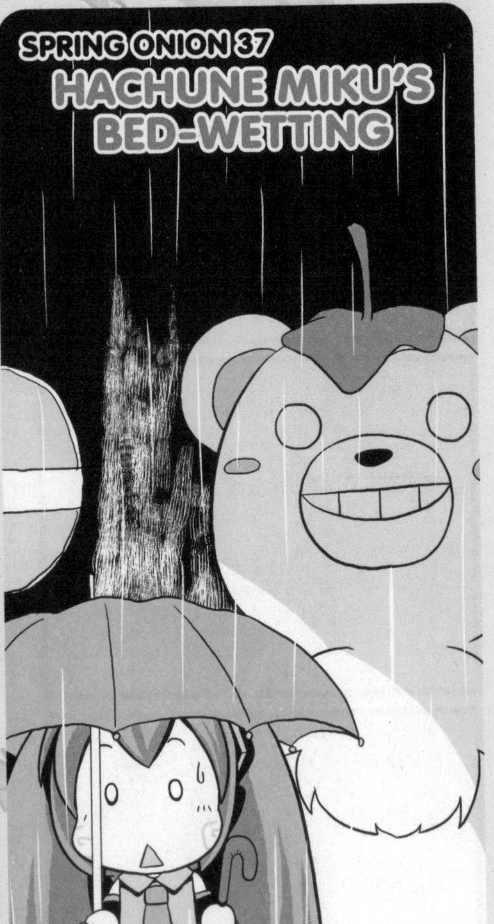
SPRING ONION 37
HACHUNE MIKU'S BED-WETTING

WET SPOT

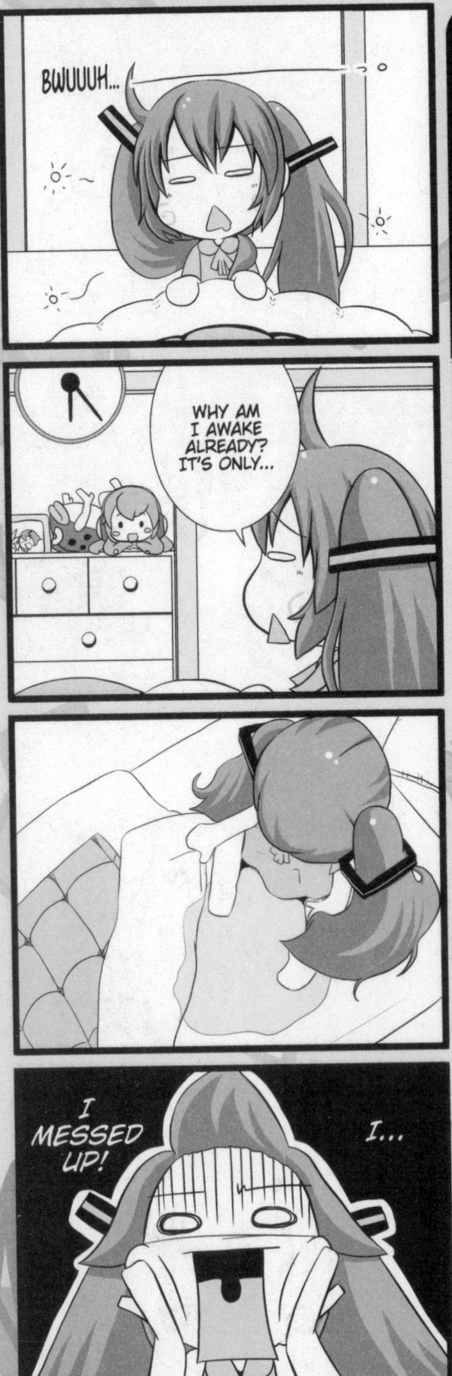
BWUUUH...
WHY AM I AWAKE ALREADY? IT'S ONLY...
I...
I MESSED UP!

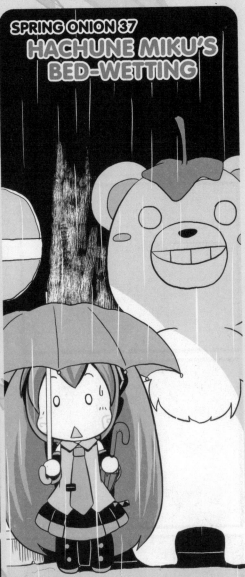

CRISIS

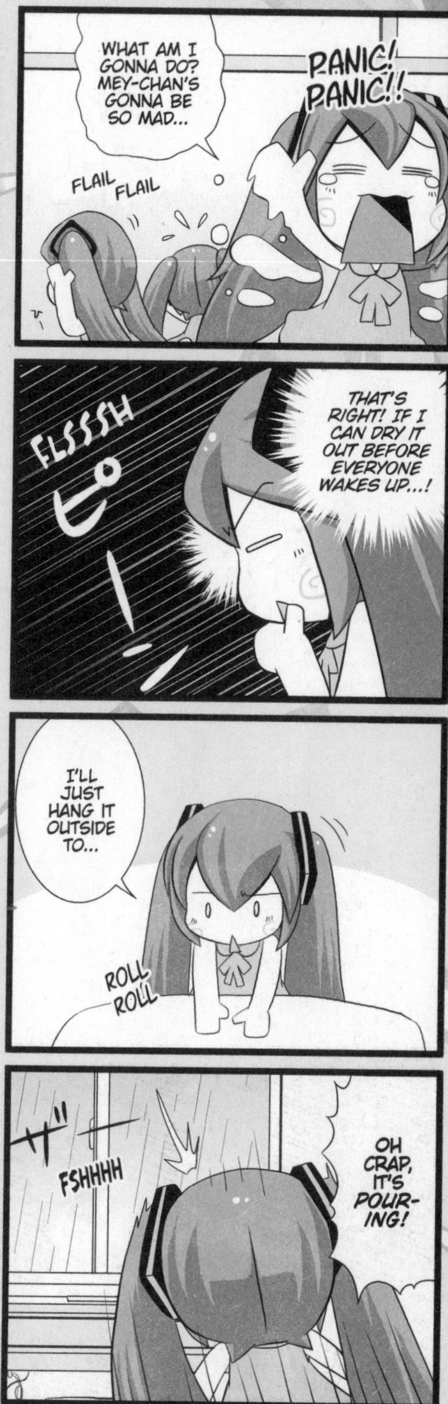
PANIC! PANIC!!
WHAT AM I GONNA DO? MEY-CHAN'S GONNA BE SO MAD...
FLAIL FLAIL
THAT'S RIGHT! IF I CAN DRY IT OUT BEFORE EVERYONE WAKES UP...!
FLSSSH
ピー
I'LL JUST HANG IT OUTSIDE TO...
ROLL ROLL
OH CRAP, IT'S POURING!
ザ
FSHHHH

DON'T PANIC, DON'T PANIC

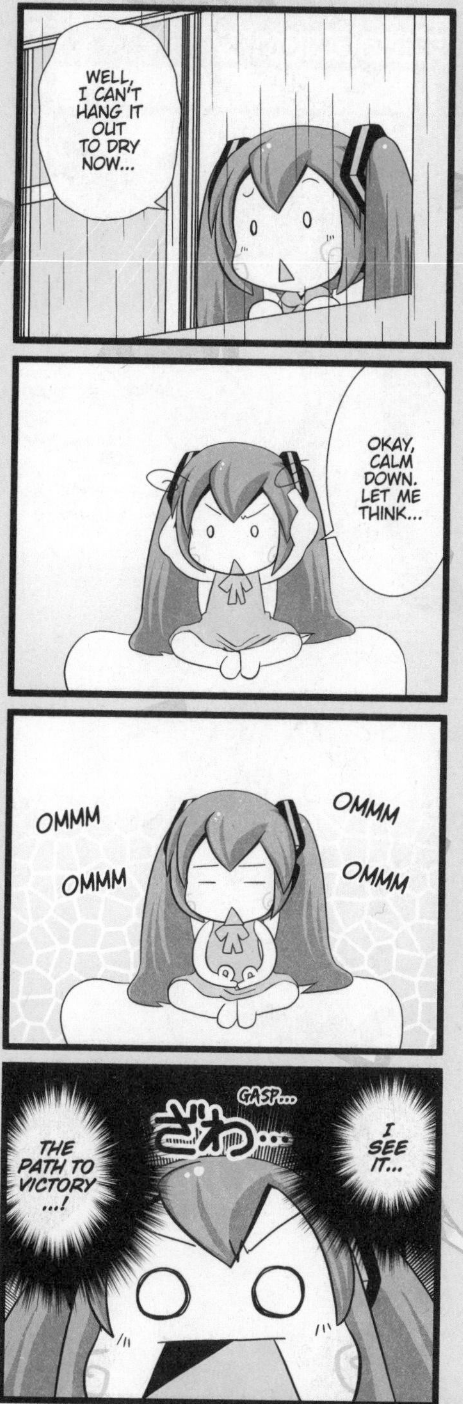
WELL, I CAN'T HANG IT OUT TO DRY NOW...
OKAY, CALM DOWN. LET ME THINK...
OMMM
OMMM
OMMM
OMMM
I SEE IT...
GASP...
ざわっ...
THE PATH TO VICTORY...!

SYNCHRONIZED

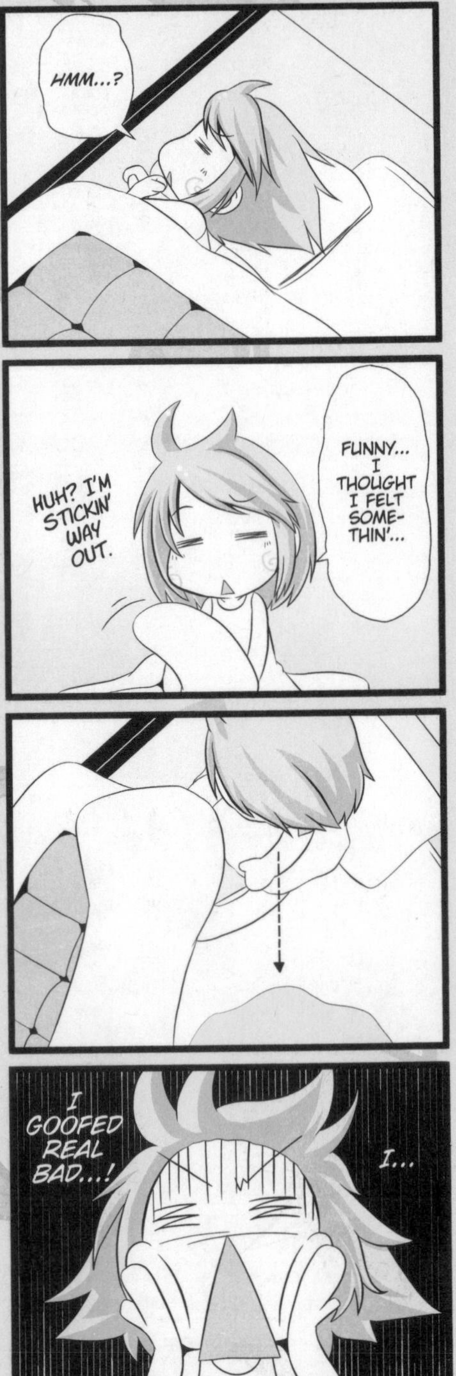
HMM...?
FUNNY... I THOUGHT I FELT SOME-THIN'...
HUH? I'M STICKIN' WAY OUT.
I...
I GOOFED REAL BAD...!

SUSPICIOUS

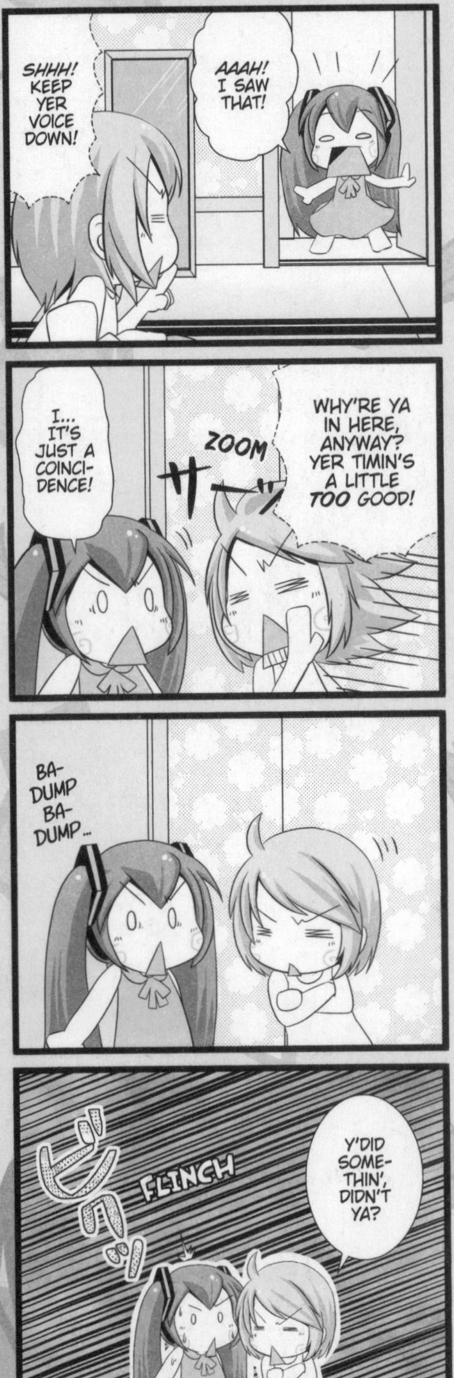
AAAH! I SAW THAT!
SHHH! KEEP YER VOICE DOWN!
WHY'RE YA IN HERE, ANYWAY? YER TIMIN'S A LITTLE *TOO* GOOD!
ZOOM
I... IT'S JUST A COINCI-DENCE!
BA-DUMP BA-DUMP...
Y'DID SOME-THIN', DIDN'T YA?
FLINCH

UNEXPECTED: PART 1

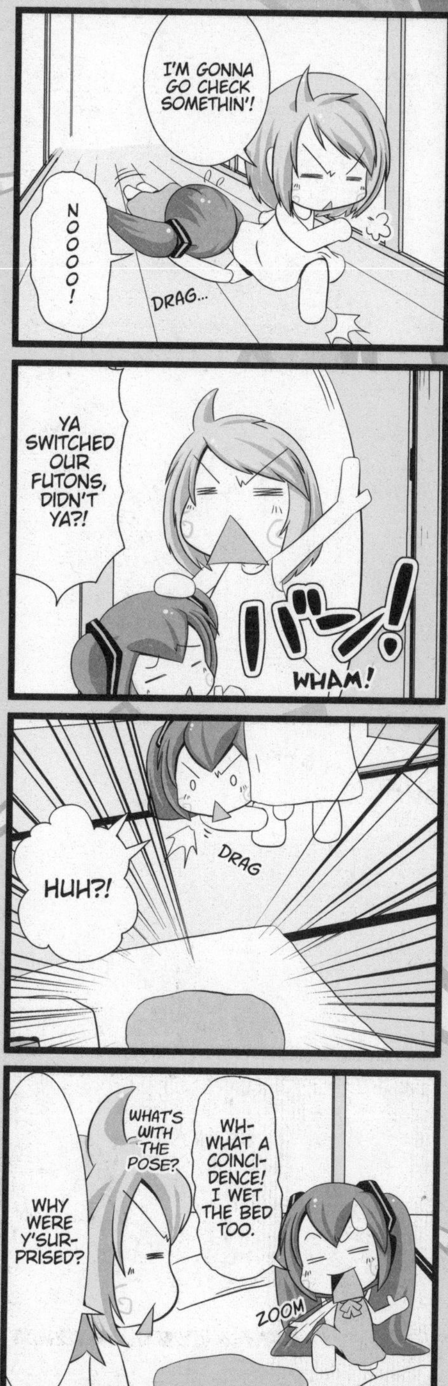
I'M GONNA GO CHECK SOMETHIN'!
NOOOOO!
DRAG...
YA SWITCHED OUR FUTONS, DIDN'T YA?!
バーン!
WHAM!
DRAG
HUH?!
WH-WHAT A COINCIDENCE! I WET THE BED TOO.
WHAT'S WITH THE POSE?
WHY WERE Y'SURPRISED?
ZOOM

DISPOSAL

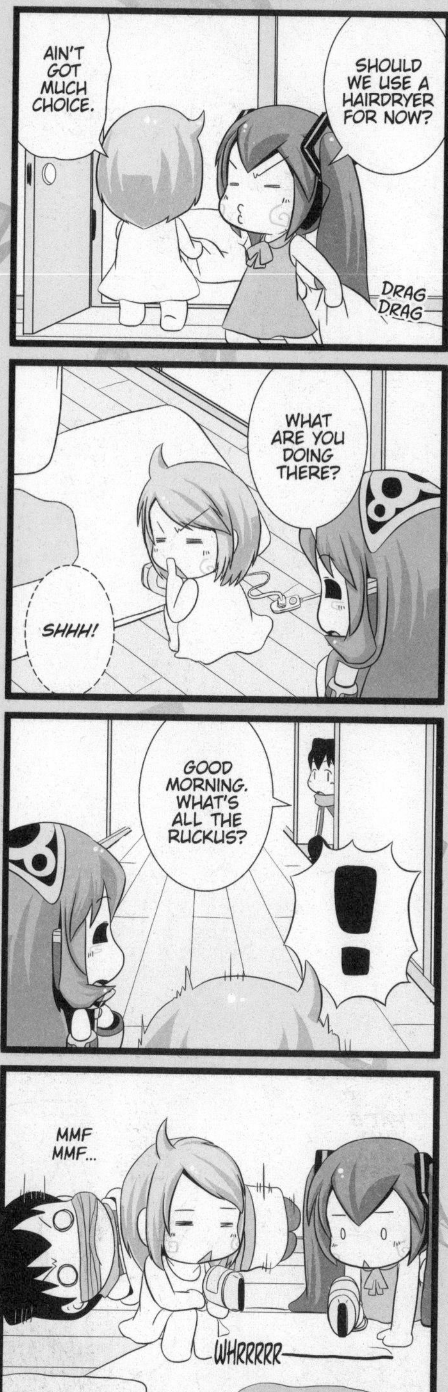
SHOULD WE USE A HAIRDRYER FOR NOW?
AIN'T GOT MUCH CHOICE.
DRAG DRAG
WHAT ARE YOU DOING THERE?
SHHH!
GOOD MORNING. WHAT'S ALL THE RUCKUS?
!
MMF MMF...
WHRRRRR—

EMBARRASSED

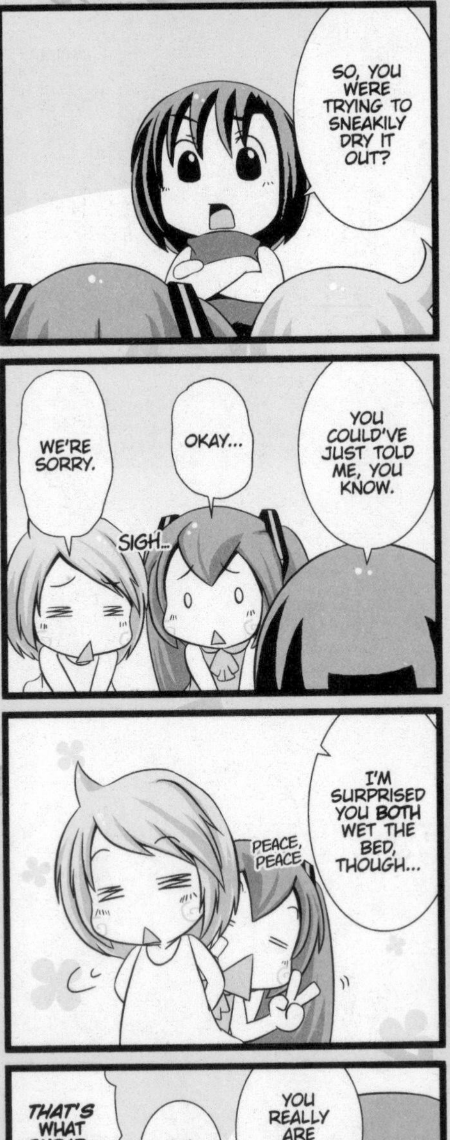

SO, YOU WERE TRYING TO SNEAKILY DRY IT OUT?
YOU COULD'VE JUST TOLD ME, YOU KNOW.
OKAY...
WE'RE SORRY.
SIGH...
I'M SURPRISED YOU BOTH WET THE BED, THOUGH...
PEACE, PEACE
YOU REALLY ARE CLOSE, HUH?
AW, JEEZ!
THAT'S WHAT EMBARRASSED YA?!

UNEXPECTED: PART 2

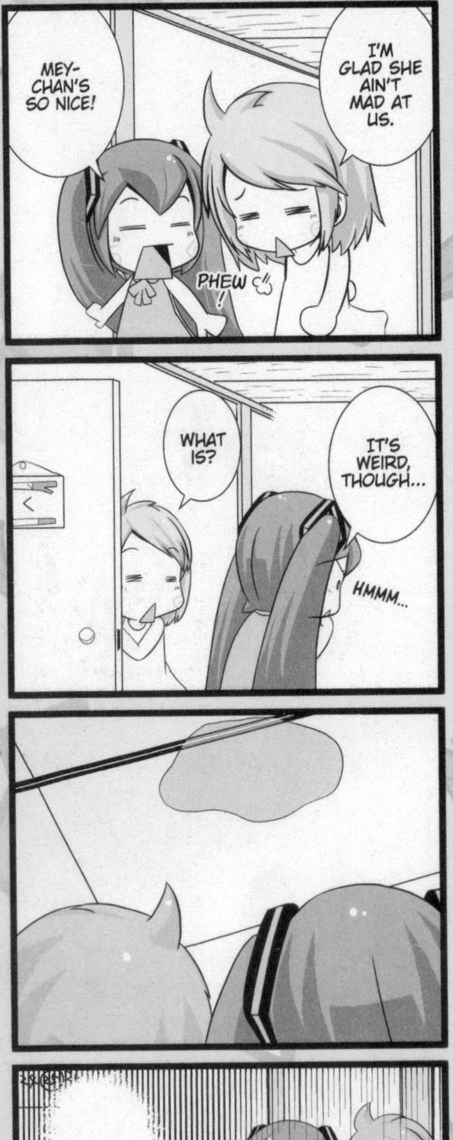

I'M GLAD SHE AIN'T MAD AT US.
MEY-CHAN'S SO NICE!
PHEW!
IT'S WEIRD, THOUGH...
WHAT IS?
HMMM...
WHAT THE HECK ...?

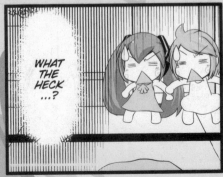

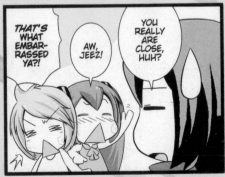

PLOT TWIST

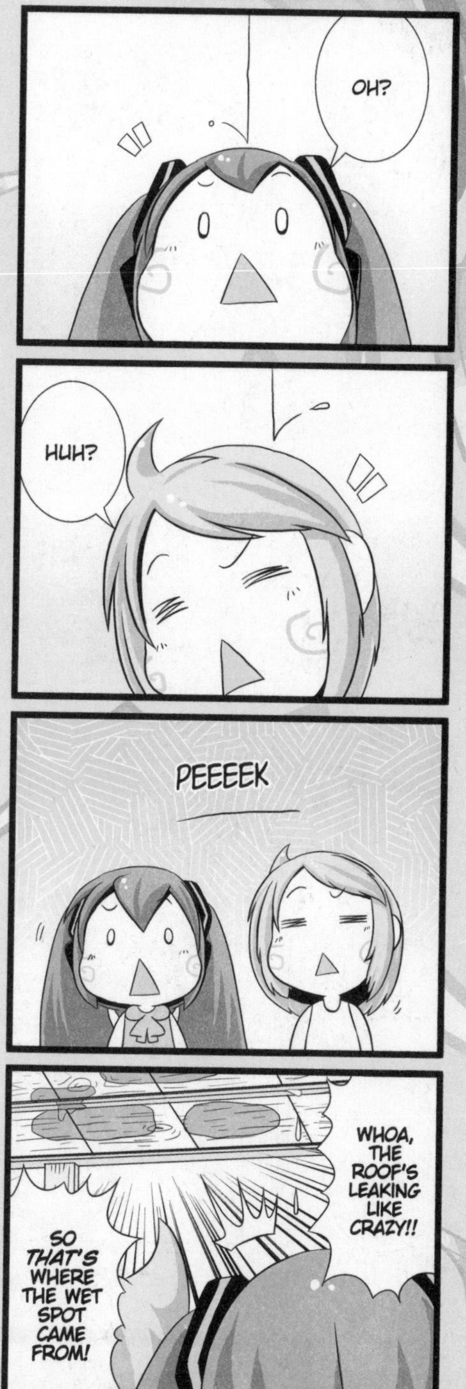
OH?
HUH?
PEEEEK
WHOA, THE ROOF'S LEAKING LIKE CRAZY!!
SO *THAT'S* WHERE THE WET SPOT CAME FROM!

RETRIBUTION

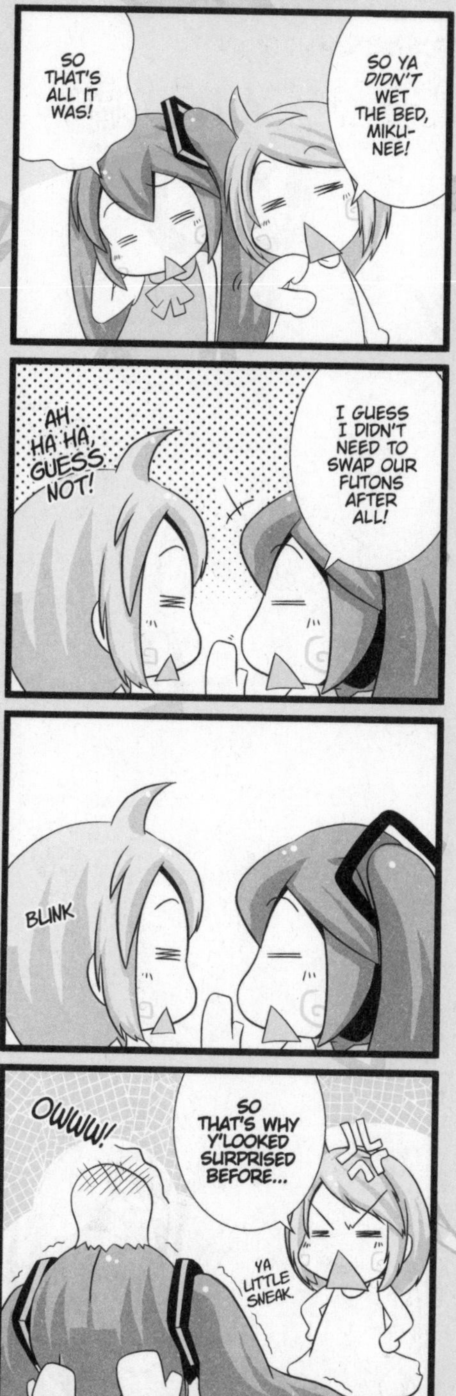
SO YA DIDN'T WET THE BED, MIKU-NEE!
SO THAT'S ALL IT WAS!
I GUESS I DIDN'T NEED TO SWAP OUR FUTONS AFTER ALL!
AH HA HA, GUESS NOT!
BLINK
SO THAT'S WHY Y'LOOKED SURPRISED BEFORE...
OWWW!
YA LITTLE SNEAK.

SPRING ONION 38

HACHUNE MIKU'S JOB

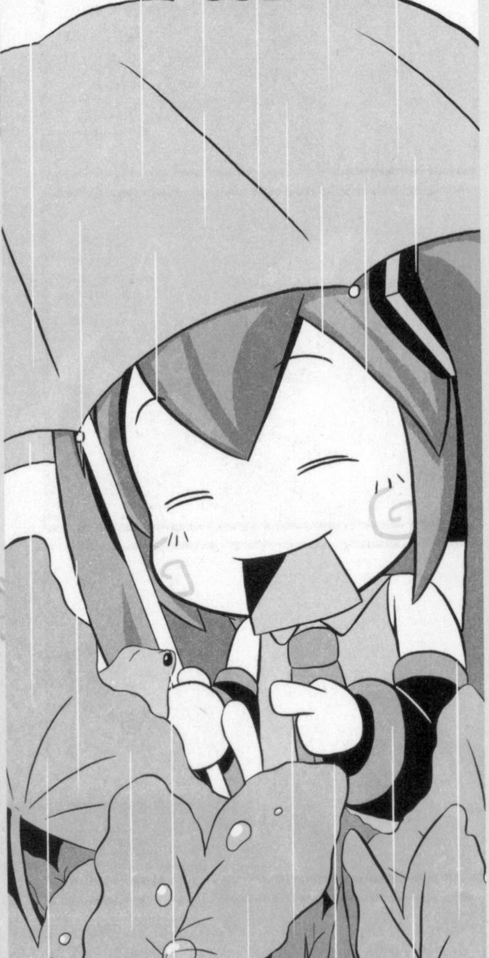

SUDDEN CLIMAX

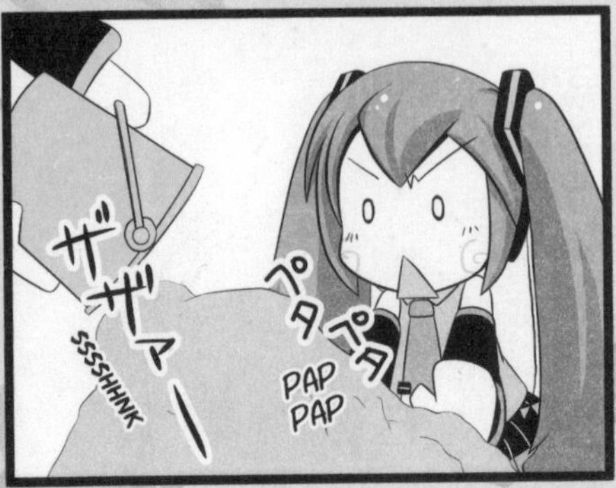
パタパタ
PAP PAP
ザザァー
SSSSHHNK

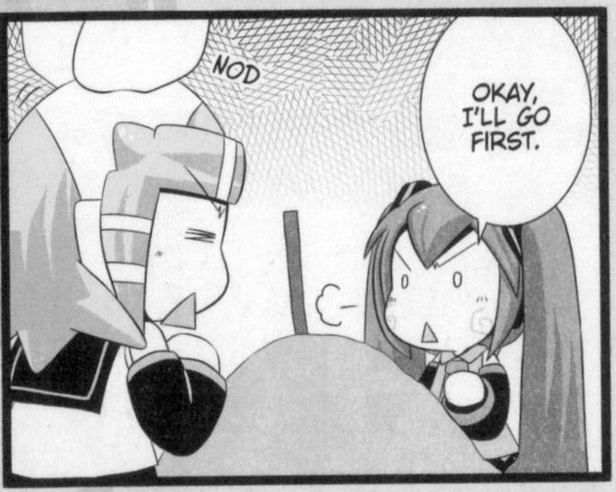
OKAY, I'LL GO FIRST.
NOD

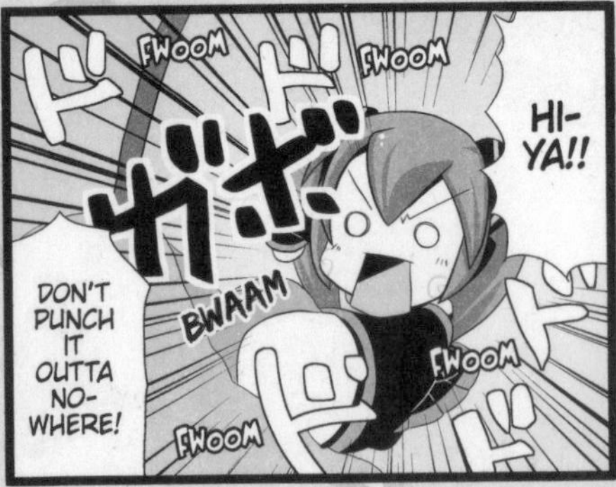
HI-YA!!
FWOOM
FWOOM
BWAAM
FWOOM
FWOOM
DON'T PUNCH IT OUTTA NO-WHERE!

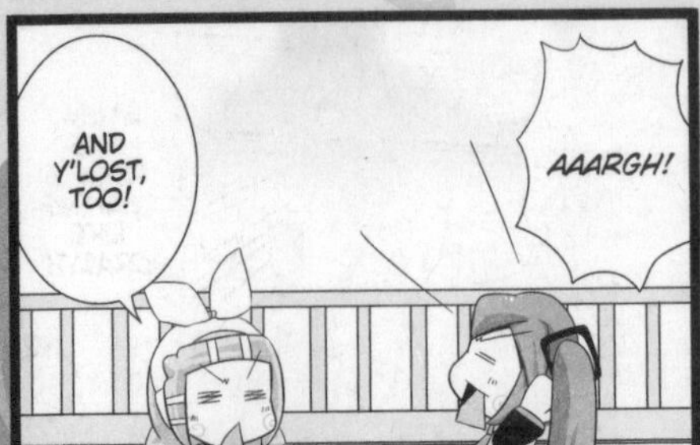
AAARGH!
AND Y'LOST, TOO!

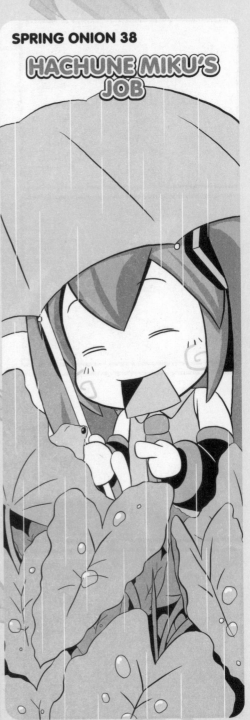

NOT GROWING AT ALL

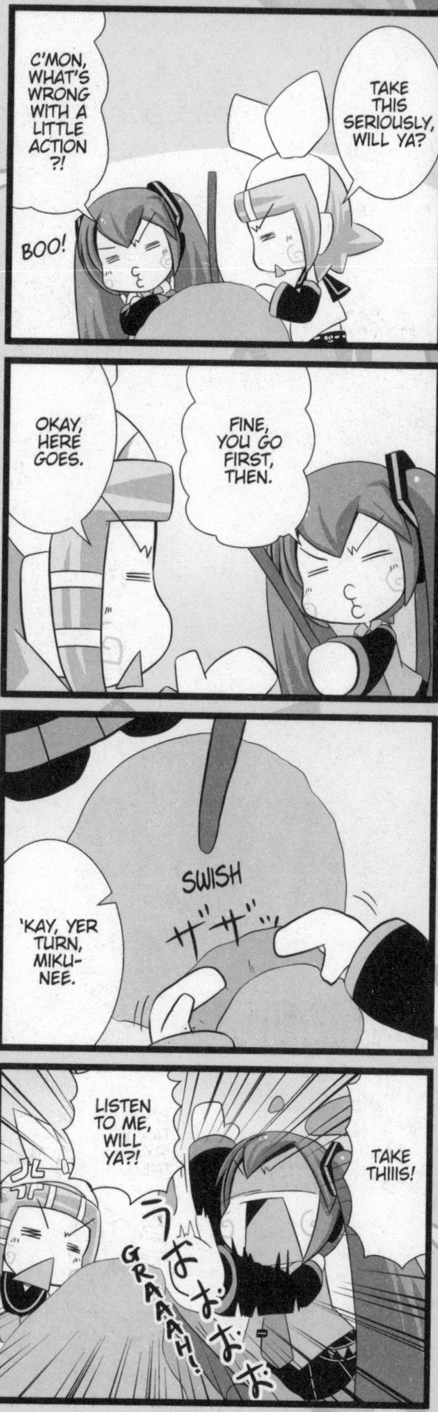
TAKE THIS SERIOUSLY, WILL YA?
C'MON, WHAT'S WRONG WITH A LITTLE ACTION?!
BOO!
FINE, YOU GO FIRST, THEN.
OKAY, HERE GOES.
SWISH
'KAY, YER TURN, MIKU-NEE.
TAKE THIIIS!
LISTEN TO ME, WILL YA?!
GRAAAH!

MISUNDERSTANDING

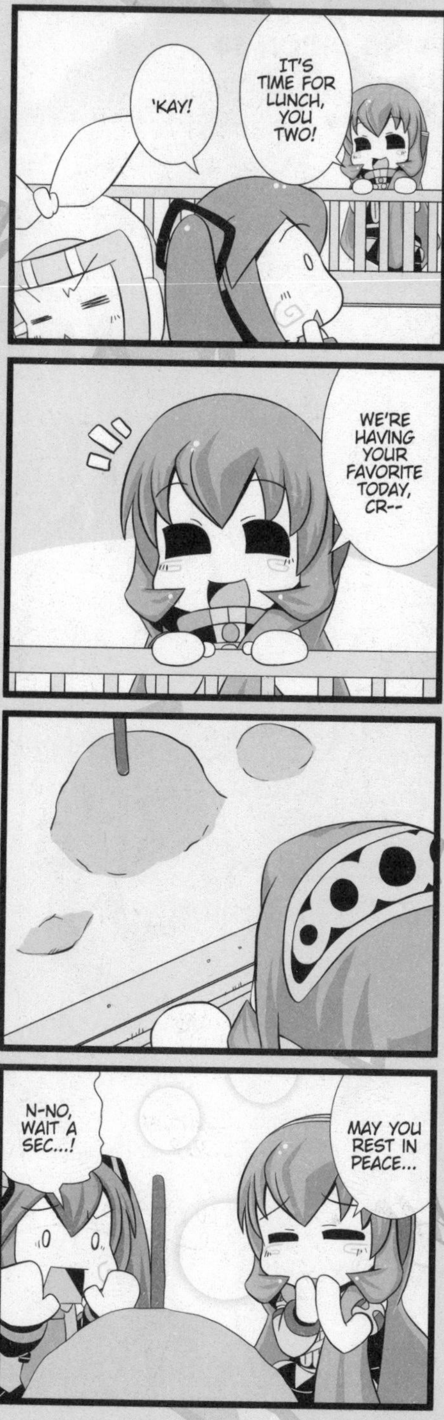
IT'S TIME FOR LUNCH, YOU TWO!
'KAY!
WE'RE HAVING YOUR FAVORITE TODAY, CR--
MAY YOU REST IN PEACE...
N-NO, WAIT A SEC...!

HUH? PART 1

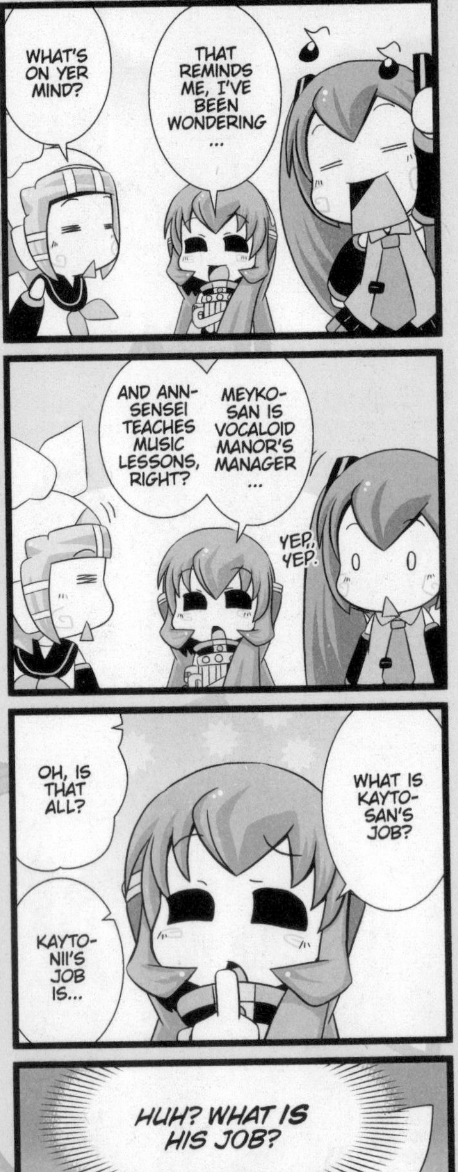
THAT REMINDS ME, I'VE BEEN WONDERING ...
WHAT'S ON YER MIND?
MEYKO-SAN IS VOCALOID MANOR'S MANAGER ...
AND ANN-SENSEI TEACHES MUSIC LESSONS, RIGHT?
YEP, YEP.
WHAT IS KAYTO-SAN'S JOB?
OH, IS THAT ALL?
KAYTO-NII'S JOB IS...
HUH? WHAT IS HIS JOB?

EVERYONE'S FAVORITE

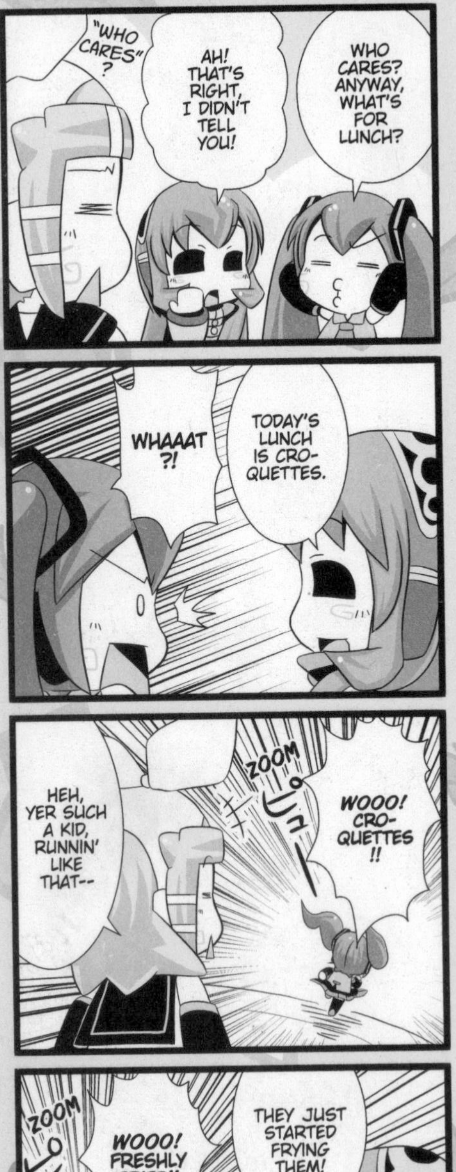
WHO CARES? ANYWAY, WHAT'S FOR LUNCH?
AH! THAT'S RIGHT, I DIDN'T TELL YOU!
"WHO CARES"?
TODAY'S LUNCH IS CRO-QUETTES.
WHAAAT ?!
WOOO! CRO-QUETTES !!
ZOOM
HEH, YER SUCH A KID, RUNNIN' LIKE THAT--
THEY JUST STARTED FRYING THEM!
WOOO! FRESHLY FRIED!!
ZOOM

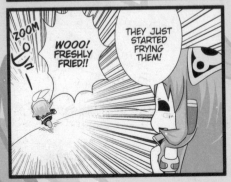

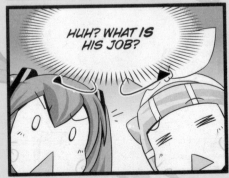

BOOBY TRAP

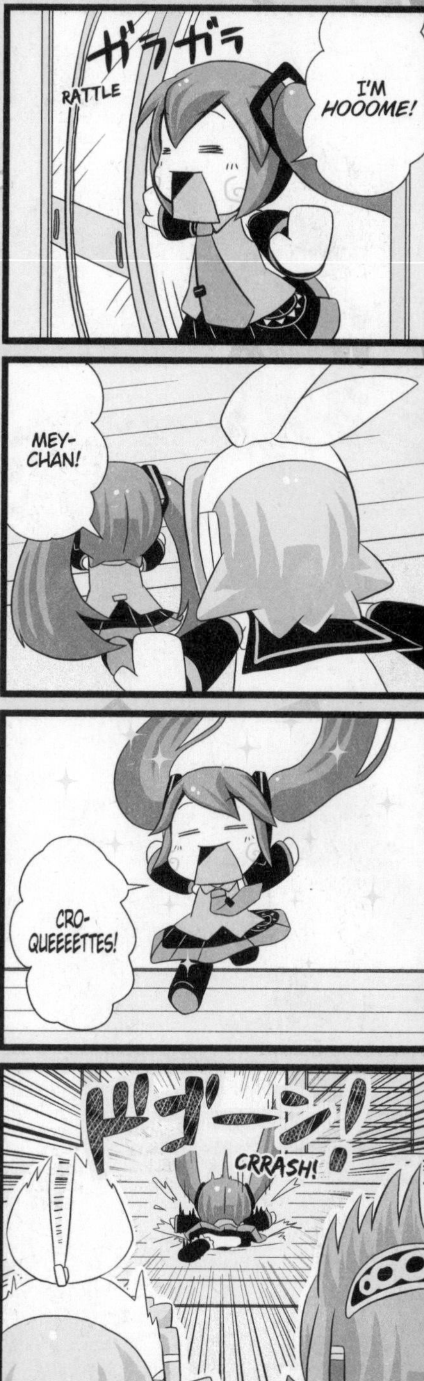
I'M HOOOME!
ガラガラ
RATTLE
MEY-CHAN!
CRO-QUEEEETTES!
ドゴーン!
CRRASH!

YOU JERKS

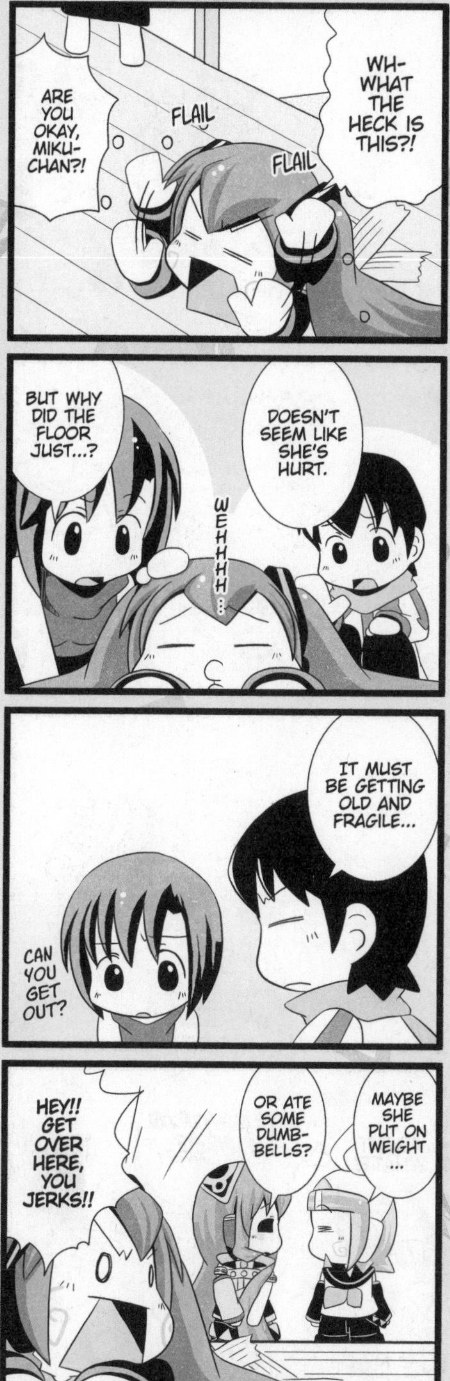
WH-WHAT THE HECK IS THIS?!
FLAIL
FLAIL
ARE YOU OKAY, MIKU-CHAN?!
DOESN'T SEEM LIKE SHE'S HURT.
WEHHHH...
BUT WHY DID THE FLOOR JUST...?
IT MUST BE GETTING OLD AND FRAGILE...
CAN YOU GET OUT?
MAYBE SHE PUT ON WEIGHT...
OR ATE SOME DUMB-BELLS?
HEY!! GET OVER HERE, YOU JERKS!!

REVERSED ROLES

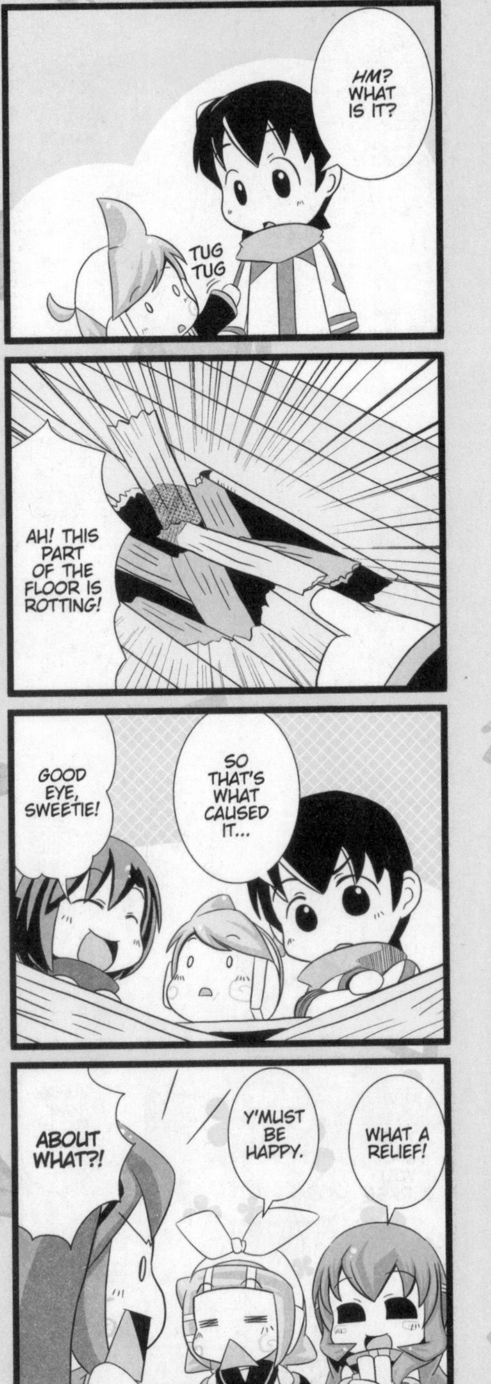
HM? WHAT IS IT?
TUG TUG
AH! THIS PART OF THE FLOOR IS ROTTING!
SO THAT'S WHAT CAUSED IT...
GOOD EYE, SWEETIE!
WHAT A RELIEF!
Y'MUST BE HAPPY.
ABOUT WHAT?!

HUH? PART 2

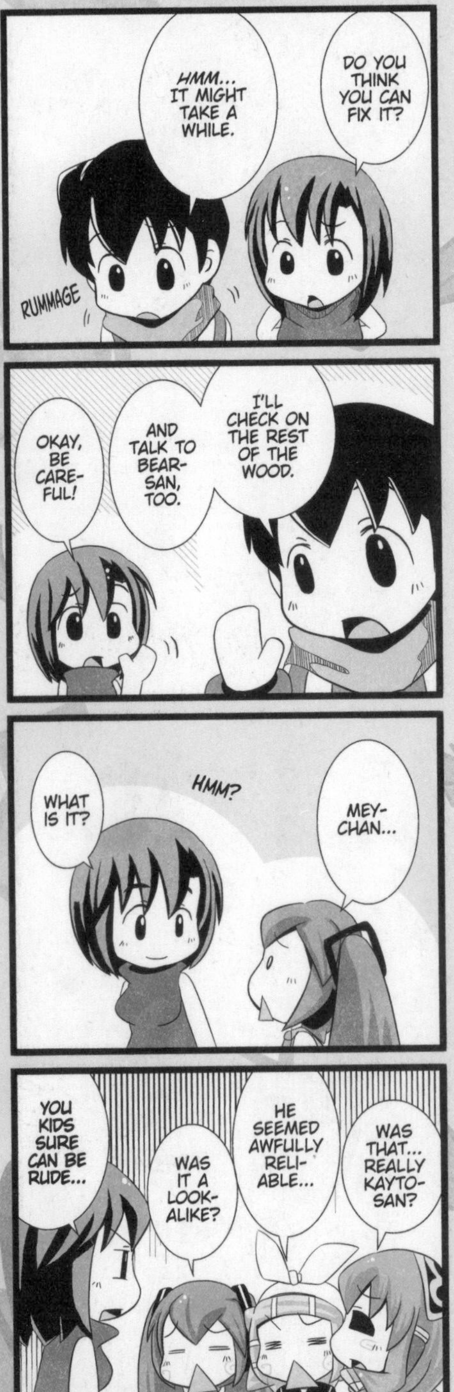
DO YOU THINK YOU CAN FIX IT?
HMM... IT MIGHT TAKE A WHILE.
RUMMAGE
I'LL CHECK ON THE REST OF THE WOOD.
AND TALK TO BEAR-SAN, TOO.
OKAY, BE CARE-FUL!
MEY-CHAN...
HMM?
WHAT IS IT?
WAS THAT... REALLY KAYTO-SAN?
HE SEEMED AWFULLY RELI-ABLE...
WAS IT A LOOK-ALIKE?
YOU KIDS SURE CAN BE RUDE...

MEMORIES

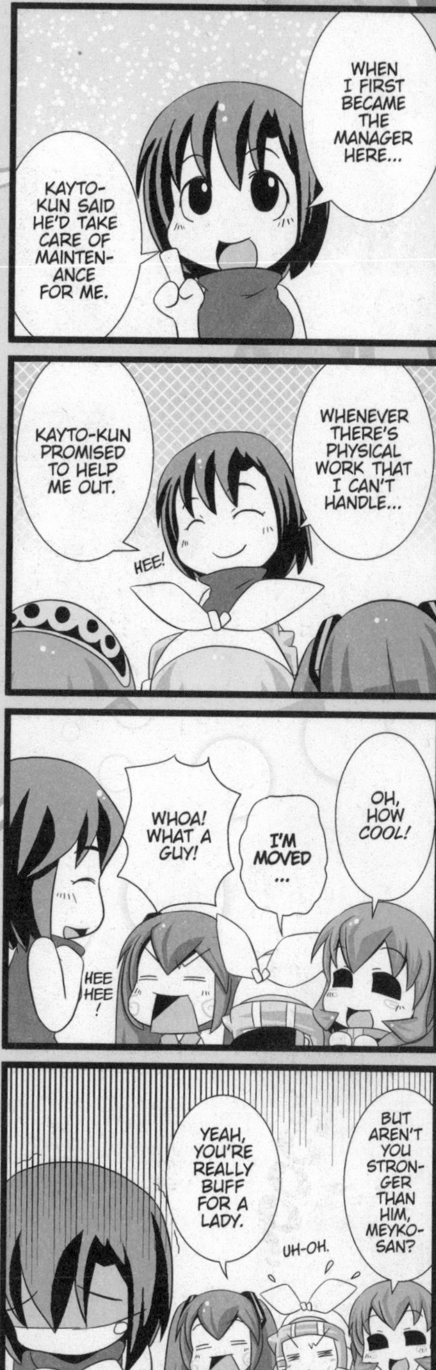

WHEN I FIRST BECAME THE MANAGER HERE...
KAYTO-KUN SAID HE'D TAKE CARE OF MAINTENANCE FOR ME.
WHENEVER THERE'S PHYSICAL WORK THAT I CAN'T HANDLE...
KAYTO-KUN PROMISED TO HELP ME OUT.
HEE!
OH, HOW COOL!
I'M MOVED...
WHOA! WHAT A GUY!
HEE HEE!
BUT AREN'T YOU STRONGER THAN HIM, MEYKO-SAN?
UH-OH.
YEAH, YOU'RE REALLY BUFF FOR A LADY.

MYSTERY

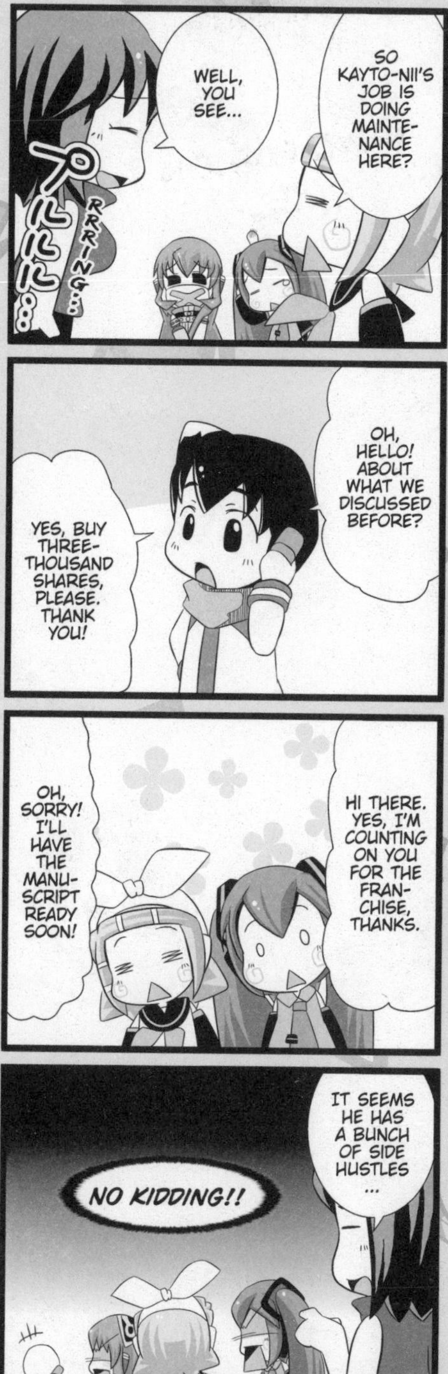

SO KAYTO-NII'S JOB IS DOING MAINTENANCE HERE?
WELL, YOU SEE...
プルルル...
RRRING...
OH, HELLO! ABOUT WHAT WE DISCUSSED BEFORE?
YES, BUY THREE-THOUSAND SHARES, PLEASE. THANK YOU!
HI THERE. YES, I'M COUNTING ON YOU FOR THE FRANCHISE, THANKS.
OH, SORRY! I'LL HAVE THE MANUSCRIPT READY SOON!
IT SEEMS HE HAS A BUNCH OF SIDE HUSTLES...
NO KIDDING!!

MOBILE VERSION LoiPara! BAND EDITION #7

SO THAT JUST LEAVES GUITAR, RIGHT?
SHOULDN'T A FOUR-PIECE BAND HAVE A KEYBOARD?
WHAT A GRAND IDEA!
HMM...
LUKA-CHAN, DON'T YOU PLAY PIANO?
I SUPPOSE, BUT ONLY A LITTLE...
OH, YER SO MODEST.
RIN-SAN!
POMF
SHOVE
I HEAR Y'WERE SO GOOD THERE WERE RUMORS ABOUT YA!
OH GOSH, UM...
LIKE WHAT?
BLUSH
LIKE "SHE'S GOT EIGHT ARMS"!
LIKE AN OCTOPUS?!
NOOO!
WIGGLE
WIGGLE

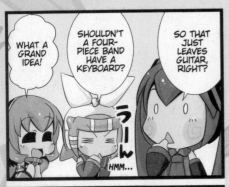

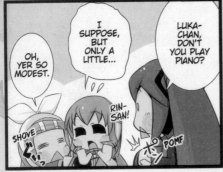

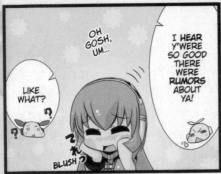

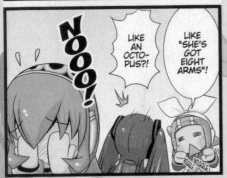

MOBILE VERSION LoiPara! BAND EDITION #8

GUESS THAT LEAVES YA ON GUITAR, MIKU-NEE.
YEAH! I GOT THIS!
IT'S ALL DECIDED, THEN!
LET'S MAKE THE BEST BAND EVER!!
UM...DO WE *HAVE* INSTRUMENTS?
URGH...

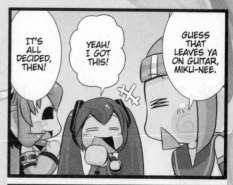

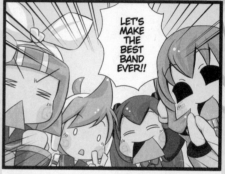

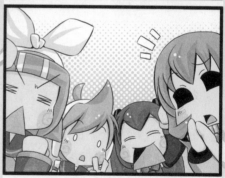

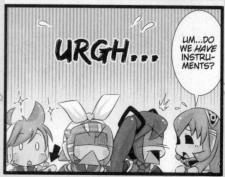

SPRING ONION 39

HACHUNE MIKU'S EYEPATCH

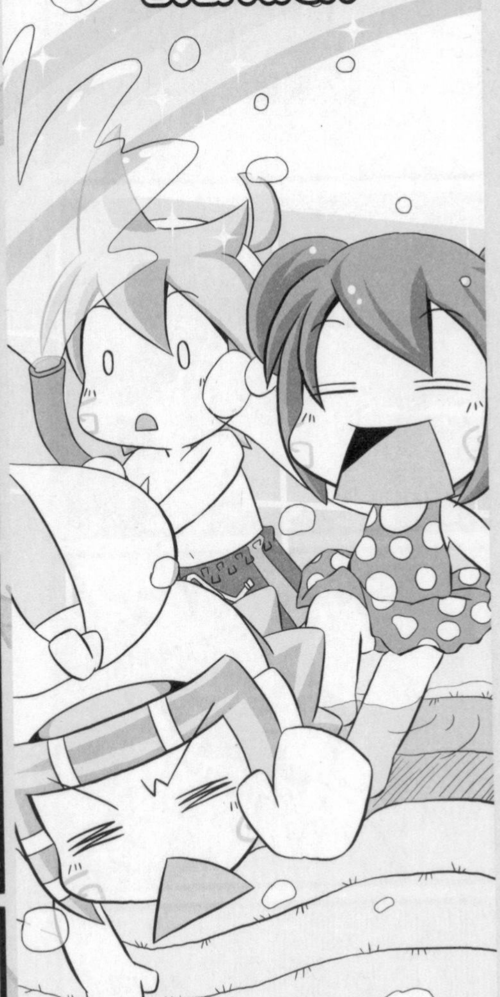

WHOOPS

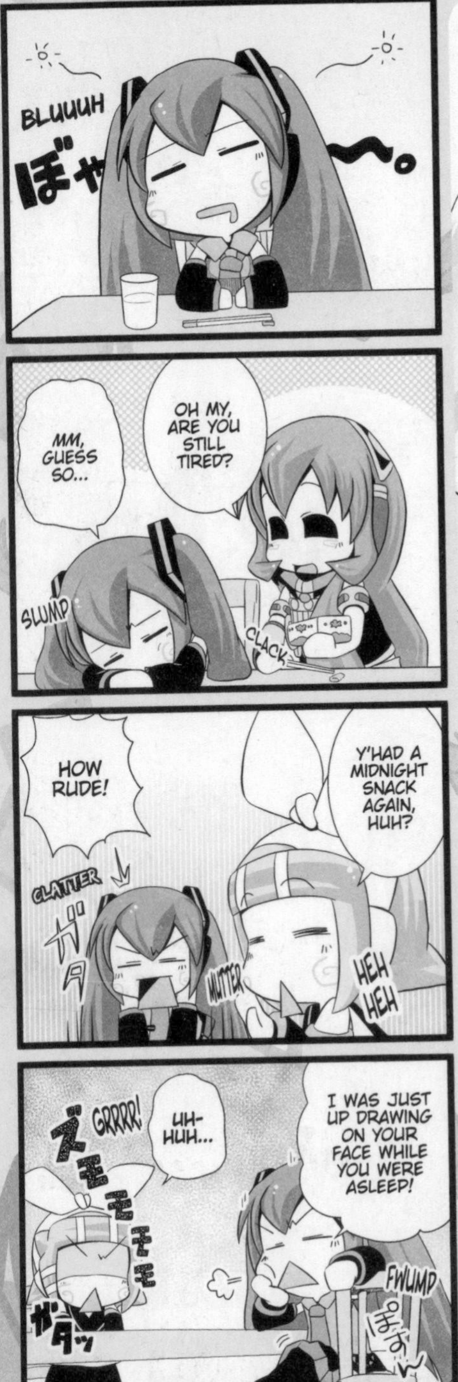
BLUUUH
ぼや〜。
OH MY, ARE YOU STILL TIRED?
MM, GUESS SO...
CLACK
SLUMP
Y'HAD A MIDNIGHT SNACK AGAIN, HUH?
HEH HEH
MUTTER
HOW RUDE!
CLATTER
ガタ
I WAS JUST UP DRAWING ON YOUR FACE WHILE YOU WERE ASLEEP!
FWUMP
ぽすん
UH-HUH...
GRRRR!
ズモモモモ
ガタッ

SQUEAK

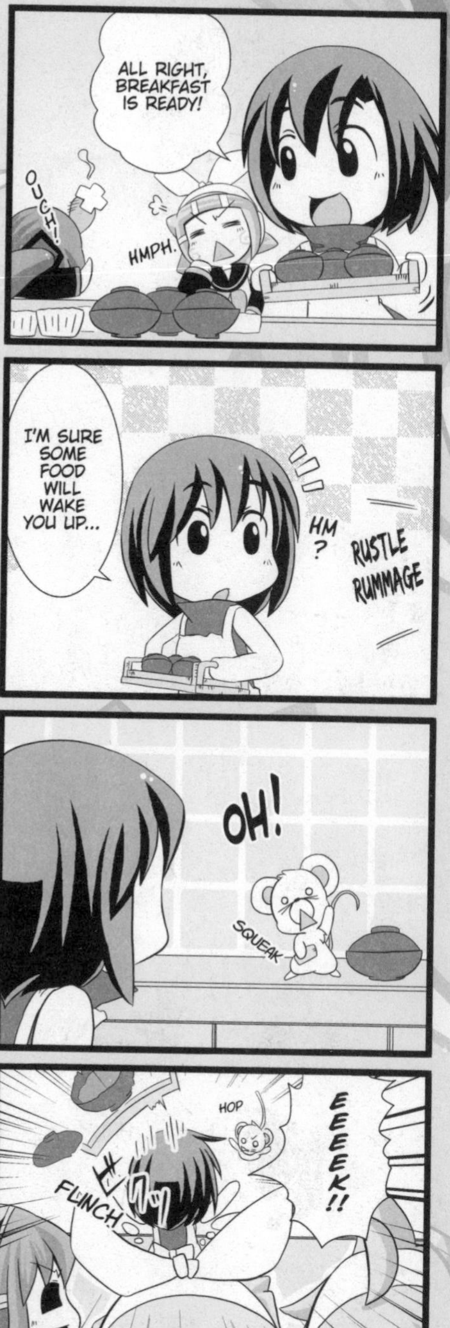
ALL RIGHT, BREAKFAST IS READY!
OUCH!
HMPH.
I'M SURE SOME FOOD WILL WAKE YOU UP...
HM?
RUSTLE RUMMAGE
OH!
SQUEAK
EEEEK!!
HOP
FLINCH

SECRET TECHNIQUE

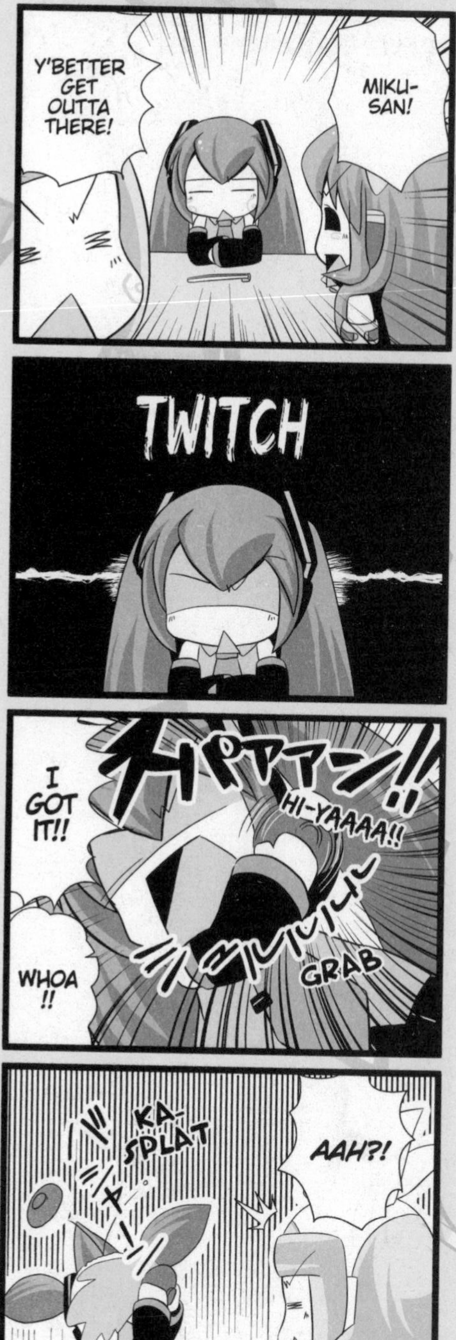
MIKU-SAN!
Y'BETTER GET OUTTA THERE!
TWITCH
HI-YAAAA!!
I GOT IT!!
GRAB
WHOA!!
AAH?!
KA-SPLAT

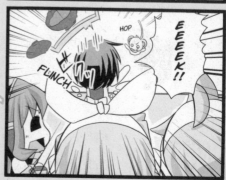

OVERKILL

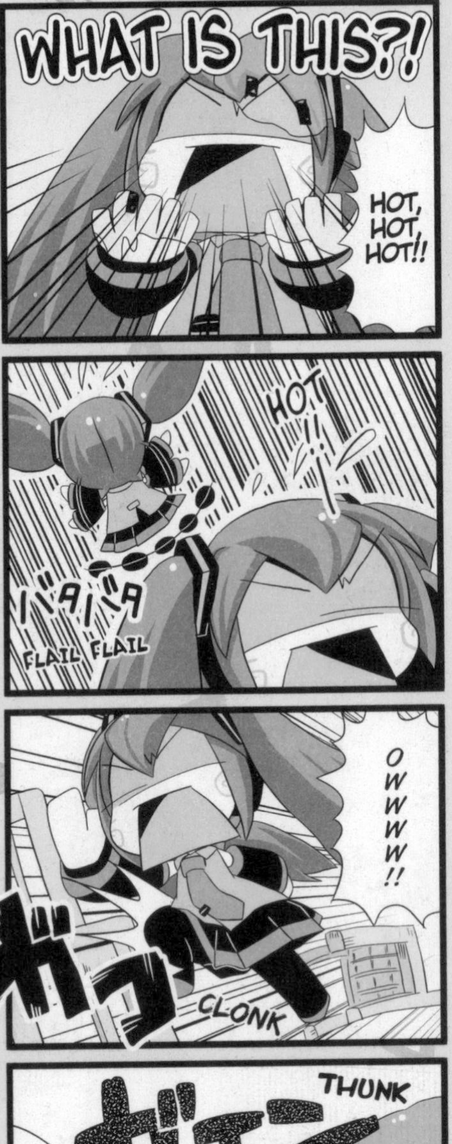
WHAT IS THIS?!
HOT, HOT, HOT!!
HOT!!
FLAIL FLAIL
OWWWWW!!
CLONK
THUNK

HUH?

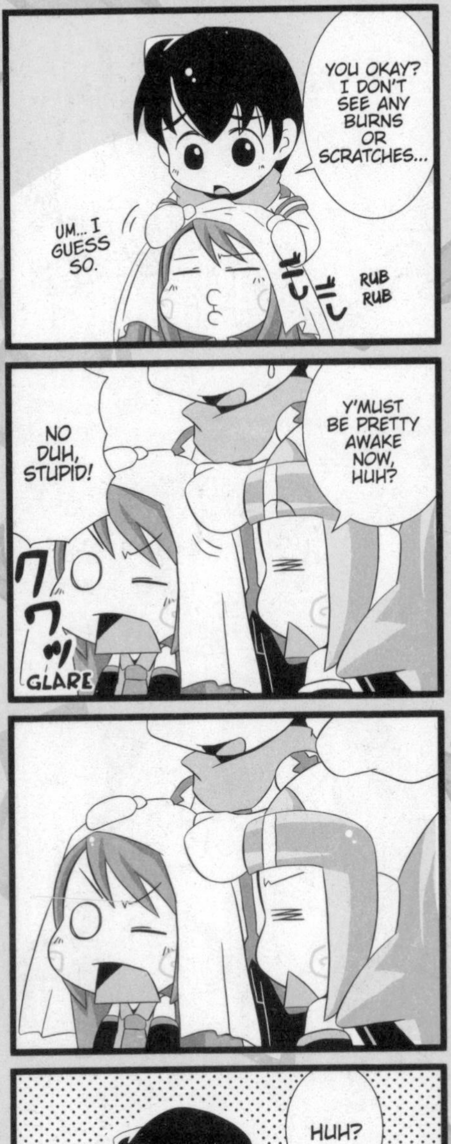
YOU OKAY? I DON'T SEE ANY BURNS OR SCRATCHES...
UM... I GUESS SO.
RUB RUB
Y'MUST BE PRETTY AWAKE NOW, HUH?
NO DUH, STUPID!
GLARE
HUH?
YOUR EYE...

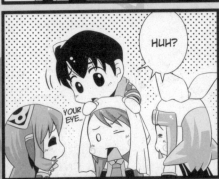

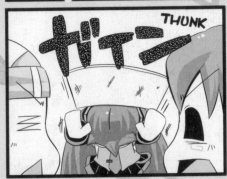

POSITIVE

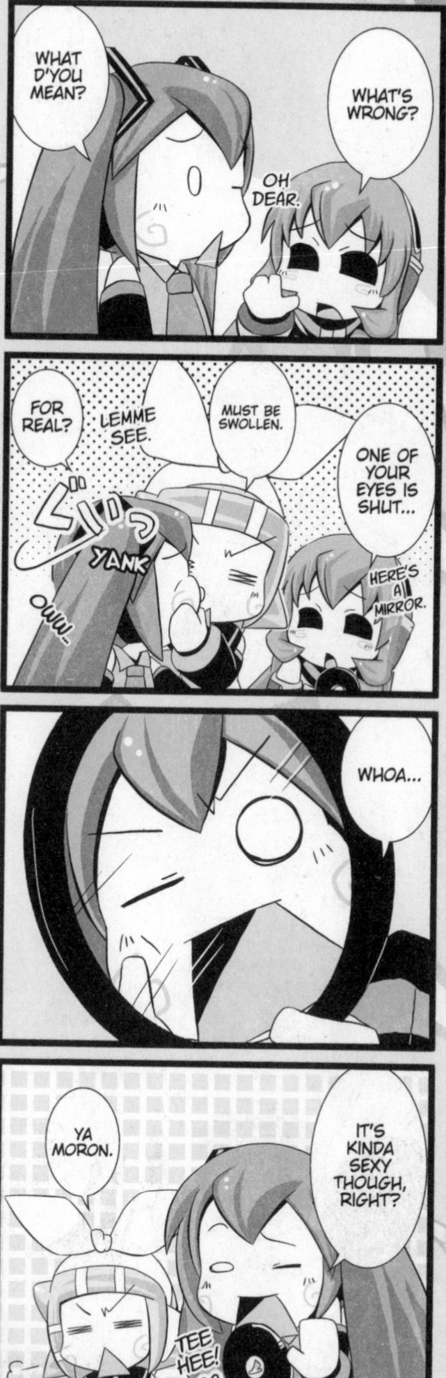
WHAT'S WRONG?
WHAT D'YOU MEAN?
OH DEAR.
ONE OF YOUR EYES IS SHUT...
MUST BE SWOLLEN.
LEMME SEE.
FOR REAL?
YANK
HERE'S A MIRROR.
OWW!
WHOA...
IT'S KINDA SEXY THOUGH, RIGHT?
YA MORON.
TEE HEE!

THEY'RE BOTH RIGHT

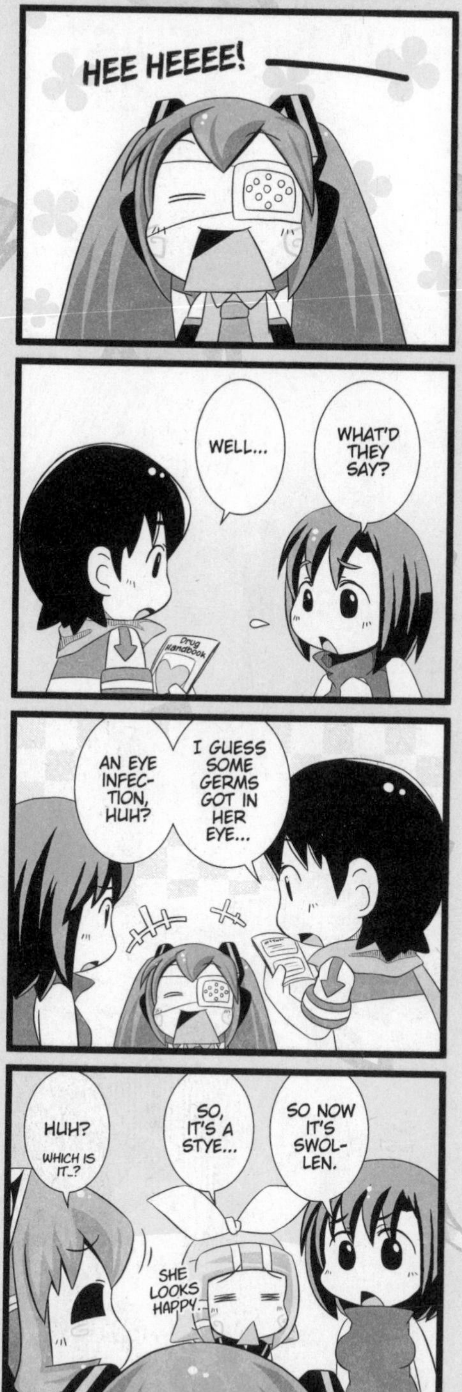
HEE HEEEE!
WHAT'D THEY SAY?
WELL...
Drug Handbook
I GUESS SOME GERMS GOT IN HER EYE...
AN EYE INFEC-TION, HUH?
SO NOW IT'S SWOL-LEN.
SO, IT'S A STYE...
HUH?
WHICH IS IT..?
SHE LOOKS HAPPY.

OUTBREAK

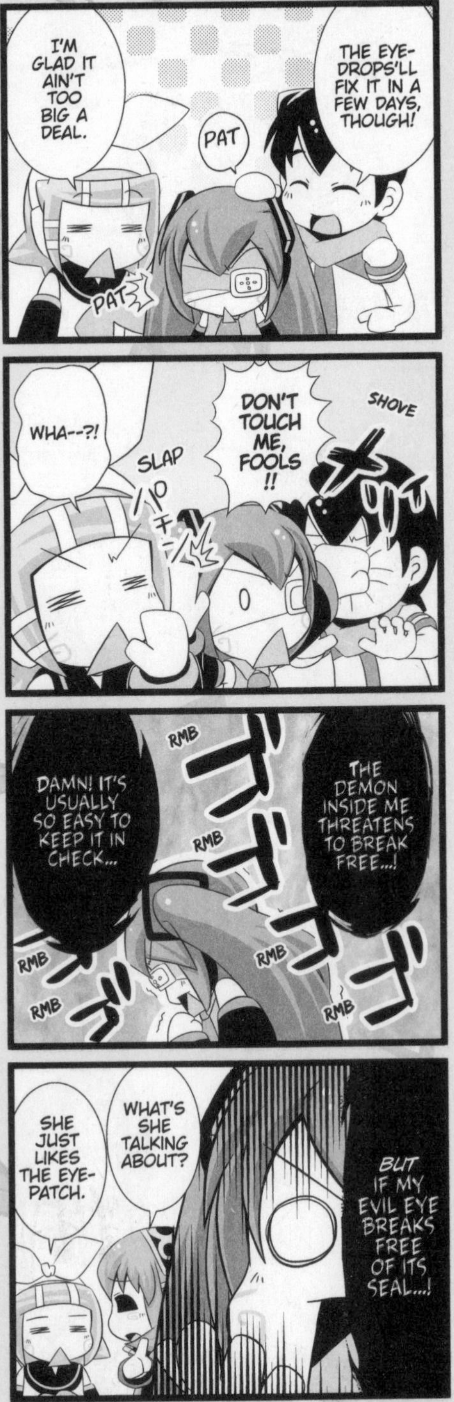
THE EYE-DROPS'LL FIX IT IN A FEW DAYS, THOUGH!
PAT
I'M GLAD IT AIN'T TOO BIG A DEAL.
PAT
SHOVE
DON'T TOUCH ME, FOOLS!!
SLAP
WHA--?!
THE DEMON INSIDE ME THREATENS TO BREAK FREE...!
RMB
DAMN! IT'S USUALLY SO EASY TO KEEP IT IN CHECK...
RMB
RMB
RMB
RMB
RMB
BUT IF MY EVIL EYE BREAKS FREE OF ITS SEAL...!
WHAT'S SHE TALKING ABOUT?
SHE JUST LIKES THE EYE-PATCH.

POKE POKE

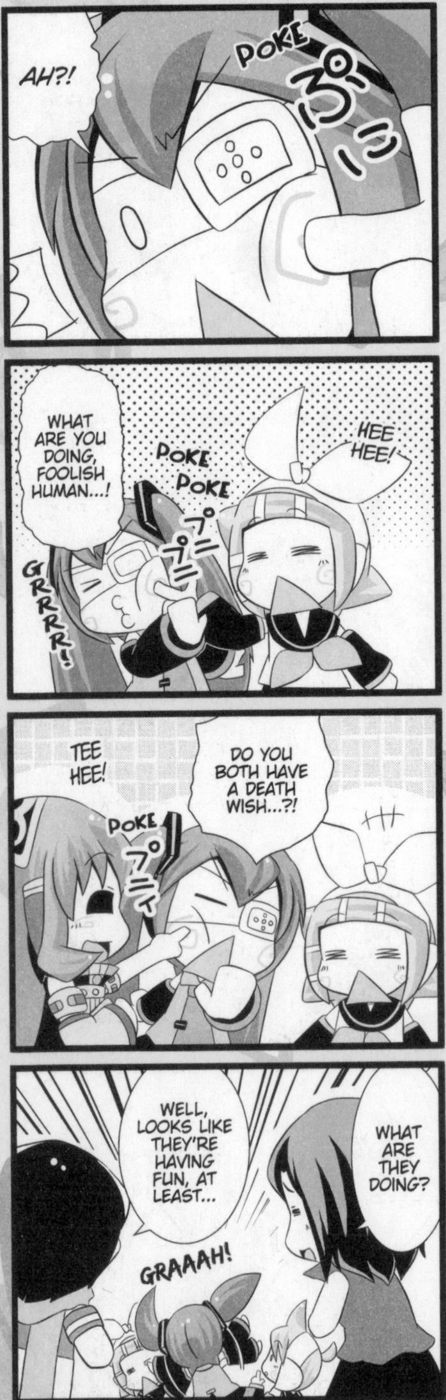
POKE
AH?!
HEE HEE!
POKE POKE
WHAT ARE YOU DOING, FOOLISH HUMAN...!
GRRRRR!
DO YOU BOTH HAVE A DEATH WISH...?!
TEE HEE!
POKE
WHAT ARE THEY DOING?
WELL, LOOKS LIKE THEY'RE HAVING FUN, AT LEAST...
GRAAAH!

COMRADES

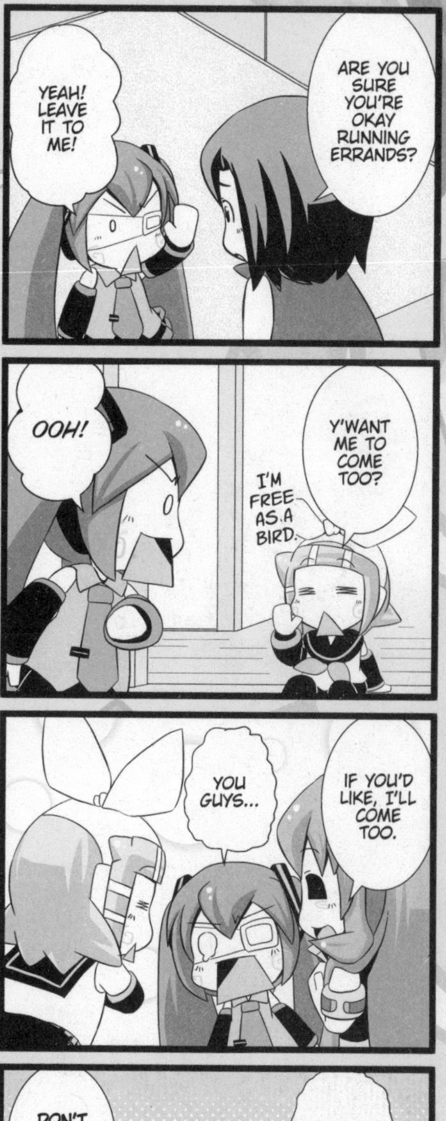
ARE YOU SURE YOU'RE OKAY RUNNING ERRANDS?
YEAH! LEAVE IT TO ME!
Y'WANT ME TO COME TOO?
I'M FREE AS A BIRD.
OOH!
IF YOU'D LIKE, I'LL COME TOO.
YOU GUYS...
MY COM-RADES!!
SOB
DON'T CALL US THAT!

THE REAL THING

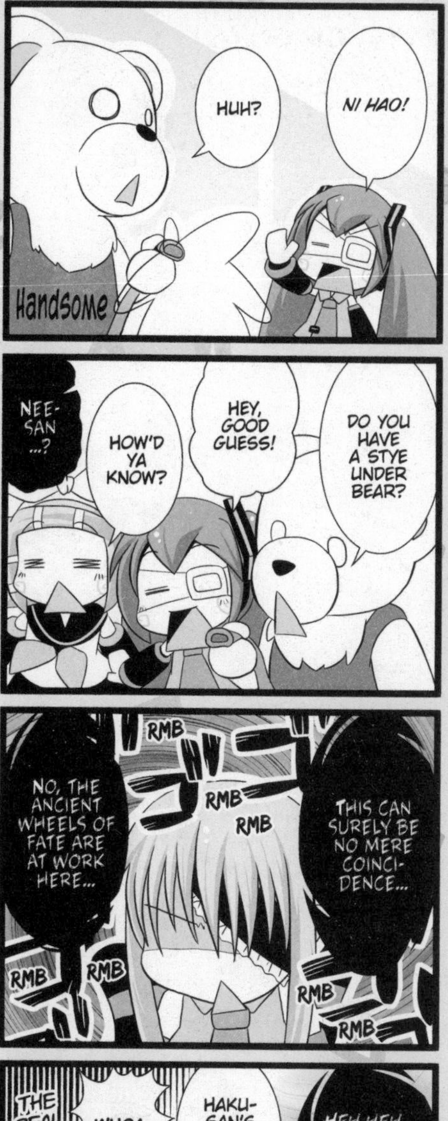
NI HAO!
HUH?
Handsome
DO YOU HAVE A STYE UNDER BEAR?
HEY, GOOD GUESS!
HOW'D YA KNOW?
NEE-SAN ...?
THIS CAN SURELY BE NO MERE COINCIDENCE...
RMB
RMB
RMB
NO, THE ANCIENT WHEELS OF FATE ARE AT WORK HERE...
RMB
RMB
RMB
RMB
HEH HEH... NOW OUR DEMONS SHALL BE JOINED AS ONE...
HAKU-SAN'S BEARING ONE TOO.
WHOA, SHE'S SCARY!
THE REAL THING!
Dark Future

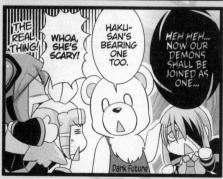

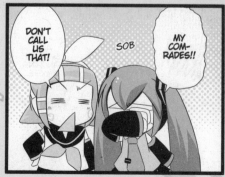

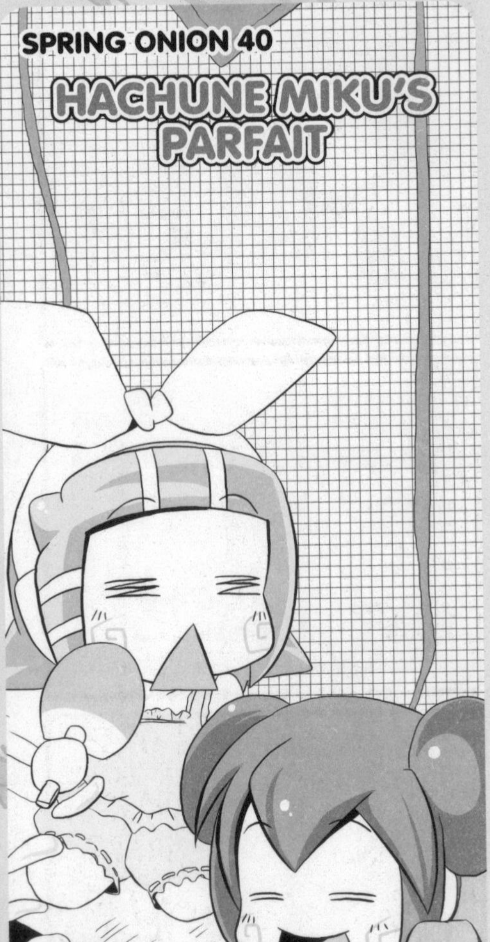
SPRING ONION 40
HACHUNE MIKU'S PARFAIT

SUDDEN THOUGHT

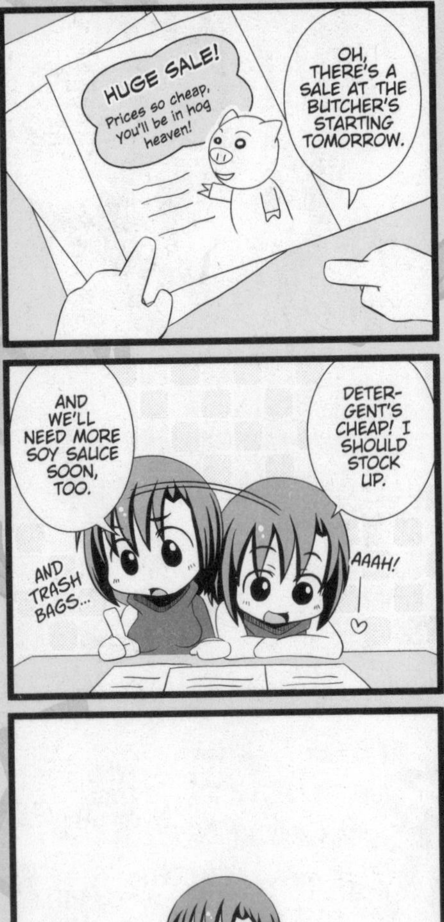
OH, THERE'S A SALE AT THE BUTCHER'S STARTING TOMORROW.
HUGE SALE! Prices so cheap, you'll be in hog heaven!
DETER-GENT'S CHEAP! I SHOULD STOCK UP.
AAAH!
AND WE'LL NEED MORE SOY SAUCE SOON, TOO.
AND TRASH BAGS...
BOY, AM I SICK OF PINCHING PENNIES...
URRGH

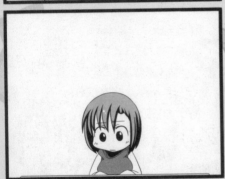

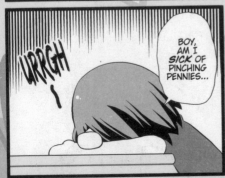

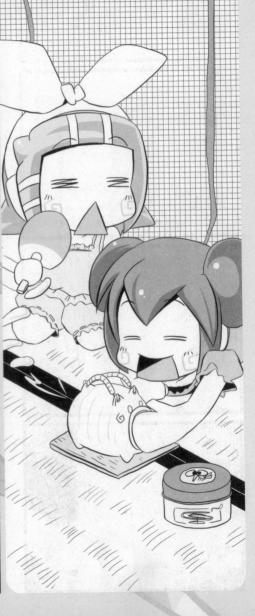

BAD TIMING

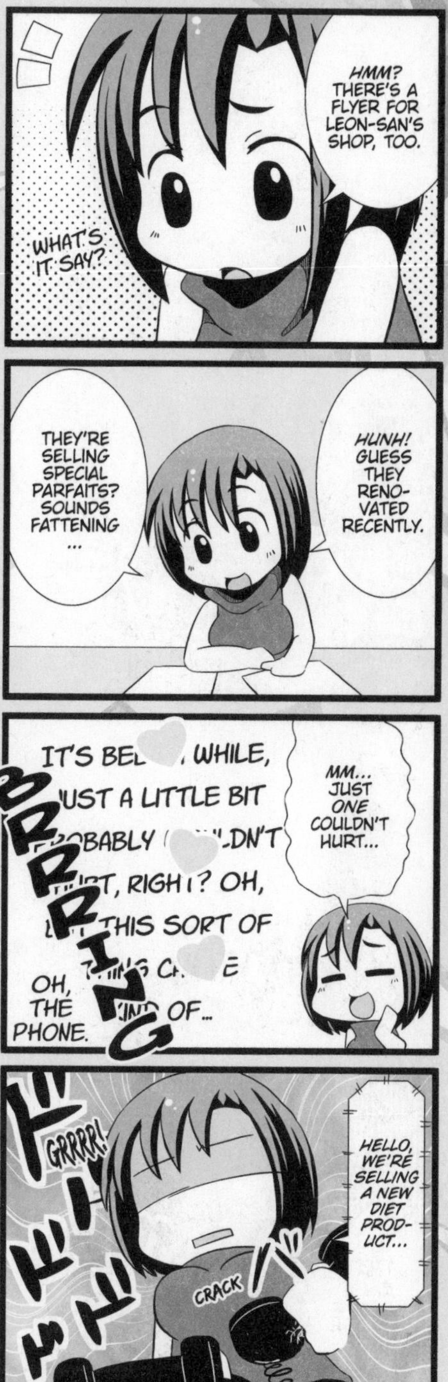
HMM? THERE'S A FLYER FOR LEON-SAN'S SHOP, TOO.
WHAT'S IT SAY?
HUNH! GUESS THEY RENO-VATED RECENTLY.
THEY'RE SELLING SPECIAL PARFAITS? SOUNDS FATTENING ...
MM... JUST ONE COULDN'T HURT...
BRRRRING
OH, THE PHONE.
HELLO, WE'RE SELLING A NEW DIET PROD-UCT...
CRACK
GRRRR!

PRIORITIES

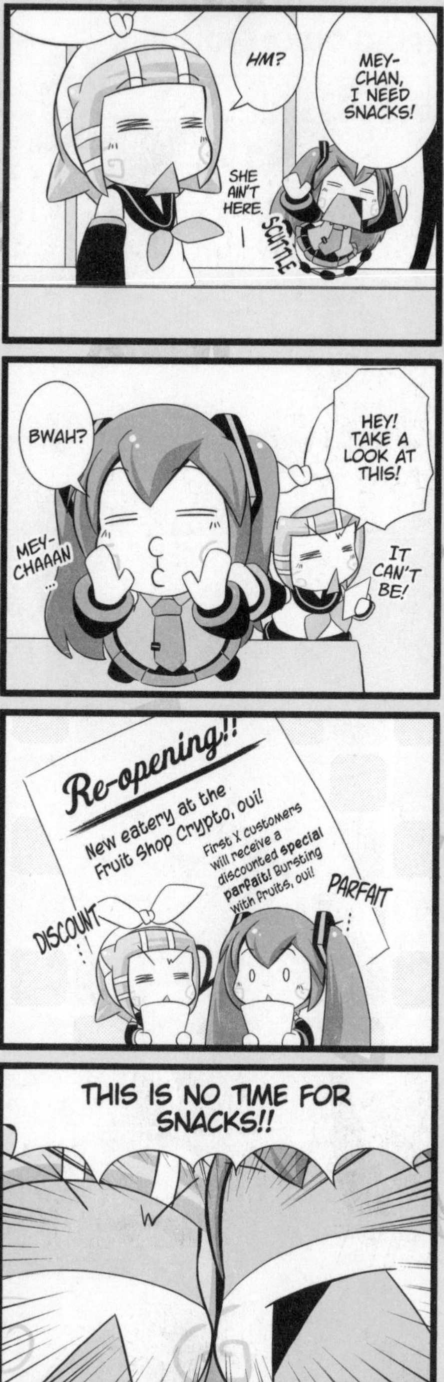
MEY-CHAN, I NEED SNACKS!
HM?
SHE AIN'T HERE.
SCUTTLE
HEY! TAKE A LOOK AT THIS!
IT CAN'T BE!
BWAH?
MEY-CHAAAN ...
Re-opening!!
New eatery at the Fruit Shop Crypto, oui!
First X customers will receive a discounted special parfait! Bursting with fruits, oui!
PARFAIT
DISCOUNT
THIS IS NO TIME FOR SNACKS!!

FORGET IT, FORGET IT

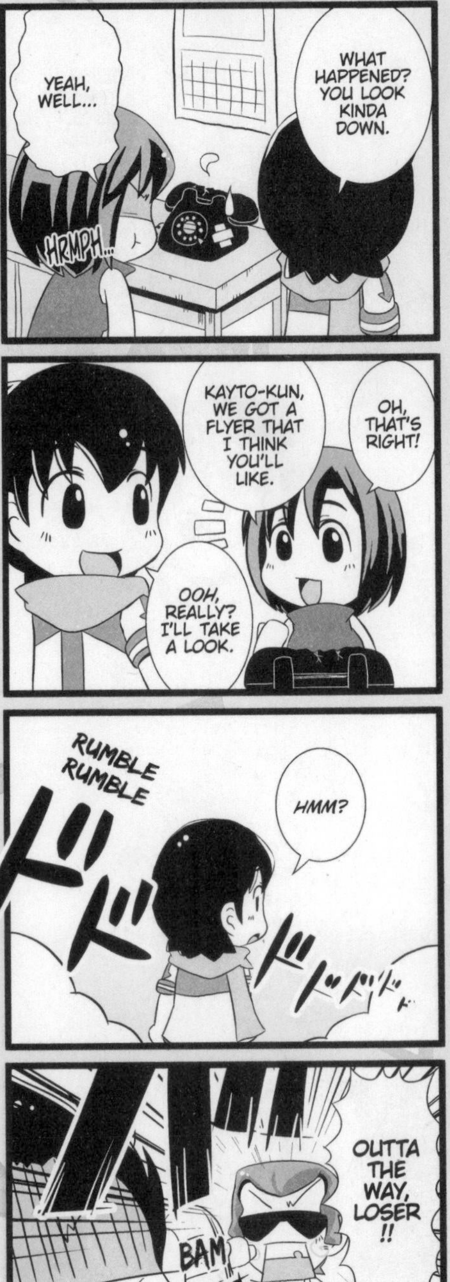
WHAT HAPPENED? YOU LOOK KINDA DOWN.
YEAH, WELL...
HRMPH...
OH, THAT'S RIGHT!
KAYTO-KUN, WE GOT A FLYER THAT I THINK YOU'LL LIKE.
OOH, REALLY? I'LL TAKE A LOOK.
RUMBLE RUMBLE
HMM?
OUTTA THE WAY, LOSER!!
BAM

NOT THAT

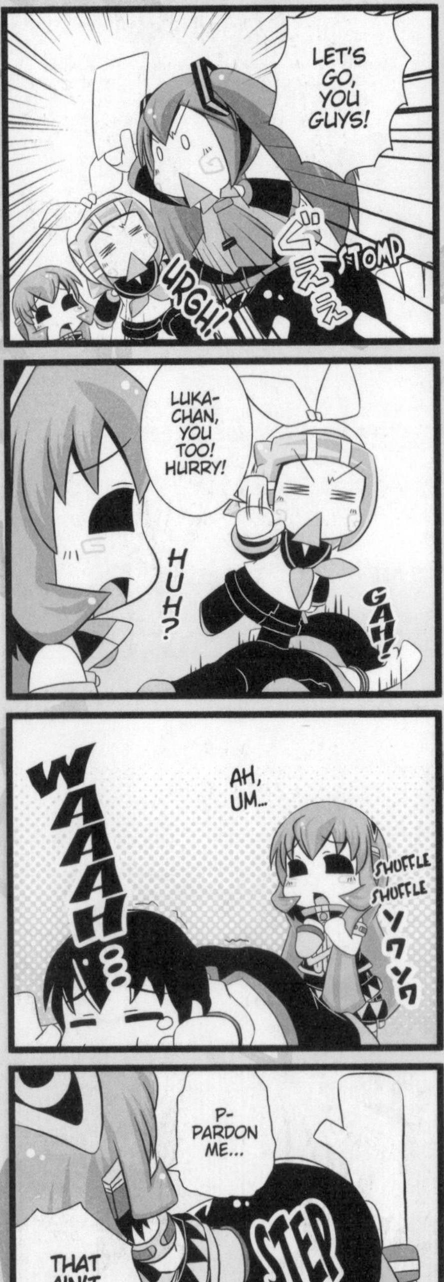
LET'S GO, YOU GUYS!
STOMP
URGH!
LUKA-CHAN, YOU TOO! HURRY!
HUH?
GAH!
AH, UM...
SHUFFLE SHUFFLE
WAAAAH...
P-PARDON ME...
STEP
THAT AIN'T WHAT I MEANT!!
C'MON!

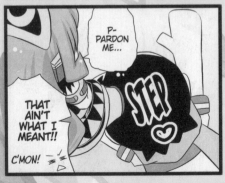

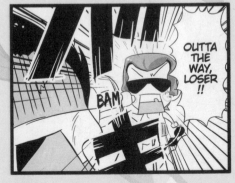

FINISHER

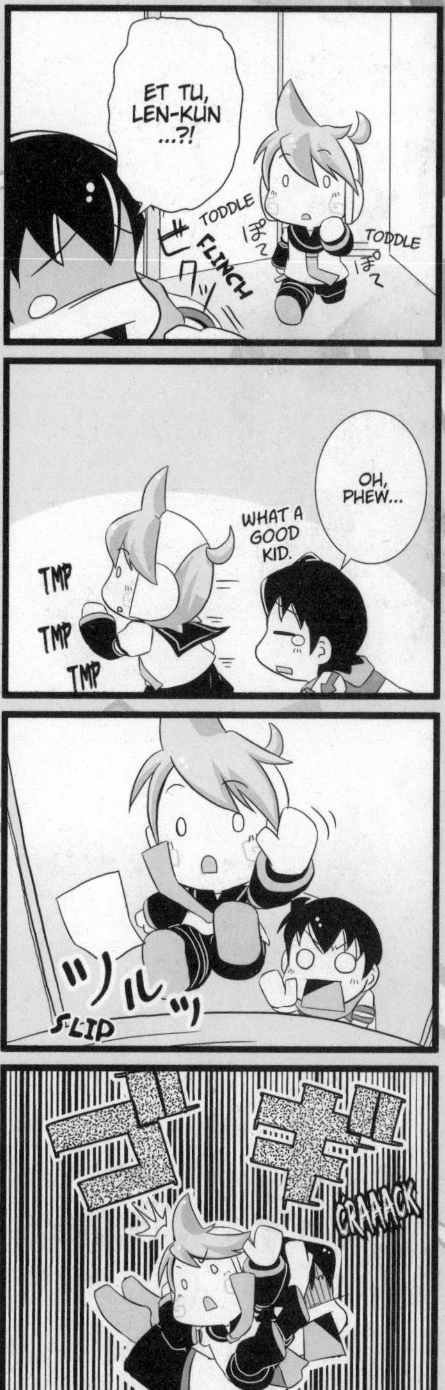
ET TU, LEN-KUN ...?!
TODDLE
TODDLE
FLINCH
OH, PHEW...
WHAT A GOOD KID.
TMP
TMP
TMP
SLIP
CRAAACK

FLYER

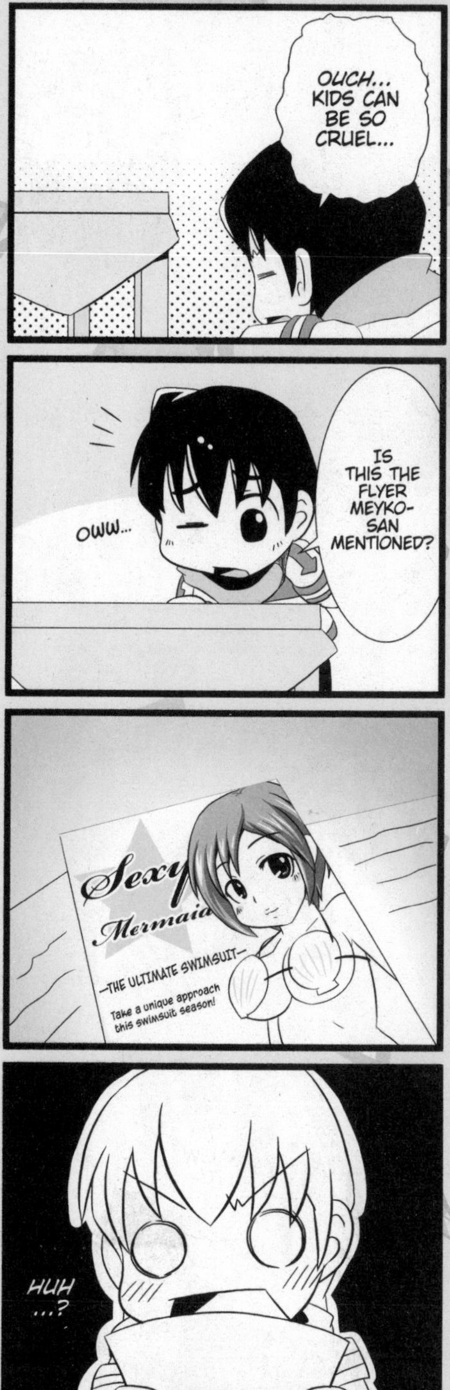
OUCH... KIDS CAN BE SO CRUEL...
IS THIS THE FLYER MEYKO-SAN MENTIONED?
OWW...
Sexy Mermaid
—THE ULTIMATE SWIMSUIT—
Take a unique approach this swimsuit season!
HUH ...?

WELL?

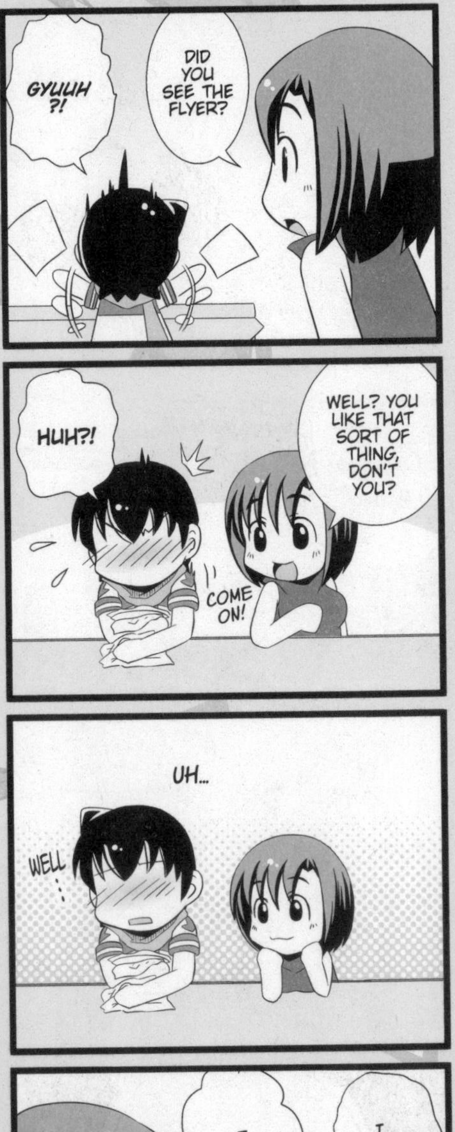
DID YOU SEE THE FLYER?
GYUUH ?!
WELL? YOU LIKE THAT SORT OF THING, DON'T YOU?
COME ON!
HUH?!
UH...
WELL...
I... DON'T DISLIKE IT...
I KNEW IT!

A MAIDEN'S FULL POWER

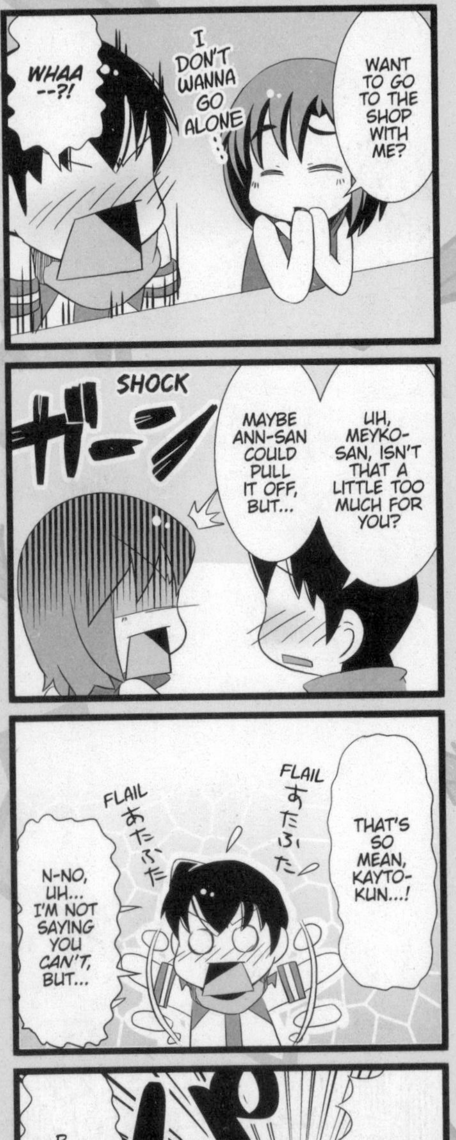
WANT TO GO TO THE SHOP WITH ME?
I DON'T WANNA GO ALONE...
WHAA--?!
UH, MEYKO-SAN, ISN'T THAT A LITTLE TOO MUCH FOR YOU?
MAYBE ANN-SAN COULD PULL IT OFF, BUT...
SHOCK
ガーン
THAT'S SO MEAN, KAYTO-KUN...!
FLAIL すたふた
FLAIL あたふた
N-NO, UH... I'M NOT SAYING YOU CAN'T, BUT...
WHAT'S WRONG WITH ONE LITTLE PARFAIT? YOU JERK!!
SLAP
P... PARFAIT ?!

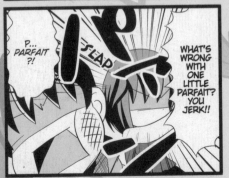

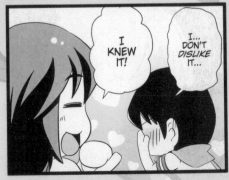

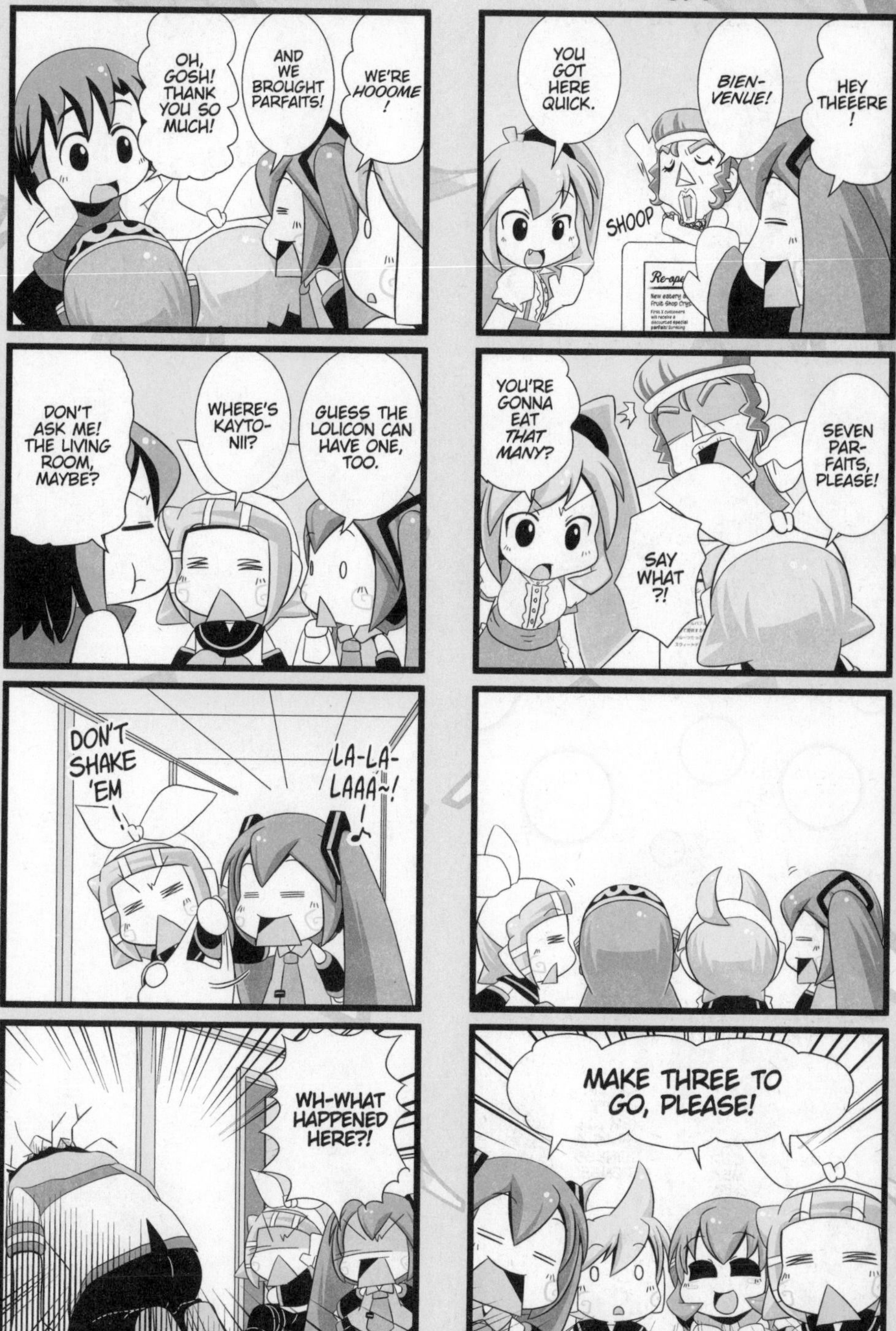
HEY THEEERE!
BIEN-VENUE!
YOU GOT HERE QUICK.
SHOOP
SEVEN PAR-FAITS, PLEASE!
YOU'RE GONNA EAT THAT MANY?
SAY WHAT ?!
MAKE THREE TO GO, PLEASE!
WE'RE HOOOME!
AND WE BROUGHT PARFAITS!
OH, GOSH! THANK YOU SO MUCH!
GUESS THE LOLICON CAN HAVE ONE, TOO.
WHERE'S KAYTO-NII?
DON'T ASK ME! THE LIVING ROOM, MAYBE?
LA-LA-LAAA~!
DON'T SHAKE 'EM!
WH-WHAT HAPPENED HERE?!

MOBILE VERSION LoiPara! BAND EDITION #9

DON'T WORRY, WE HAVE INSTRUMENTS RIGHT HERE!
TA-DAAA!
WHOA!
Y'GOT EVERYTHING!
I CAN TEACH YOU THE BASICS OF MUSIC, TOO.
THAT'S OUR MEY-CHAN FOR YOU!
MEYKO-SAN, YER A STAND-UP GAL!
BOO-HOO!
BUT THESE ARE BRAND NEW, AREN'T THEY?
WHAT ABOUT YER BUDGET?
OH, YOU KIDS SHOULDN'T WORRY ABOUT THAT STUFF!
WE CAN WRITE THEM ALL OFF AS A BUSINESS EXPENSE!
GRIN
THAT'S OUR MEY-CHAN.
SURE IS.

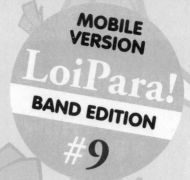

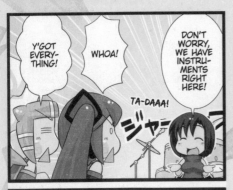

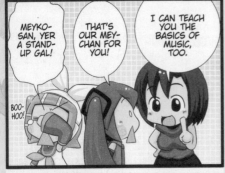

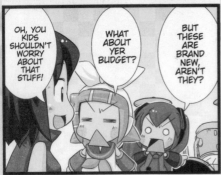

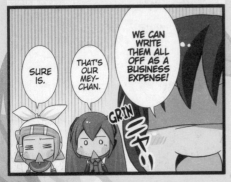

MOBILE VERSION

LoiPara!

BAND EDITION

#10

HUH? LEN-KUN'S BASS DOESN'T LOOK NEW...
HM?
YER RIGHT! AND THE COLOR LOOKS FAMILIAR...
THAT'S A HAND-ME-DOWN FROM ME.
FOR REAL?!
YOU CAN PLAY AN INSTRUMENT, KAYTO-NII?
I'M GREAT WITH INSTRUMENTS AND ALL KINDS OF GEAR!
WOBBLE WOBBLE
I'LL TEACH YOU ALL THERE IS TO KNOW!
STREEETCH
バーン
YEAH, NO THANKS.
YER CREEPIN' ME OUT.
SHOCK
ガーン
SHOO SHOO!

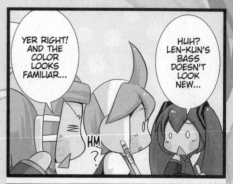

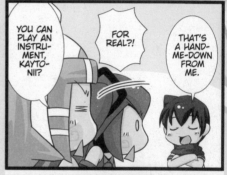

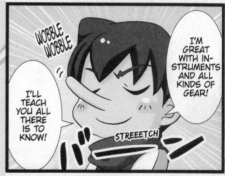

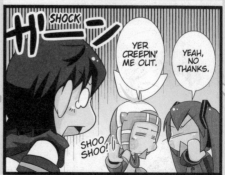

SPRING ONION 41

HACHUNE MIKU'S CONVENTIONS

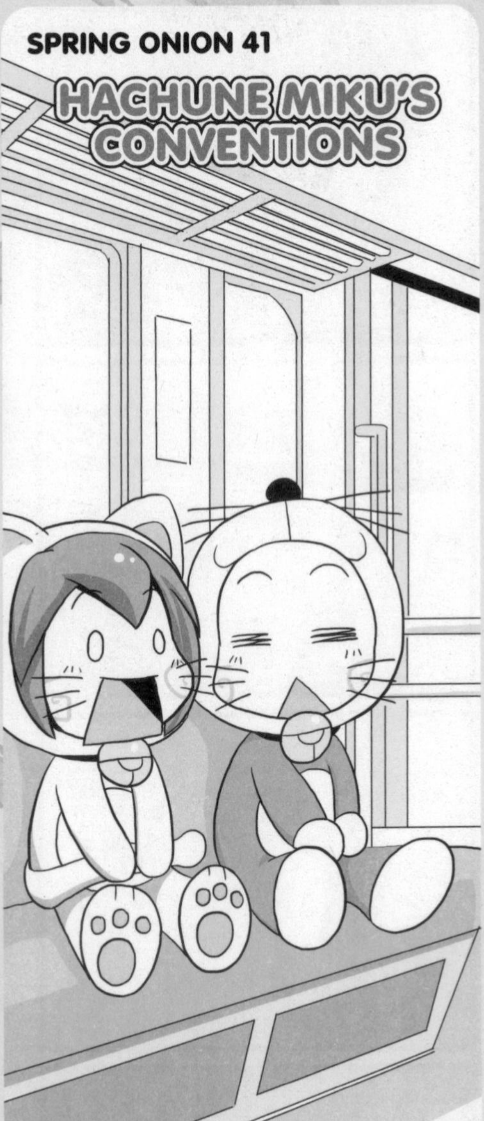

PREPARATIONS

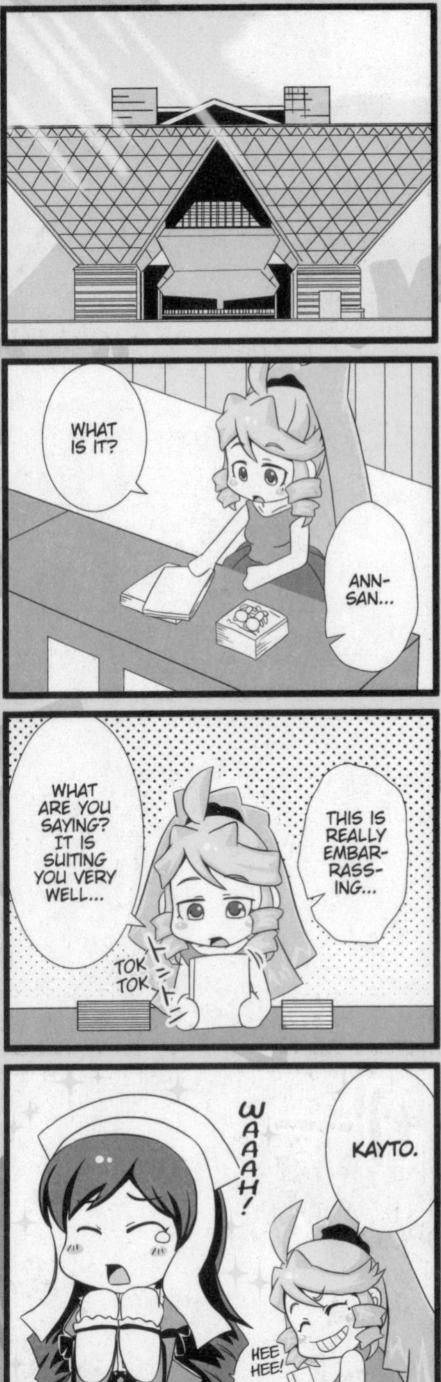
ANN-SAN...
WHAT IS IT?
THIS IS REALLY EMBARRASSING...
WHAT ARE YOU SAYING? IT IS SUITING YOU VERY WELL...
TOK TOK
KAYTO.
WAAAAH!
HEE HEE!

I CANNOT TELL A LIE

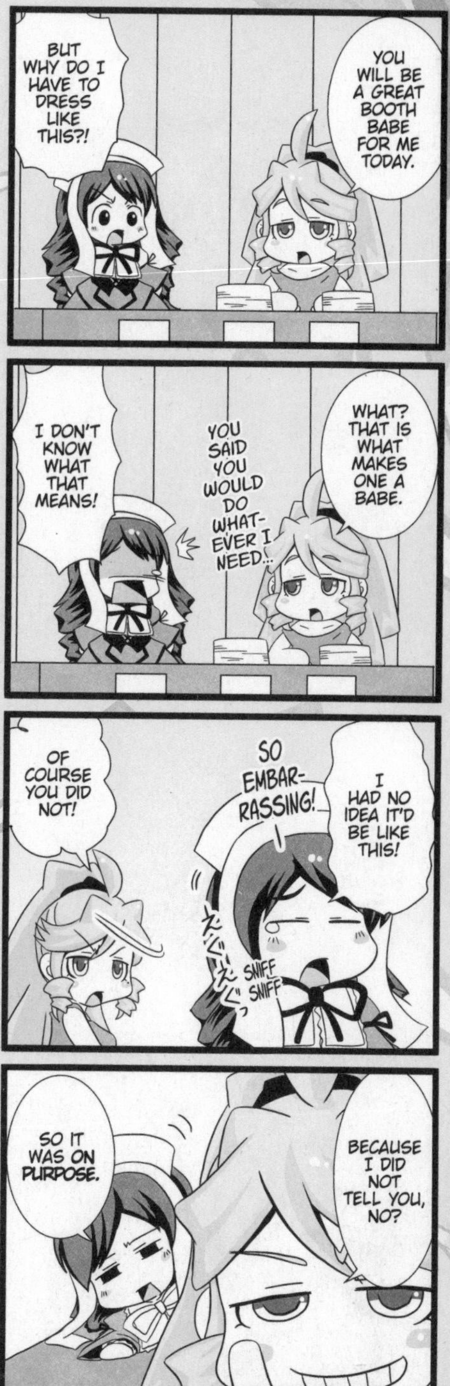
YOU WILL BE A GREAT BOOTH BABE FOR ME TODAY.
BUT WHY DO I HAVE TO DRESS LIKE THIS?!
WHAT? THAT IS WHAT MAKES ONE A BABE.
YOU SAID YOU WOULD DO WHAT-EVER I NEED...
I DON'T KNOW WHAT THAT MEANS!
I HAD NO IDEA IT'D BE LIKE THIS!
SO EMBAR-RASSING!
SNIFF SNIFF
OF COURSE YOU DID NOT!
BECAUSE I DID NOT TELL YOU, NO?
SO IT WAS ON PURPOSE.

LOOK!

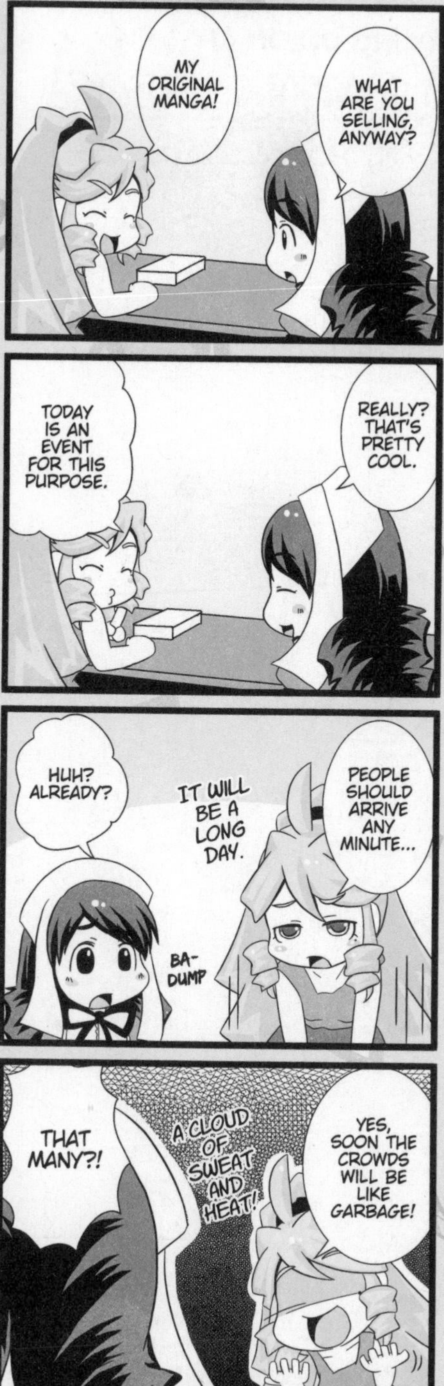
WHAT ARE YOU SELLING, ANYWAY?
MY ORIGINAL MANGA!
REALLY? THAT'S PRETTY COOL.
TODAY IS AN EVENT FOR THIS PURPOSE.
PEOPLE SHOULD ARRIVE ANY MINUTE...
IT WILL BE A LONG DAY.
BA-DUMP
HUH? ALREADY?
YES, SOON THE CROWDS WILL BE LIKE GARBAGE!
A CLOUD OF SWEAT AND HEAT!
THAT MANY?!

STARING

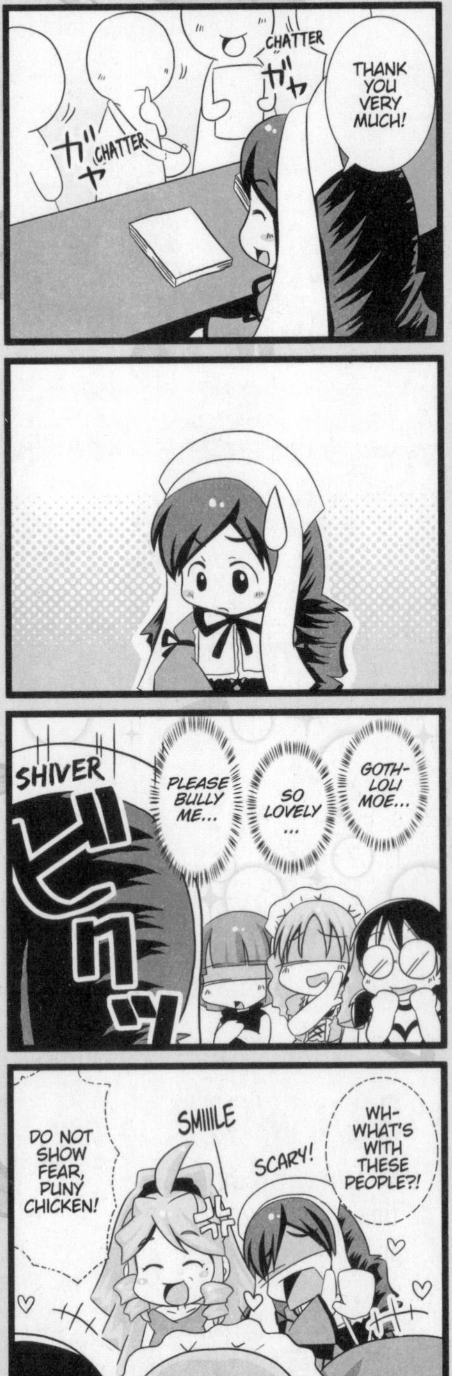
THANK YOU VERY MUCH!
CHATTER
CHATTER
PLEASE BULLY ME...
SO LOVELY ...
GOTH-LOLI MOE...
SHIVER
WH-WHAT'S WITH THESE PEOPLE?!
SCARY!
SMIIILE
DO NOT SHOW FEAR, PUNY CHICKEN!

LANGUAGE

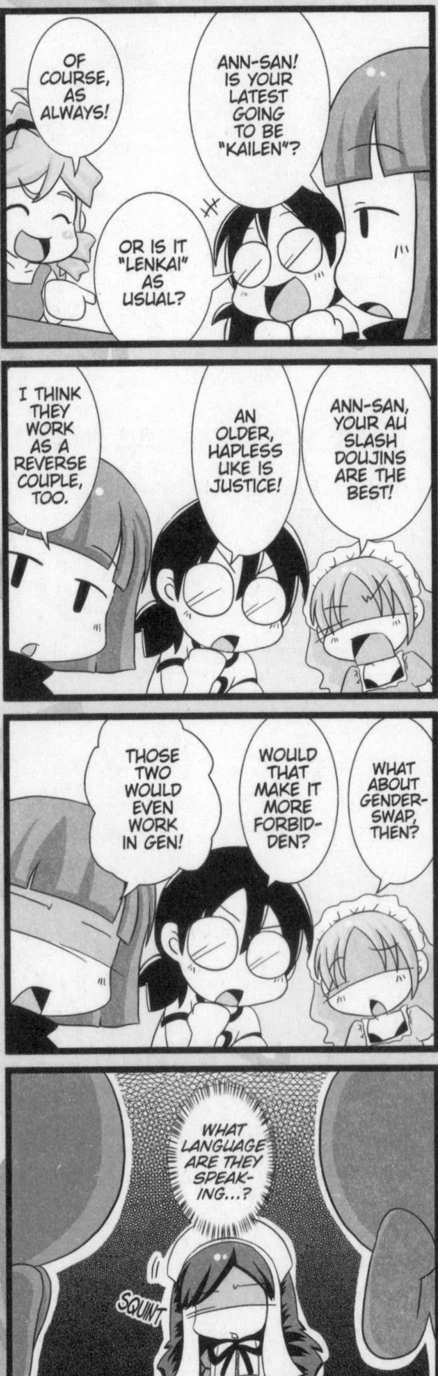
ANN-SAN! IS YOUR LATEST GOING TO BE "KAILEN"?
OR IS IT "LENKAI" AS USUAL?
OF COURSE, AS ALWAYS!
ANN-SAN, YOUR AU SLASH DOUJINS ARE THE BEST!
AN OLDER, HAPLESS UKE IS JUSTICE!
I THINK THEY WORK AS A REVERSE COUPLE, TOO.
WHAT ABOUT GENDER-SWAP, THEN?
WOULD THAT MAKE IT MORE FORBIDDEN?
THOSE TWO WOULD EVEN WORK IN GEN!
WHAT LANGUAGE ARE THEY SPEAKING...?
SQUINT

SKETCHBOOK

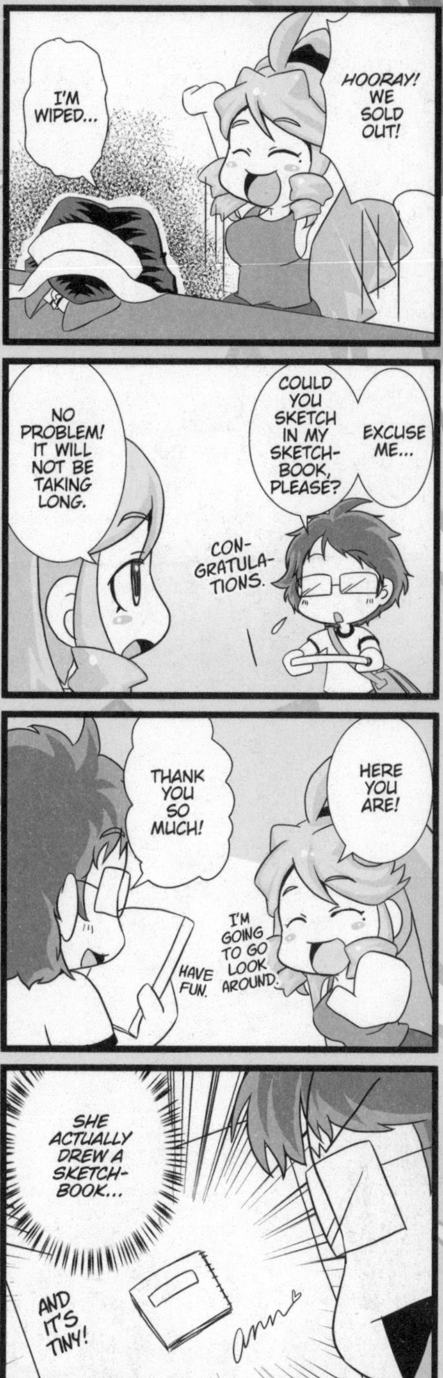
HOORAY! WE SOLD OUT!
I'M WIPED...
EXCUSE ME...
COULD YOU SKETCH IN MY SKETCH-BOOK, PLEASE?
NO PROBLEM! IT WILL NOT BE TAKING LONG.
CON-GRATULA-TIONS.
HERE YOU ARE!
THANK YOU SO MUCH!
I'M GOING TO GO LOOK AROUND.
HAVE FUN.
SHE ACTUALLY DREW A SKETCH-BOOK...
AND IT'S TINY!

WELCOME

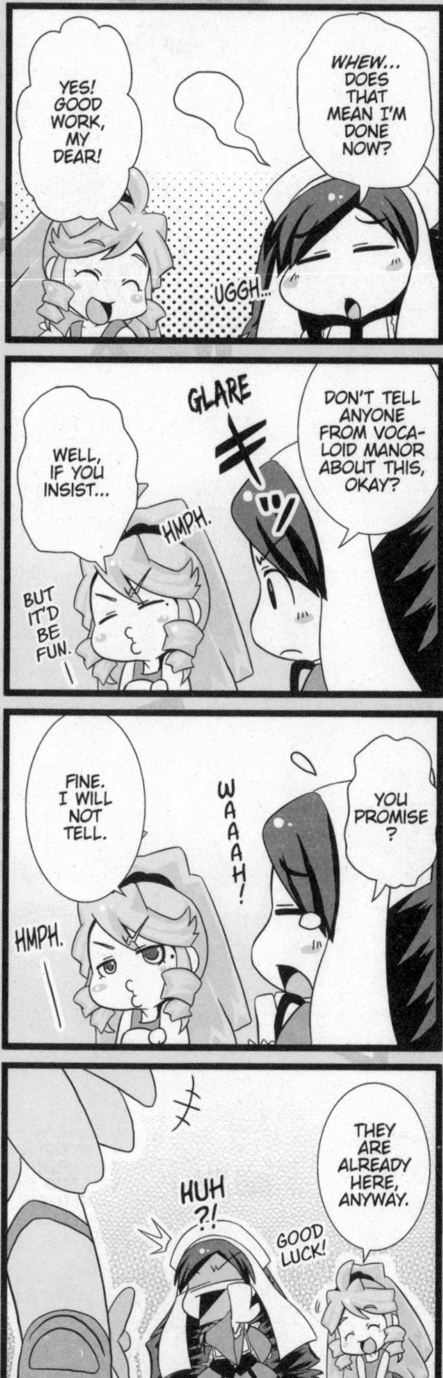
WHEW... DOES THAT MEAN I'M DONE NOW?
YES! GOOD WORK, MY DEAR!
UGGH...
DON'T TELL ANYONE FROM VOCA-LOID MANOR ABOUT THIS, OKAY?
GLARE
WELL, IF YOU INSIST...
HMPH.
BUT IT'D BE FUN.
YOU PROMISE?
WAAAAH!
FINE. I WILL NOT TELL.
HMPH.
THEY ARE ALREADY HERE, ANYWAY.
GOOD LUCK!
HUH?!

WHEN IN ROME

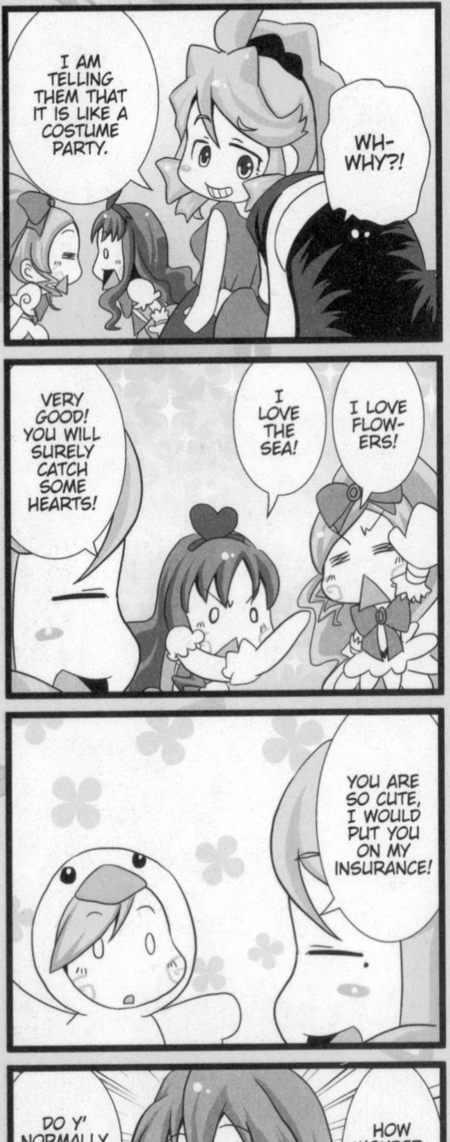
WH- WHY?!
I AM TELLING THEM THAT IT IS LIKE A COSTUME PARTY.
I LOVE FLOW- ERS!
I LOVE THE SEA!
VERY GOOD! YOU WILL SURELY CATCH SOME HEARTS!
YOU ARE SO CUTE, I WOULD PUT YOU ON MY INSURANCE!
HOW WONDER- FUL! IT'S A PERFECT MATCH!
DO Y' NORMALLY WEAR CONTACTS ?
SHE'S HAVING FUN!
YOU LOOK LIKE A KNOW-IT- ALL!
SHE'S HAVIN' FUN!

DIRECT HIT

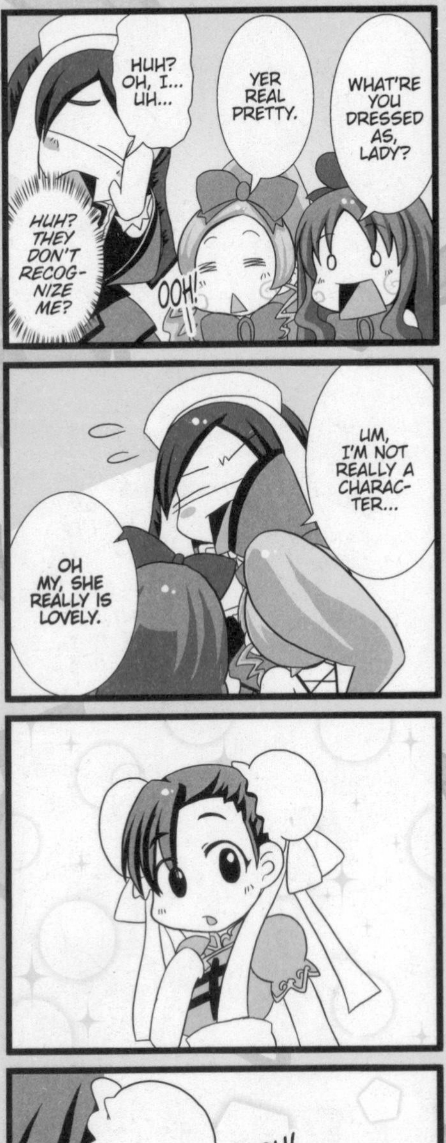
WHAT'RE YOU DRESSED AS, LADY?
YER REAL PRETTY.
HUH? OH, I... UH...
OOH!
HUH? THEY DON'T RECOG- NIZE ME?
UM, I'M NOT REALLY A CHARAC- TER...
OH MY, SHE REALLY IS LOVELY.
OOH!

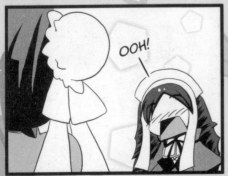

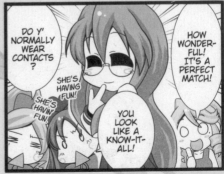

I'M SURE

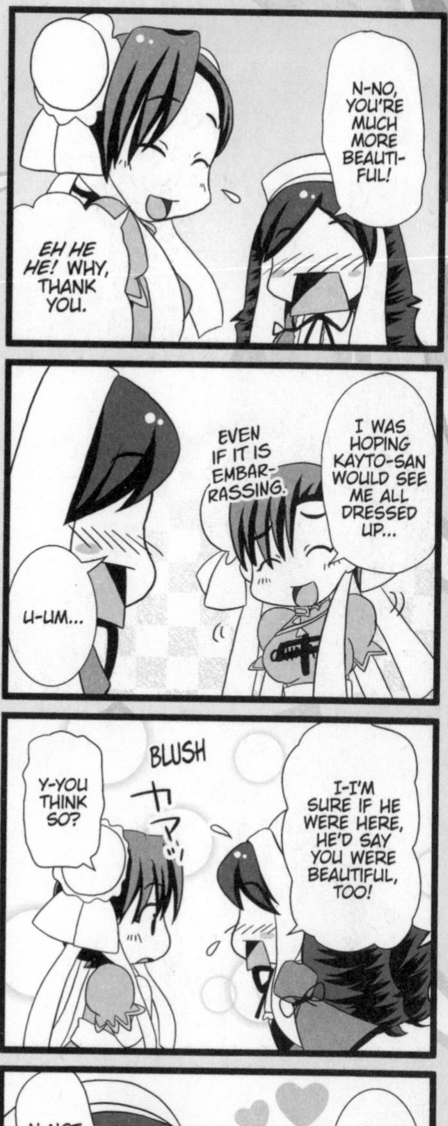
N-NO, YOU'RE MUCH MORE BEAUTI-FUL!
EH HE HE! WHY, THANK YOU.
I WAS HOPING KAYTO-SAN WOULD SEE ME ALL DRESSED UP...
EVEN IF IT IS EMBAR-RASSING.
U-UM...
I-I'M SURE IF HE WERE HERE, HE'D SAY YOU WERE BEAUTIFUL, TOO!
BLUSH
Y-YOU THINK SO?
THANK YOU.
N-NOT AT ALL...

DRAG

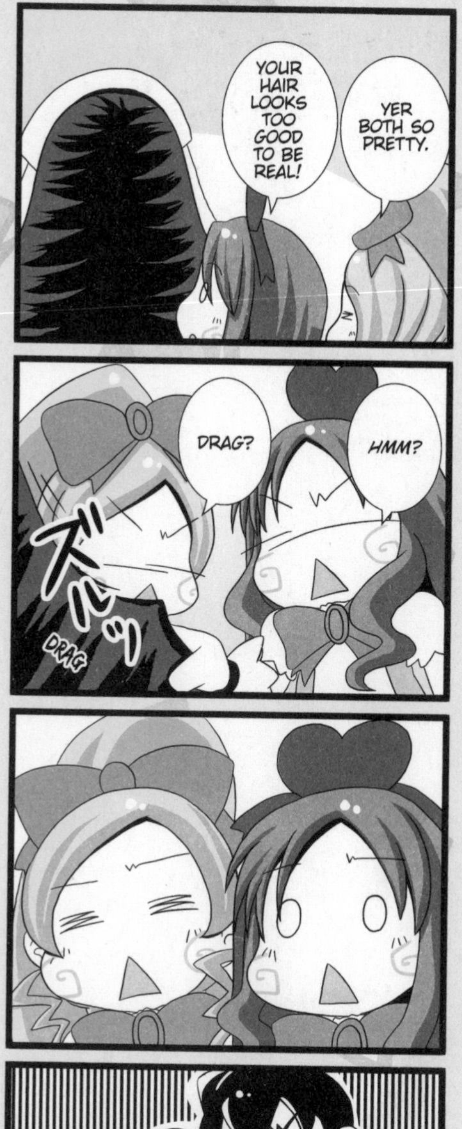
YER BOTH SO PRETTY.
YOUR HAIR LOOKS TOO GOOD TO BE REAL!
HMM?
DRAG?
DRAG

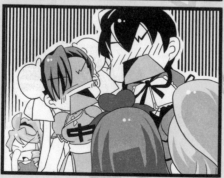

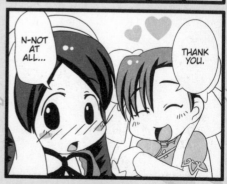

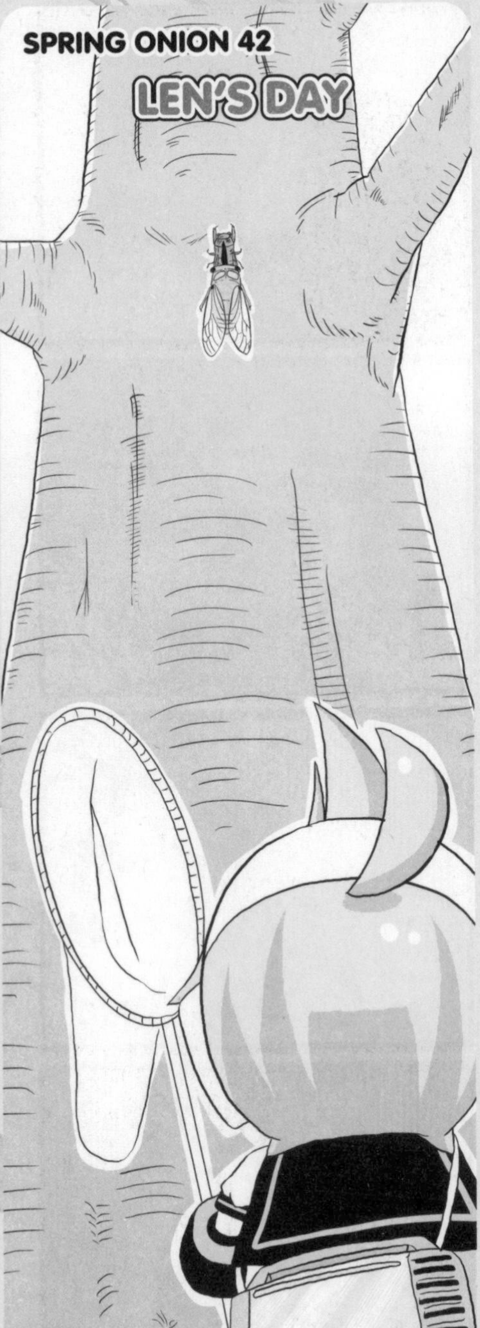
SPRING ONION 42
LEN'S DAY

GOING OUT

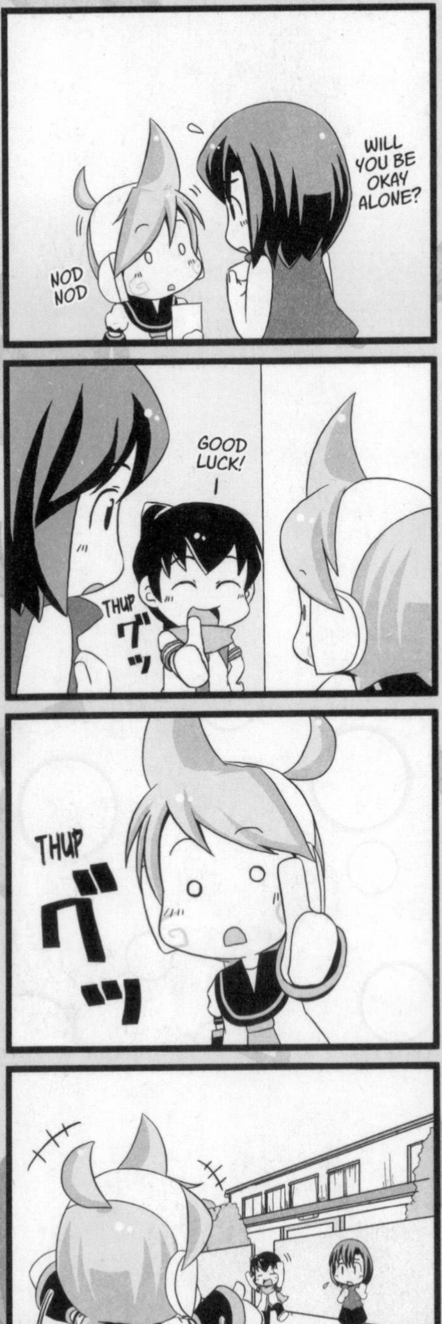
WILL YOU BE OKAY ALONE?
NOD NOD
GOOD LUCK!
THUP
グッ
THUP
ベッ

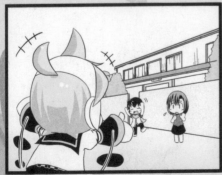

CHEERFUL

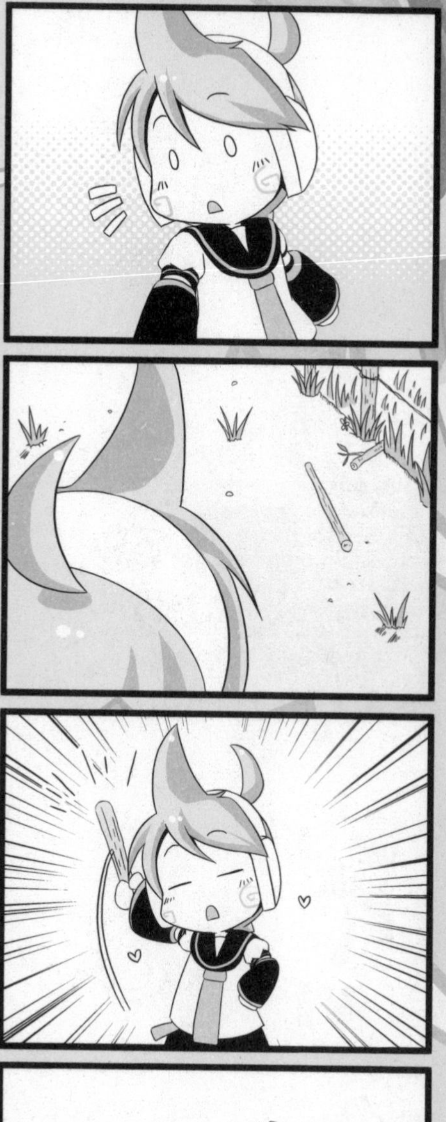

BAD LUCK

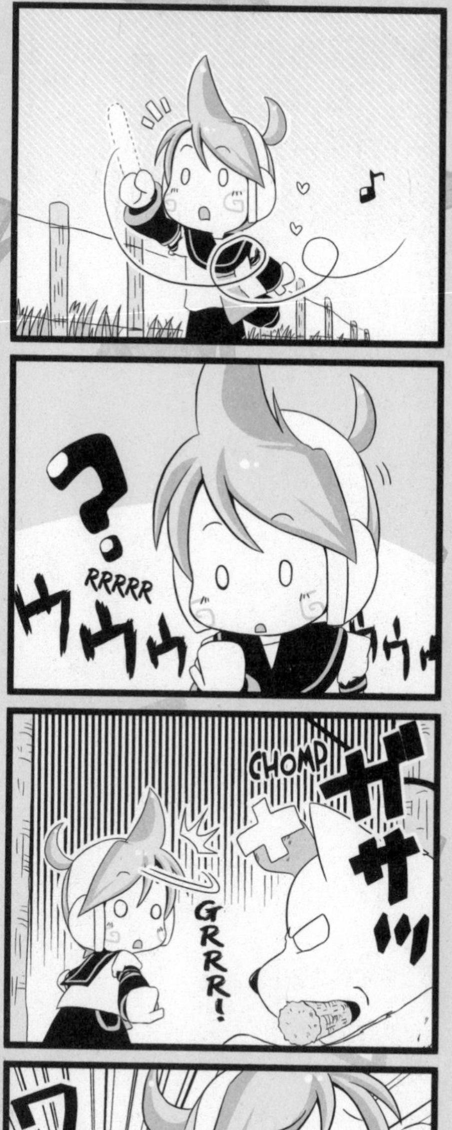
?
RRRRR
CHOMP
ガサッ
GRRRR!
RUFF! RUFF!
DASH

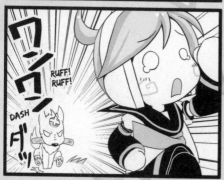

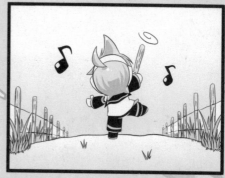

PLEASANTRIES

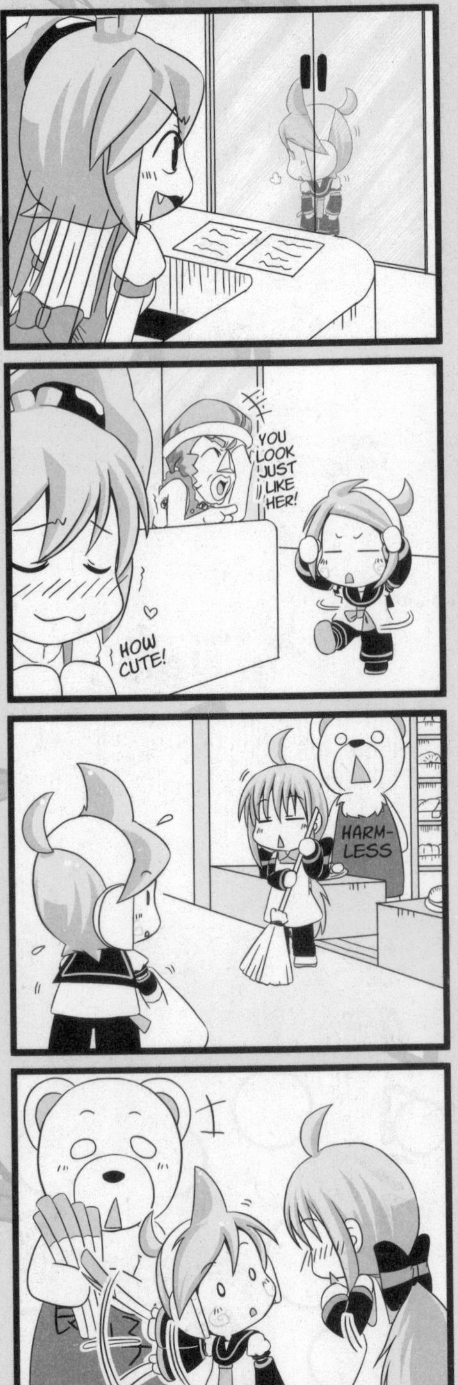
YOU LOOK JUST LIKE HER!
HOW CUTE!
HARM-LESS

TROUBLE

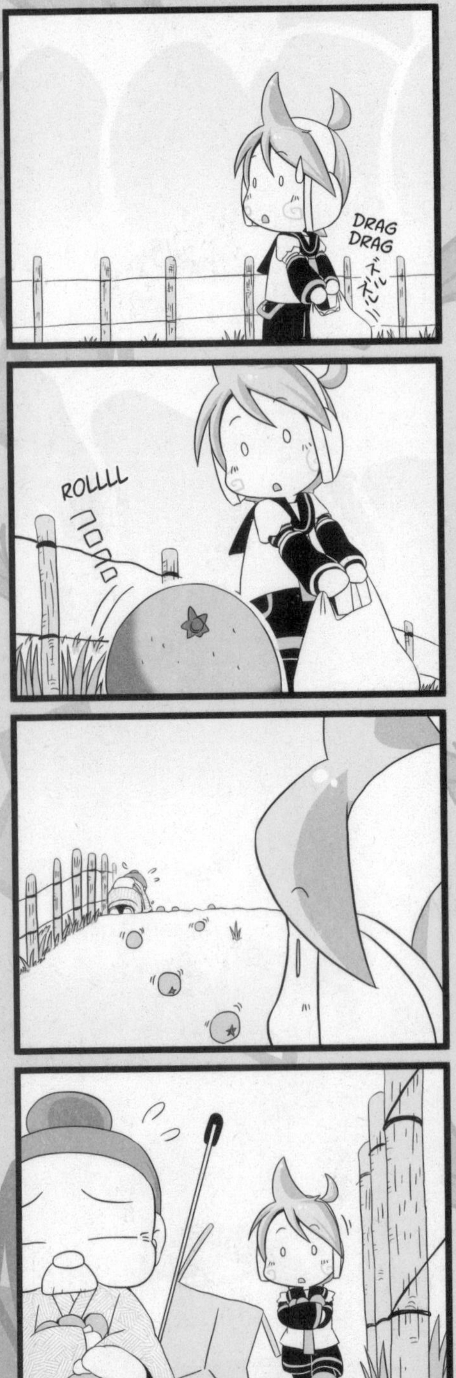
DRAG DRAG
ズルズル
ROLLLL
コロコロ

LOST ITEM

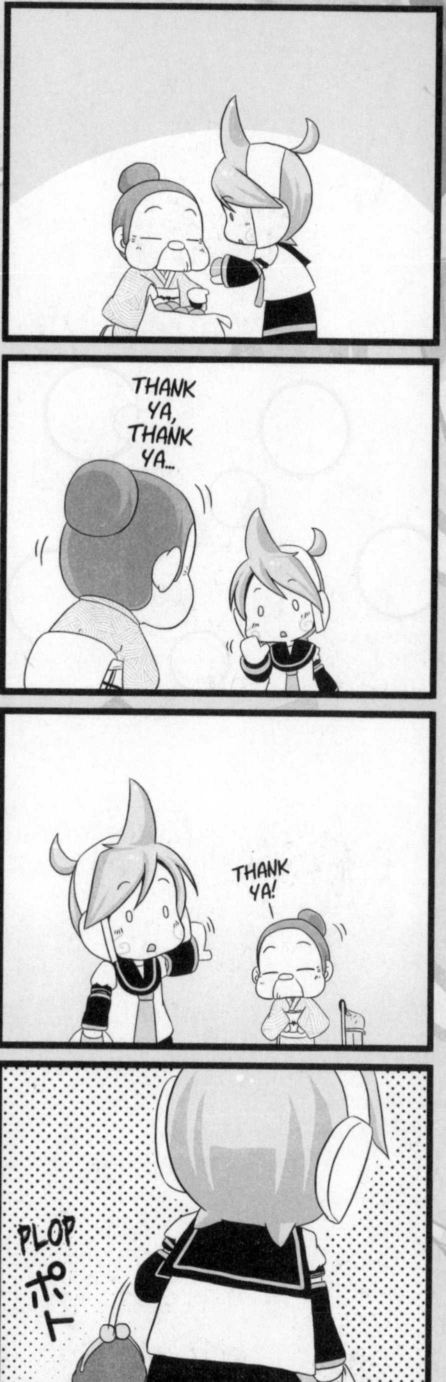
THANK YA, THANK YA...
THANK YA!
PLOP
ポト

OHO?

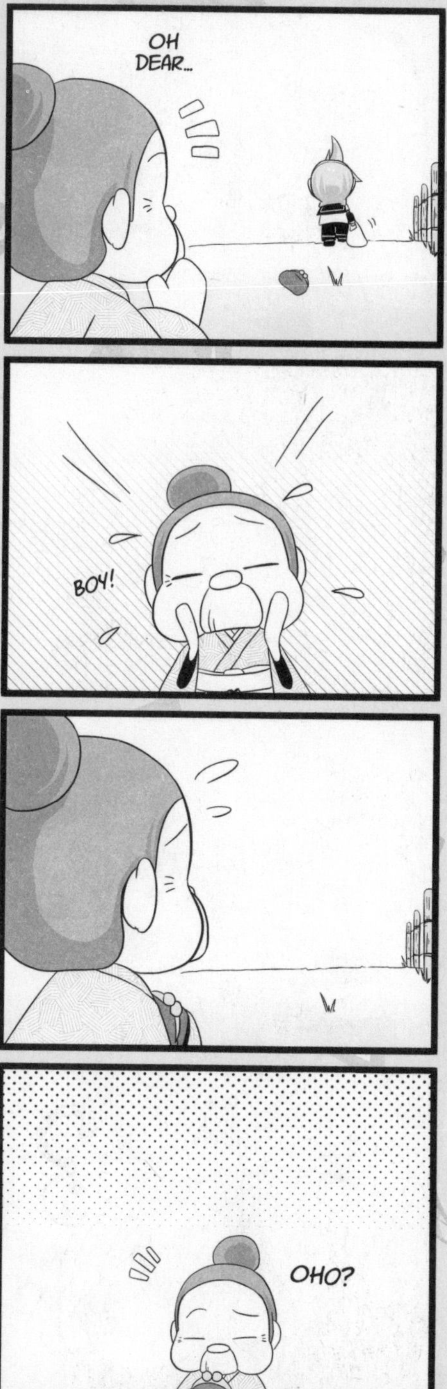
OH DEAR...
BOY!
OHO?

OH NO

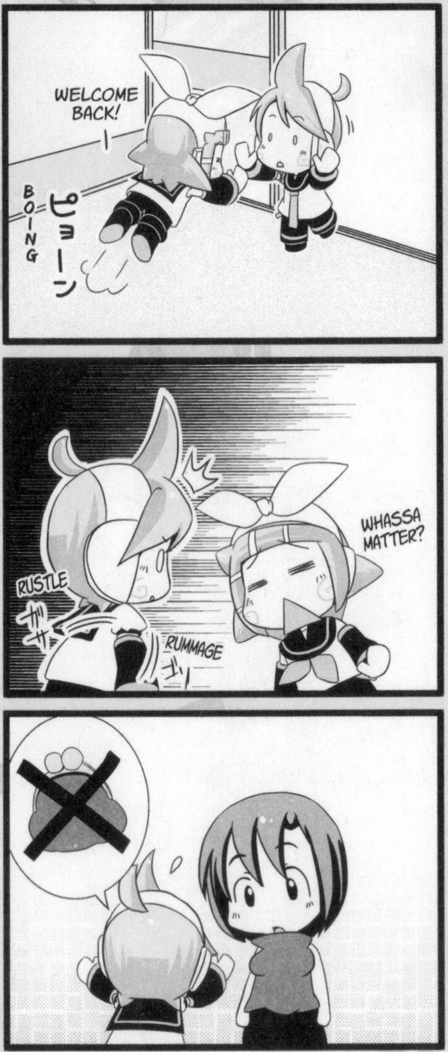
WELCOME BACK!
BOING
ピョーン
WHASSA MATTER?
RUSTLE
RUMMAGE
DON'T YOU WORRY!

GOOD JOB

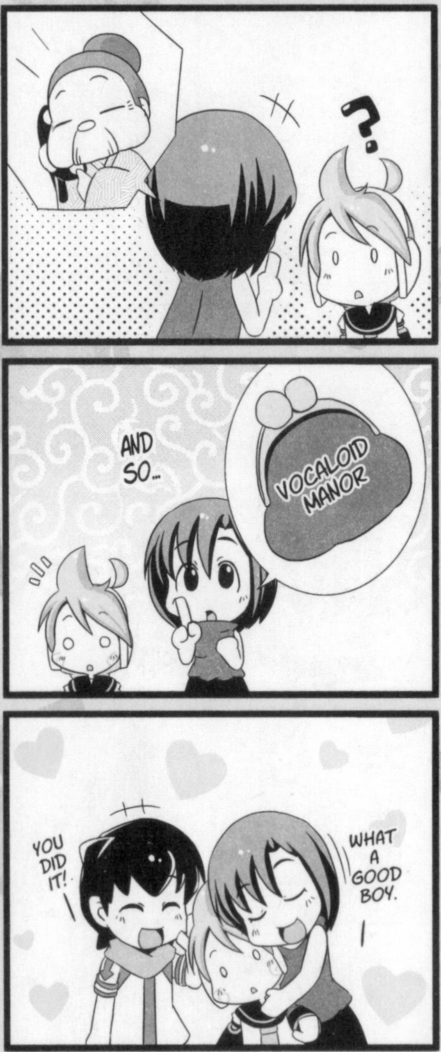
VOCALOID MANOR
AND SO...
WHAT A GOOD BOY.
YOU DID IT!
NICE ONE.
GOOD ON YA!

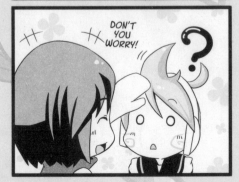

THANKS

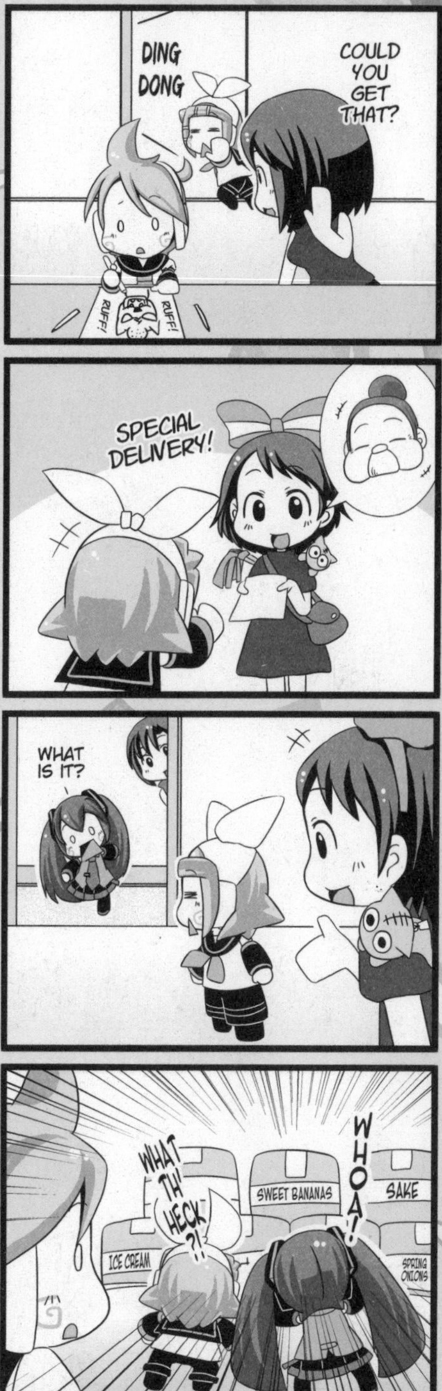
COULD YOU GET THAT?
DING DONG
RUFF! RUFF!
SPECIAL DELIVERY!
WHAT IS IT?
WHOA!
WHAT TH' HECK?!
SAKE
SWEET BANANAS
SPRING ONIONS
ICE CREAM

GREAT JOB

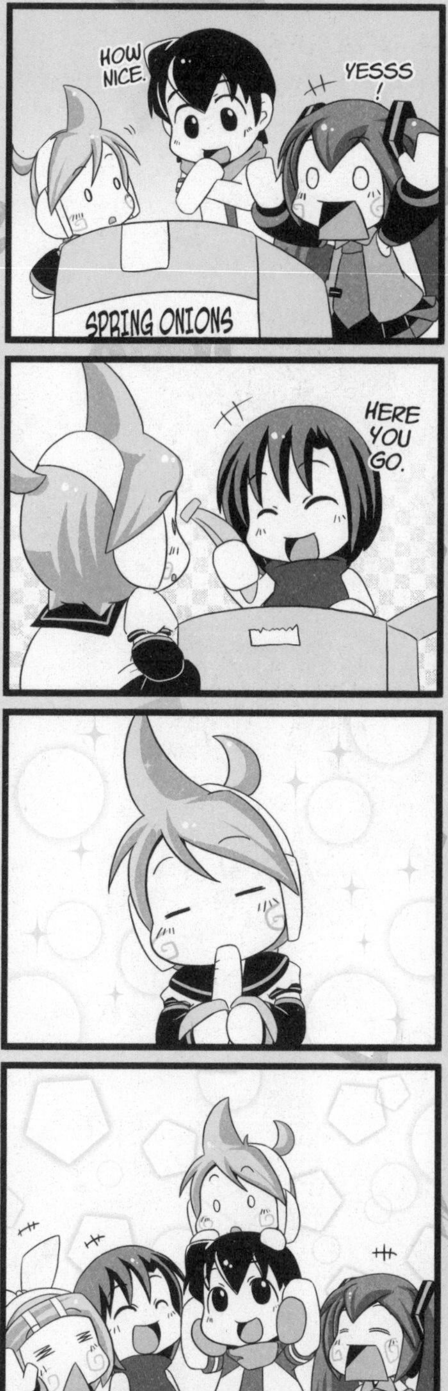
YESSS!
HOW NICE.
SPRING ONIONS
HERE YOU GO.

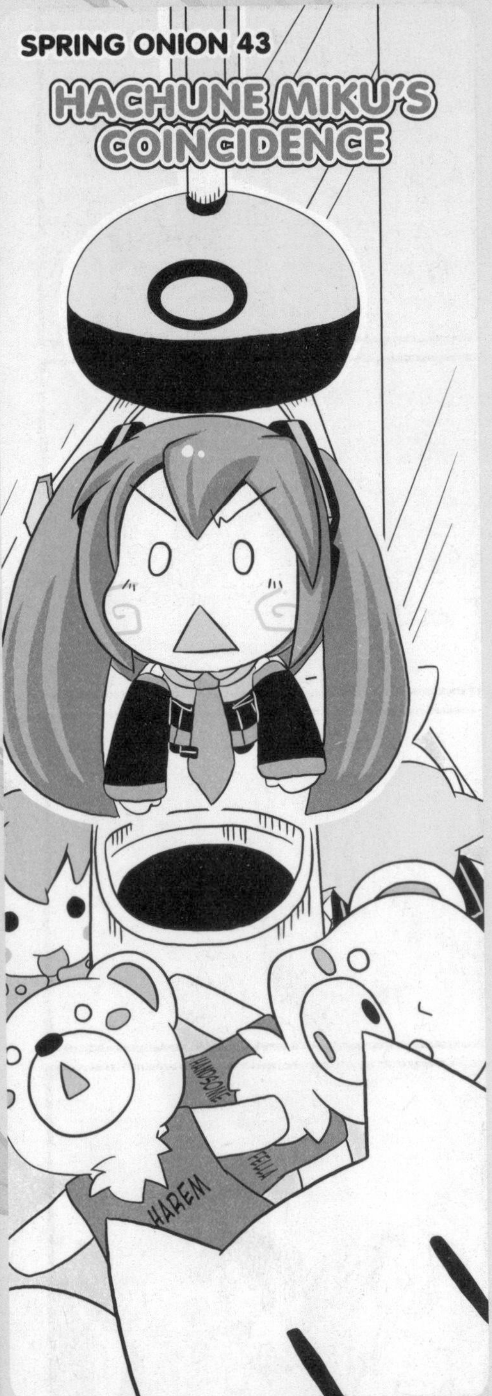
SPRING ONION 43
HACHUNE MIKU'S COINCIDENCE
HANDSOME
FELLA
HAREM

PHRASING

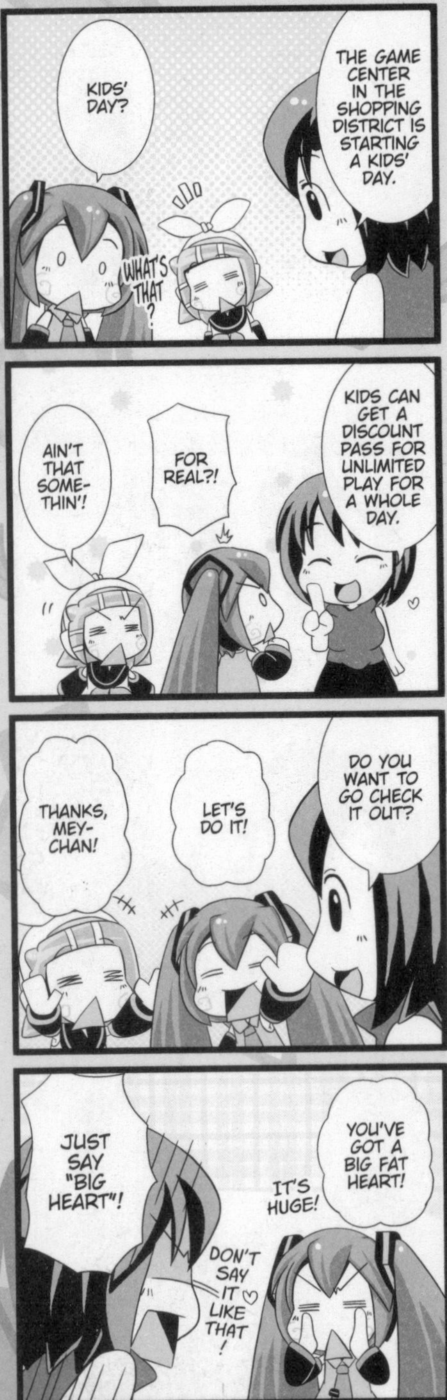
THE GAME CENTER IN THE SHOPPING DISTRICT IS STARTING A KIDS' DAY.
KIDS' DAY?
WHAT'S THAT?
KIDS CAN GET A DISCOUNT PASS FOR UNLIMITED PLAY FOR A WHOLE DAY.
FOR REAL?!
AIN'T THAT SOME-THIN'!
DO YOU WANT TO GO CHECK IT OUT?
LET'S DO IT!
THANKS, MEY-CHAN!
YOU'VE GOT A BIG FAT HEART!
IT'S HUGE!
JUST SAY "BIG HEART"!
DON'T SAY IT ♡ LIKE THAT!

EXTRA KID

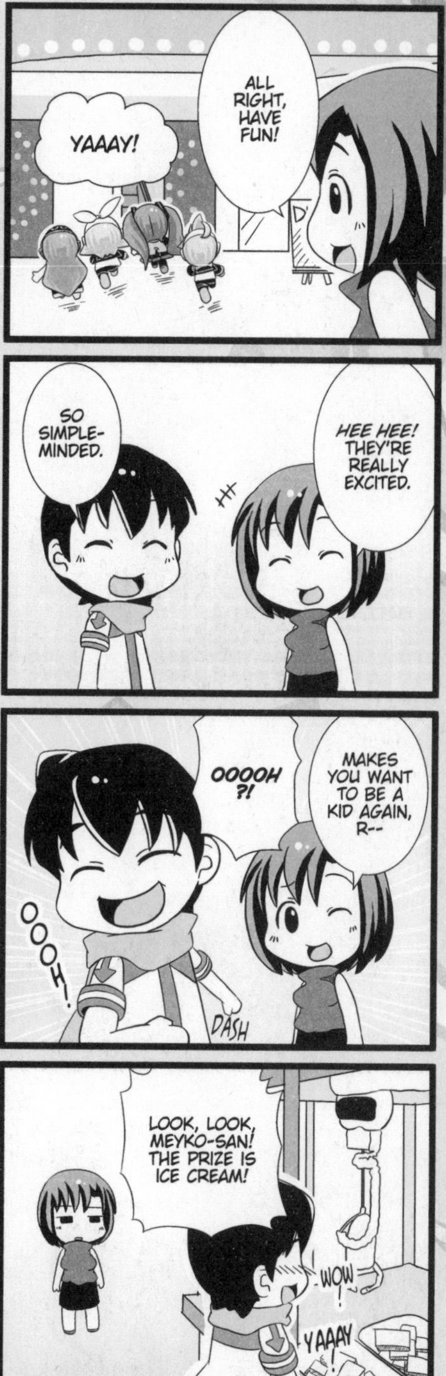
ALL RIGHT, HAVE FUN!
YAAAY!
HEE HEE! THEY'RE REALLY EXCITED.
SO SIMPLE-MINDED.
MAKES YOU WANT TO BE A KID AGAIN, R--
OOOOH ?!
OOOH!
DASH
LOOK, LOOK, MEYKO-SAN! THE PRIZE IS ICE CREAM!
WOW!
YAAAY!

LEAVE IT TO MEYKO-SAN

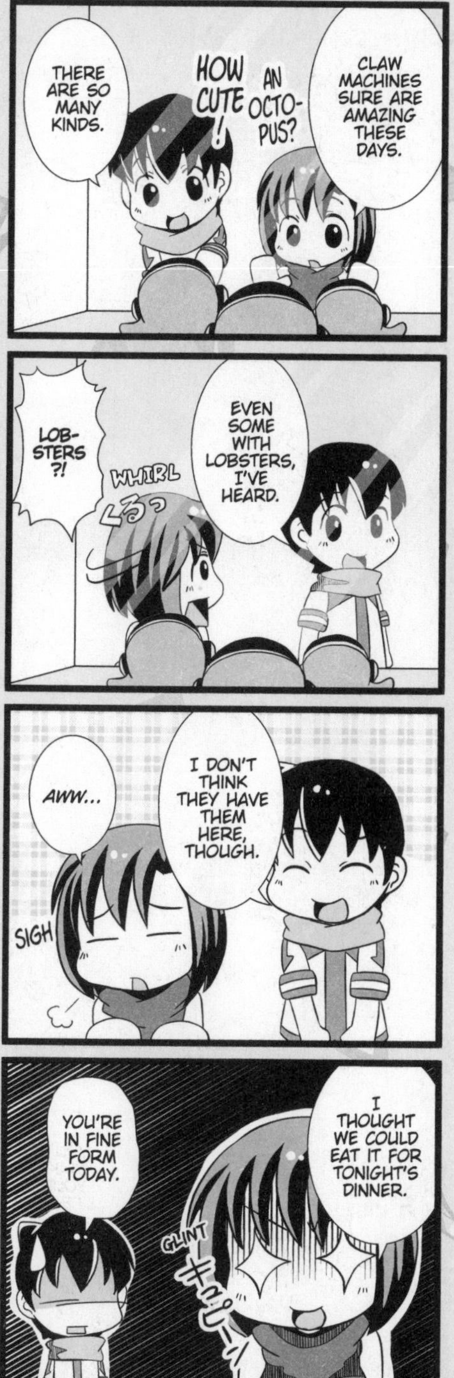
CLAW MACHINES SURE ARE AMAZING THESE DAYS.
AN OCTO-PUS?
HOW CUTE!
THERE ARE SO MANY KINDS.
EVEN SOME WITH LOBSTERS, I'VE HEARD.
WHIRL
くるっ
LOBSTERS ?!
I DON'T THINK THEY HAVE THEM HERE, THOUGH.
AWW...
SIGH
I THOUGHT WE COULD EAT IT FOR TONIGHT'S DINNER.
GLINT
YOU'RE IN FINE FORM TODAY.

EASY

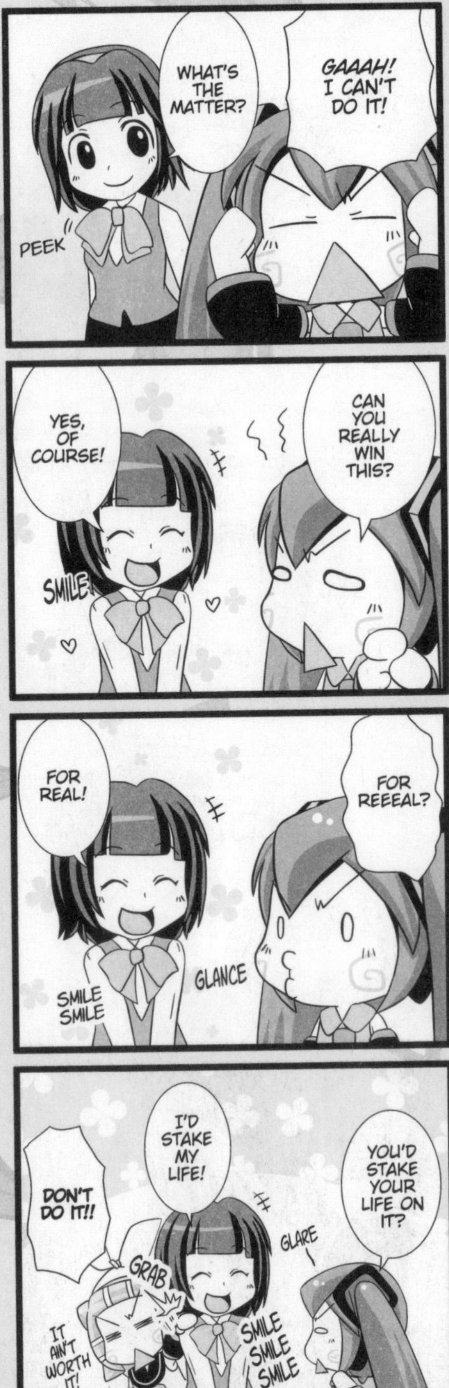
GAAAH! I CAN'T DO IT!
WHAT'S THE MATTER?
PEEK
CAN YOU REALLY WIN THIS?
YES, OF COURSE!
SMILE
FOR REEEAL?
FOR REAL!
GLANCE
SMILE SMILE
YOU'D STAKE YOUR LIFE ON IT?
I'D STAKE MY LIFE!
GLARE
DON'T DO IT!!
GRAB
SMILE SMILE SMILE
IT AIN'T WORTH IT!

SECRET TECHNIQUE

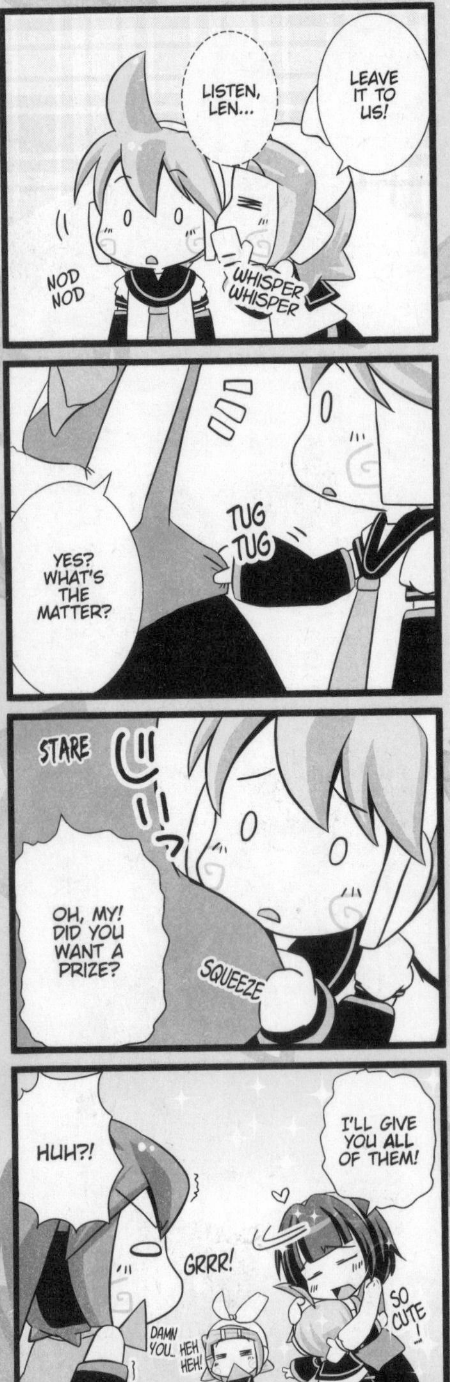
LEAVE IT TO US!
LISTEN, LEN...
WHISPER WHISPER
NOD NOD
TUG TUG
YES? WHAT'S THE MATTER?
STARE
SQUEEZE
OH, MY! DID YOU WANT A PRIZE?
I'LL GIVE YOU ALL OF THEM!
SO CUTE!
HUH?!
GRRR!
HEH HEH!
DAMN YOU...

BATTLE

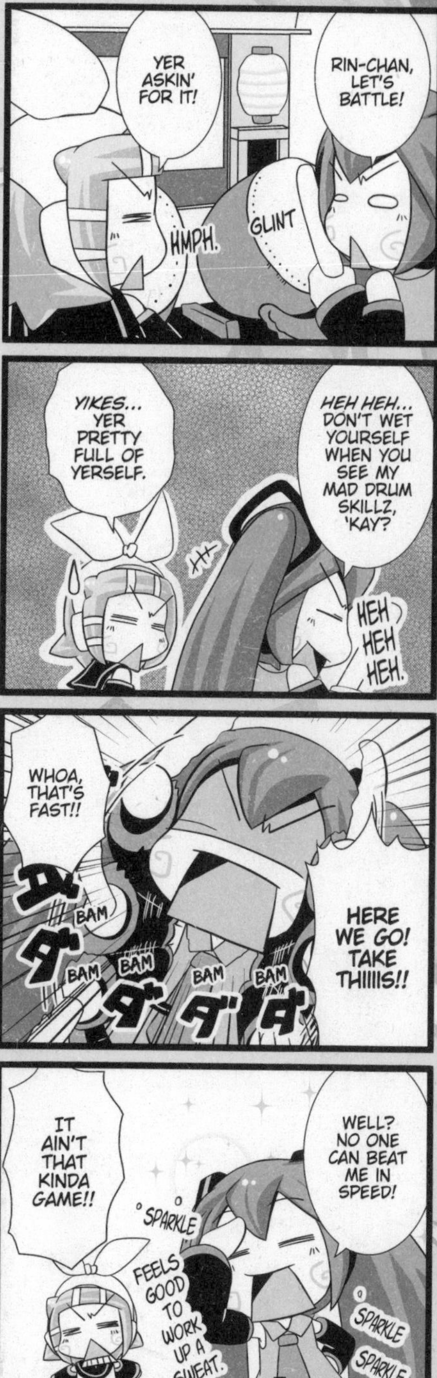
RIN-CHAN, LET'S BATTLE!
YER ASKIN' FOR IT!
GLINT
HMPH.
HEH HEH... DON'T WET YOURSELF WHEN YOU SEE MY MAD DRUM SKILLZ, 'KAY?
YIKES... YER PRETTY FULL OF YERSELF.
HEH HEH HEH.
HERE WE GO! TAKE THIIIIS!!
WHOA, THAT'S FAST!!
BAM
BAM
BAM
BAM
BAM
WELL? NO ONE CAN BEAT ME IN SPEED!
IT AIN'T THAT KINDA GAME!!
SPARKLE
SPARKLE
SPARKLE
FEELS GOOD TO WORK UP A SWEAT.

STOCK PHRASE

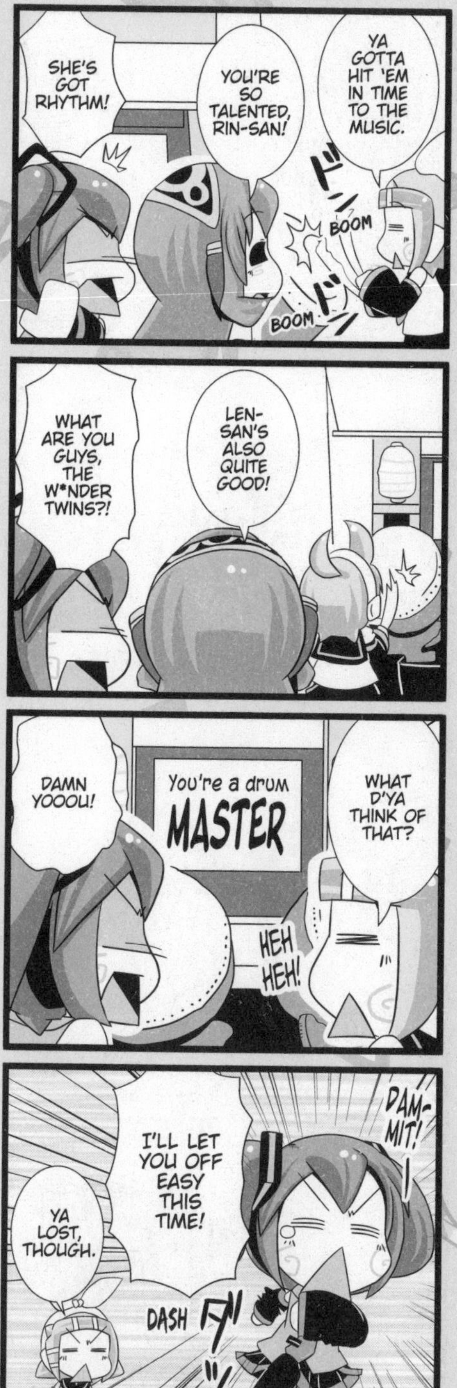
YA GOTTA HIT 'EM IN TIME TO THE MUSIC.
BOOM
BOOM
YOU'RE SO TALENTED, RIN-SAN!
SHE'S GOT RHYTHM!
LEN-SAN'S ALSO QUITE GOOD!
WHAT ARE YOU GUYS, THE W*NDER TWINS?!
WHAT D'YA THINK OF THAT?
You're a drum MASTER
HEH HEH!
DAMN YOOOU!
DAM-MIT!
I'LL LET YOU OFF EASY THIS TIME!
YA LOST, THOUGH.
DASH

GOOD LUCK, LUKA

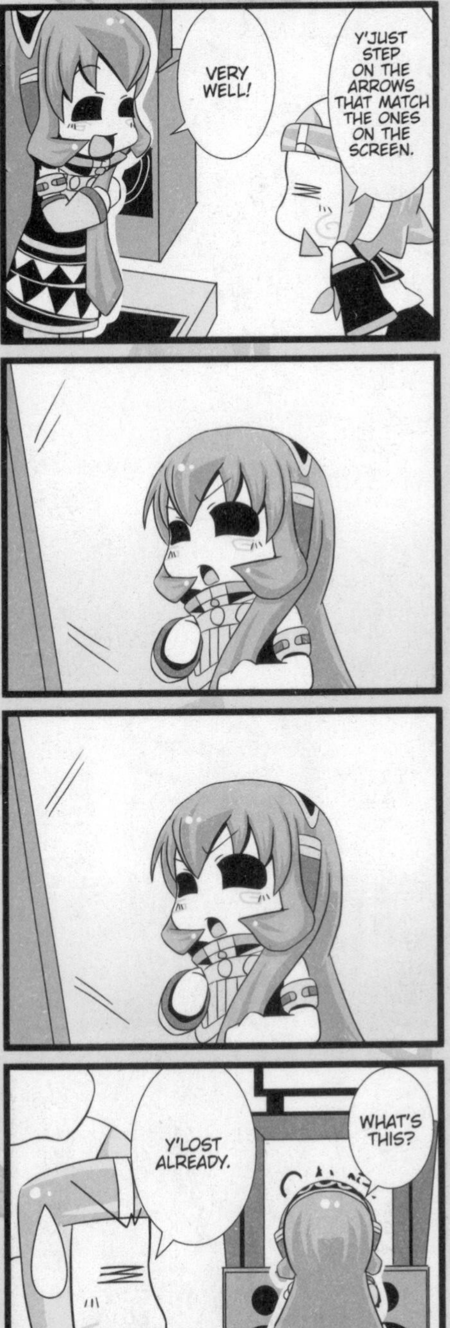
Y'JUST STEP ON THE ARROWS THAT MATCH THE ONES ON THE SCREEN.
VERY WELL!
WHAT'S THIS?
Y'LOST ALREADY.

FRAMERATE

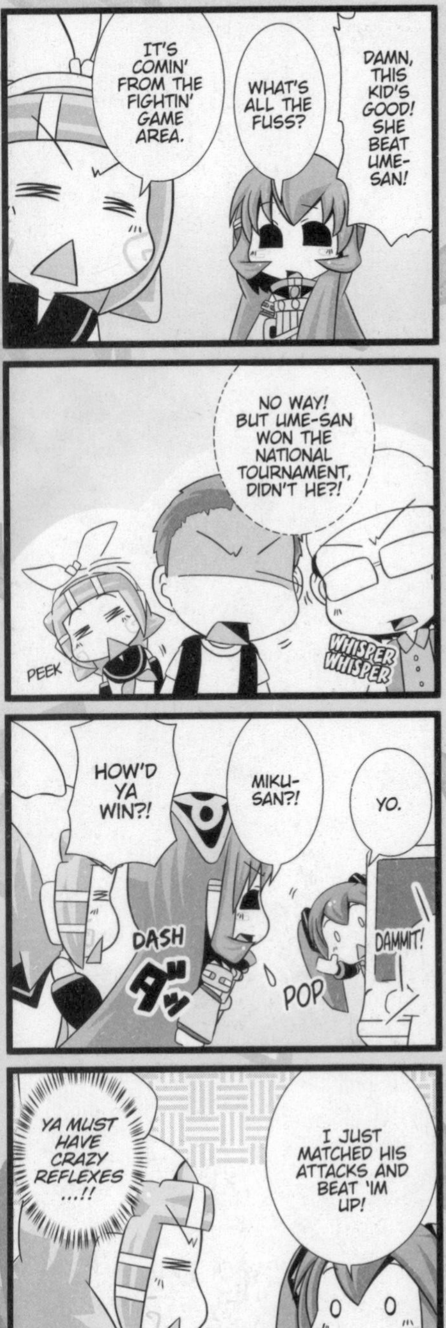
DAMN, THIS KID'S GOOD! SHE BEAT UME-SAN!
WHAT'S ALL THE FUSS?
IT'S COMIN' FROM THE FIGHTIN' GAME AREA.
NO WAY! BUT UME-SAN WON THE NATIONAL TOURNAMENT, DIDN'T HE?!
WHISPER WHISPER
PEEK
YO.
MIKU-SAN?!
HOW'D YA WIN?!
DAMMIT!
DASH
ダッ
POP
I JUST MATCHED HIS ATTACKS AND BEAT 'IM UP!
YA MUST HAVE CRAZY REFLEXES ...!!
TSK TSK!

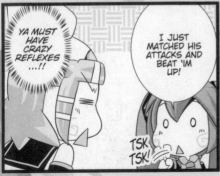

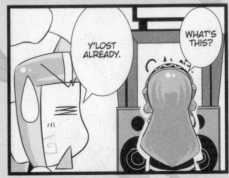

NO WAY

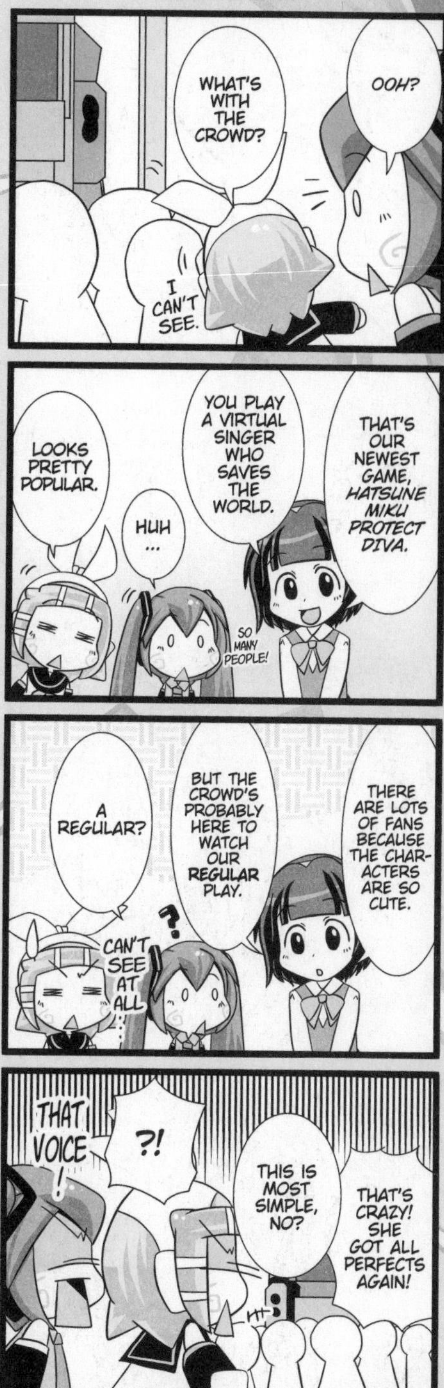
OOH?
WHAT'S WITH THE CROWD?
I CAN'T SEE.
THAT'S OUR NEWEST GAME, HATSUNE MIKU PROTECT DIVA.
YOU PLAY A VIRTUAL SINGER WHO SAVES THE WORLD.
LOOKS PRETTY POPULAR.
HUH ...
SO MANY PEOPLE!
THERE ARE LOTS OF FANS BECAUSE THE CHAR-ACTERS ARE SO CUTE.
BUT THE CROWD'S PROBABLY HERE TO WATCH OUR REGULAR PLAY.
A REGULAR?
?
CAN'T SEE AT ALL...
THAT'S CRAZY! SHE GOT ALL PERFECTS AGAIN!
THIS IS MOST SIMPLE, NO?
?!
THAT VOICE!

NOPE

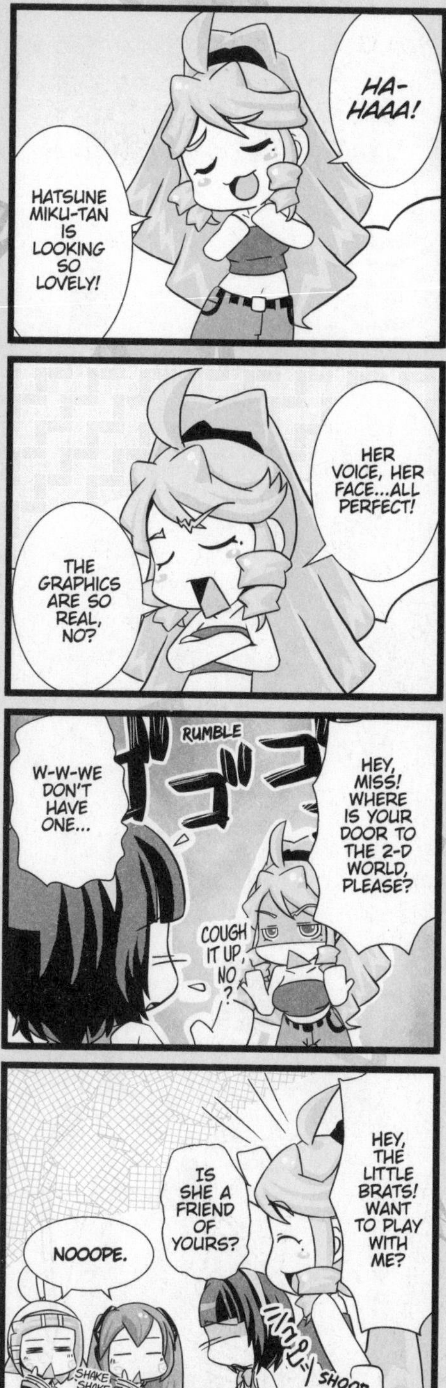
HA-HAAA!
HATSUNE MIKU-TAN IS LOOKING SO LOVELY!
HER VOICE, HER FACE...ALL PERFECT!
THE GRAPHICS ARE SO REAL, NO?
HEY, MISS! WHERE IS YOUR DOOR TO THE 2-D WORLD, PLEASE?
RUMBLE
COUGH IT UP, NO?
W-W-WE DON'T HAVE ONE...
HEY, THE LITTLE BRATS! WANT TO PLAY WITH ME?
IS SHE A FRIEND OF YOURS?
NOOOPE.
SHOOP
SHAKE SHAKE

SPRING ONION 44

HACHUNE MIKU'S YONAGO TOUR

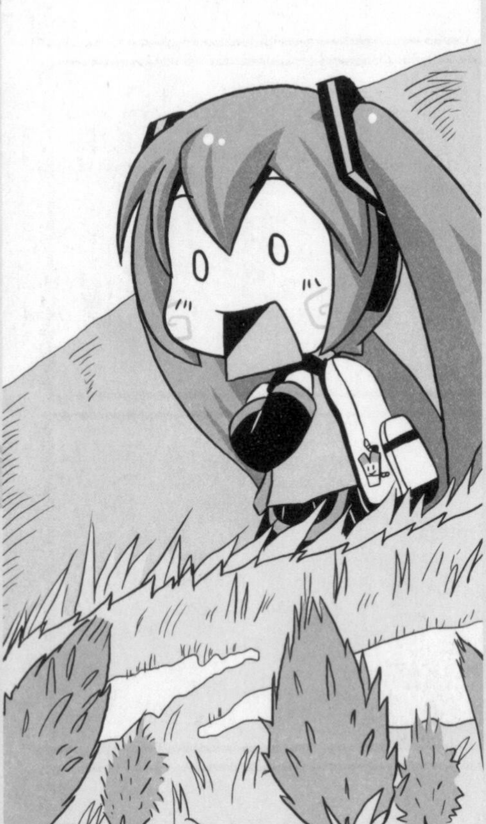

GUESTS

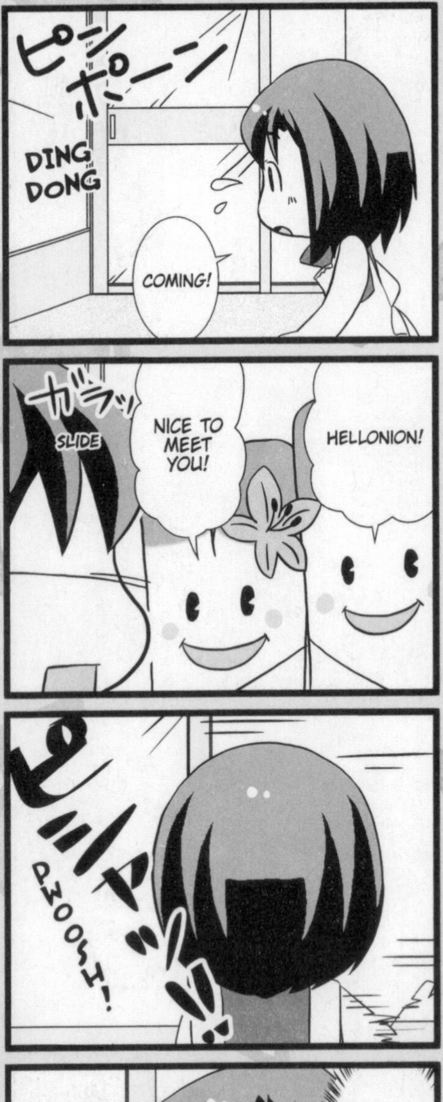
ピンポーン
DING DONG
COMING!
HELLONION!
NICE TO MEET YOU!
ガラッ
SLIDE
ピシャッ
PWOOSH!
TALKING SPRING ONIONS?!
HELLO-OOO?
KNOCK KNOCK

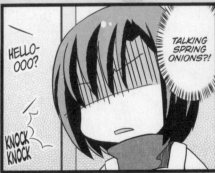

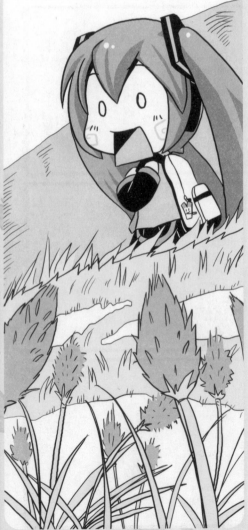

INTRODUCTIONS

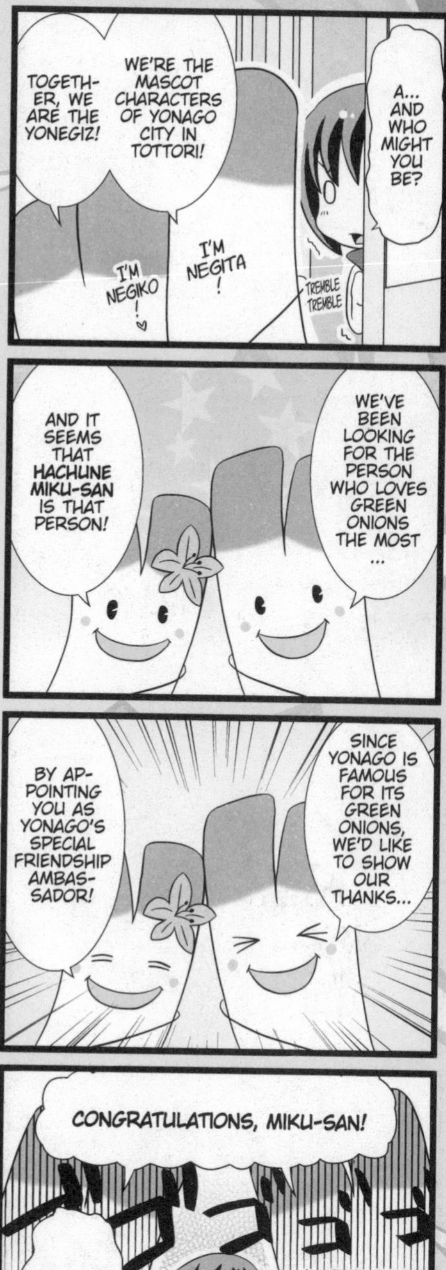
A... AND WHO MIGHT YOU BE?
WE'RE THE MASCOT CHARACTERS OF YONAGO CITY IN TOTTORI!
TOGETH-ER, WE ARE THE YONEGIZ!
TREMBLE TREMBLE
I'M NEGITA!
I'M NEGIKO! ♡
WE'VE BEEN LOOKING FOR THE PERSON WHO LOVES GREEN ONIONS THE MOST ...
AND IT SEEMS THAT HACHUNE MIKU-SAN IS THAT PERSON!
SINCE YONAGO IS FAMOUS FOR ITS GREEN ONIONS, WE'D LIKE TO SHOW OUR THANKS...
BY AP-POINTING YOU AS YONAGO'S SPECIAL FRIENDSHIP AMBAS-SADOR!
CONGRATULATIONS, MIKU-SAN!
LOOOM
I...I'M NOT MIKU!!

FIRST MEETING

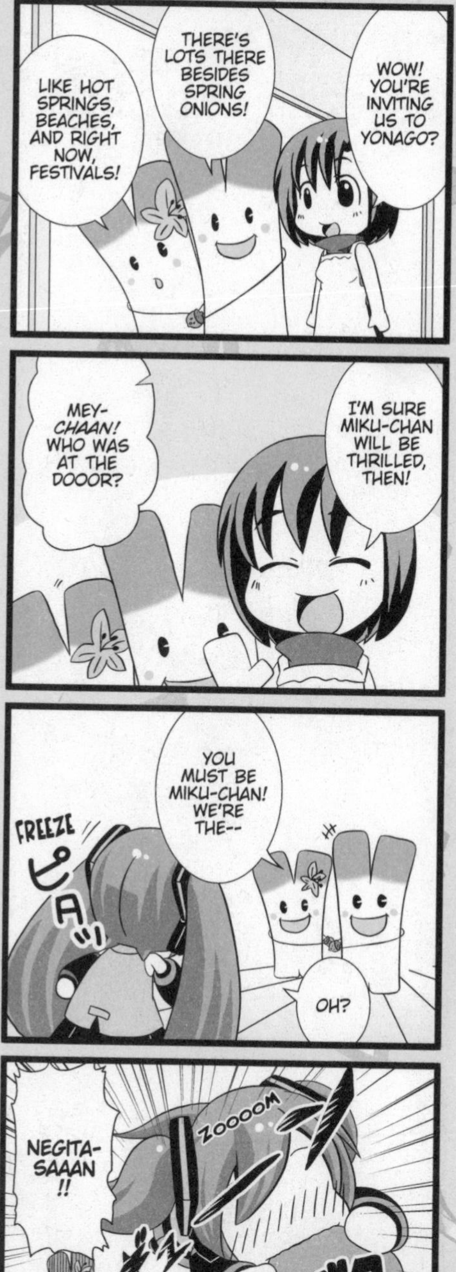
WOW! YOU'RE INVITING US TO YONAGO?
THERE'S LOTS THERE BESIDES SPRING ONIONS!
LIKE HOT SPRINGS, BEACHES, AND RIGHT NOW, FESTIVALS!
I'M SURE MIKU-CHAN WILL BE THRILLED, THEN!
MEY-CHAAN! WHO WAS AT THE DOOOR?
YOU MUST BE MIKU-CHAN! WE'RE THE--
FREEZE
OH?
ZOOOOM
CHOMP
NEGITA-SAAAN!!

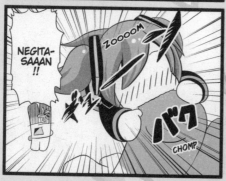

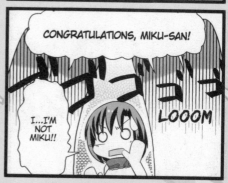

ARRIVAL

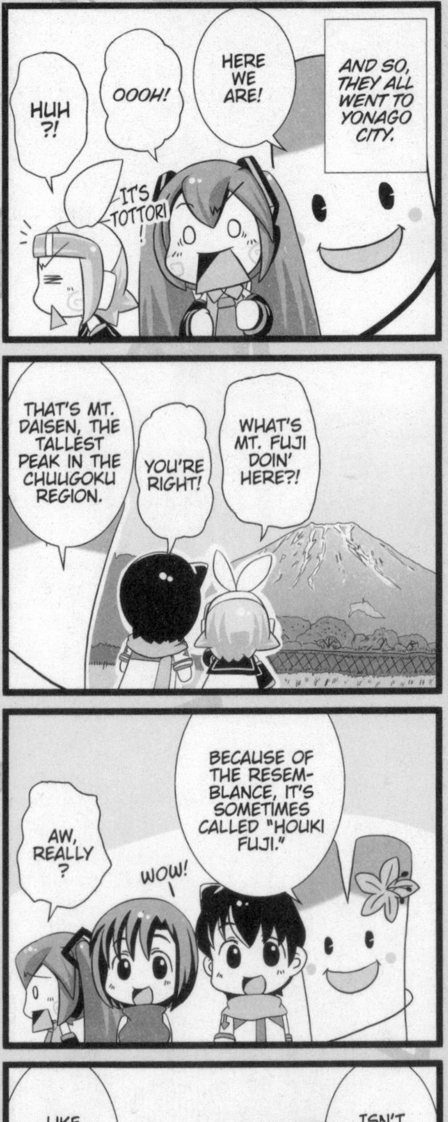
AND SO, THEY ALL WENT TO YONAGO CITY.
HERE WE ARE!
OOOH!
IT'S TOTTORI!
HUH?!
WHAT'S MT. FUJI DOIN' HERE?!
YOU'RE RIGHT!
THAT'S MT. DAISEN, THE TALLEST PEAK IN THE CHUUGOKU REGION.
BECAUSE OF THE RESEMBLANCE, IT'S SOMETIMES CALLED "HOUKI FUJI."
WOW!
AW, REALLY?
ISN'T THAT A LITTLE MEAN?
TURN
くるっ
LIKE "HOUKI PROVINCE," NOT "HOKEY."

SPEEDY

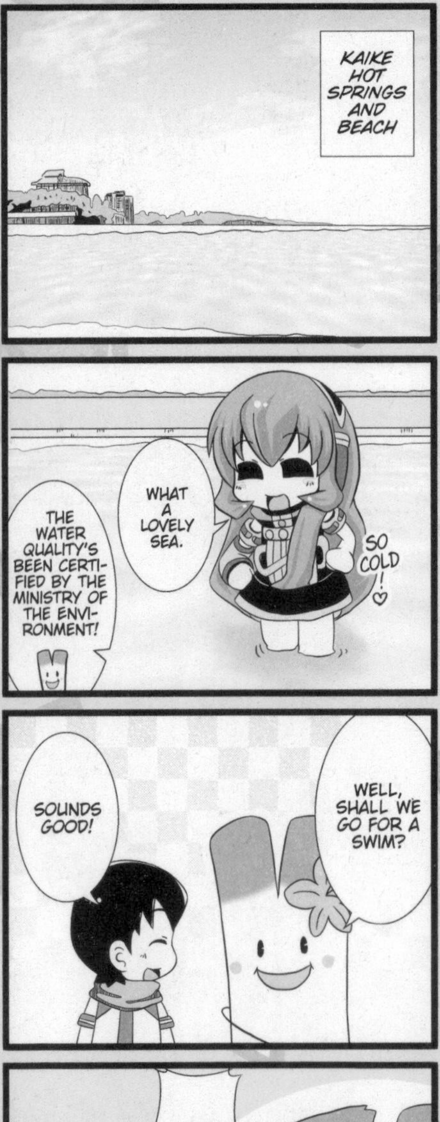
KAIKE HOT SPRINGS AND BEACH
SO COLD! ♡
WHAT A LOVELY SEA.
THE WATER QUALITY'S BEEN CERTIFIED BY THE MINISTRY OF THE ENVIRONMENT!
WELL, SHALL WE GO FOR A SWIM?
SOUNDS GOOD!
SO FAST!!
ギュイーン
ZOOM
HERE IT COMES!
YES'M!
WAH!
FLINCH

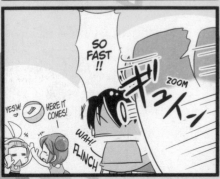

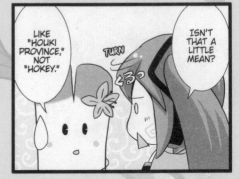

SUMMER TRADITION

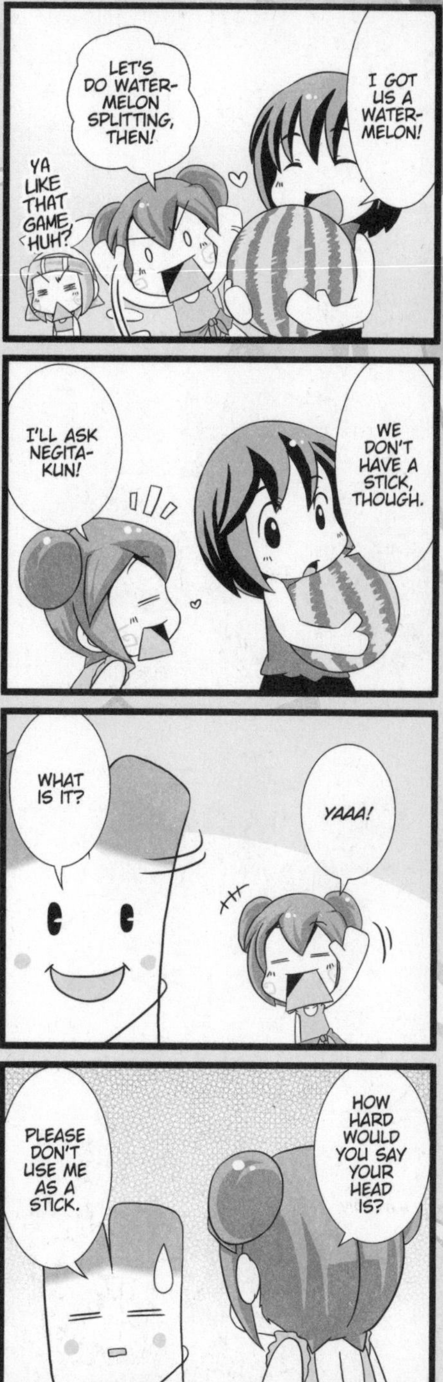
I GOT US A WATER-MELON!
LET'S DO WATER-MELON SPLITTING, THEN!
YA LIKE THAT GAME, HUH?
WE DON'T HAVE A STICK, THOUGH.
I'LL ASK NEGITA-KUN!
YAAA!
WHAT IS IT?
HOW HARD WOULD YOU SAY YOUR HEAD IS?
PLEASE DON'T USE ME AS A STICK.

A LITTLE LONGER

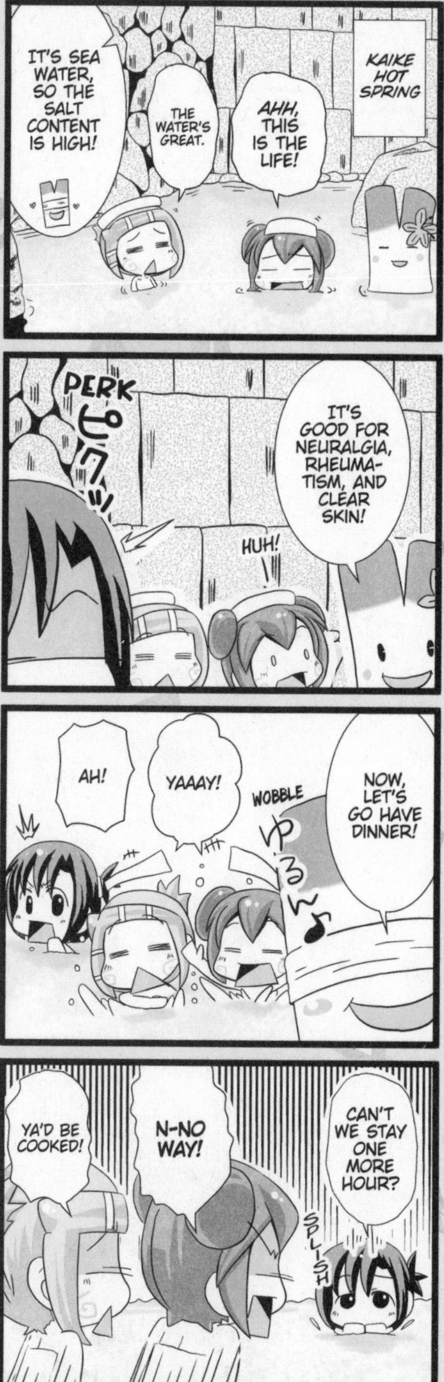
KAIKE HOT SPRING
AHH, THIS IS THE LIFE!
THE WATER'S GREAT.
IT'S SEA WATER, SO THE SALT CONTENT IS HIGH!
IT'S GOOD FOR NEURALGIA, RHEUMATISM, AND CLEAR SKIN!
HUH!
PERK
ピクッ
NOW, LET'S GO HAVE DINNER!
WOBBLE
ゆるん
YAAAY!
AH!
CAN'T WE STAY ONE MORE HOUR?
SPLISH
N-NO WAY!
YA'D BE COOKED!

CRUNCHY

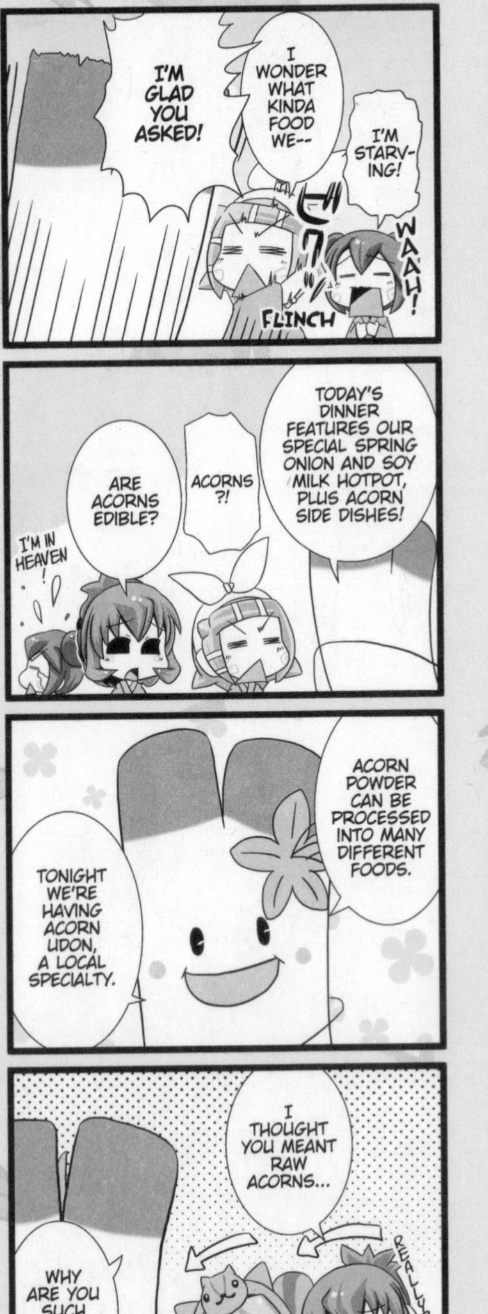

I'M STARV-ING!
I WONDER WHAT KINDA FOOD WE--
I'M GLAD YOU ASKED!
WAAH!
FLINCH
TODAY'S DINNER FEATURES OUR SPECIAL SPRING ONION AND SOY MILK HOTPOT, PLUS ACORN SIDE DISHES!
ACORNS ?!
ARE ACORNS EDIBLE?
I'M IN HEAVEN!
ACORN POWDER CAN BE PROCESSED INTO MANY DIFFERENT FOODS.
TONIGHT WE'RE HAVING ACORN UDON, A LOCAL SPECIALTY.
I THOUGHT YOU MEANT RAW ACORNS...
REALLY?
WHY ARE YOU SUCH WILD ANIMALS?
CRUNCH CRUNCH CRUNCH

AGAIN

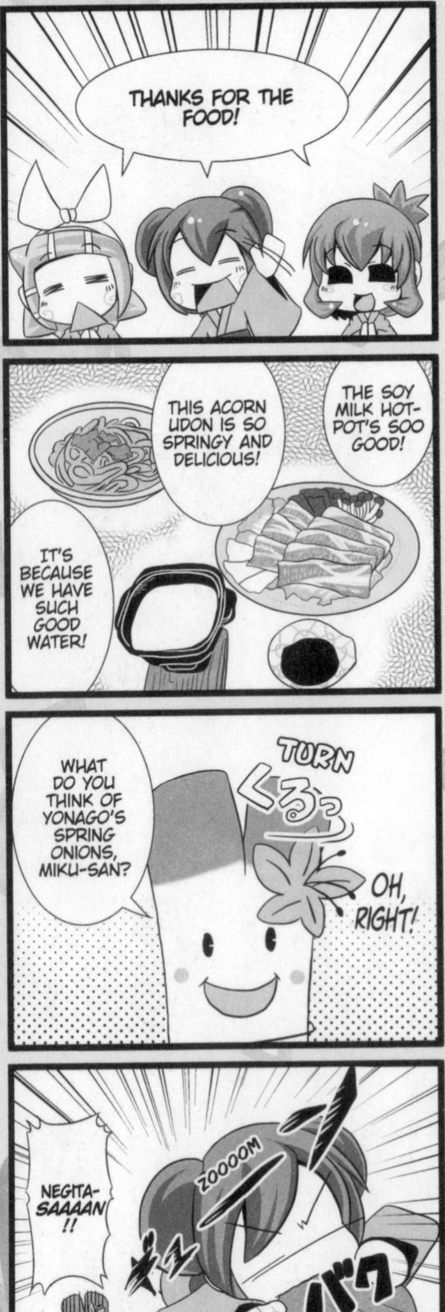

THANKS FOR THE FOOD!
THE SOY MILK HOT-POT'S SOO GOOD!
THIS ACORN UDON IS SO SPRINGY AND DELICIOUS!
IT'S BECAUSE WE HAVE SUCH GOOD WATER!
TURN
くるっ
OH, RIGHT!
WHAT DO YOU THINK OF YONAGO'S SPRING ONIONS, MIKU-SAN?
ZOOOOM
NEGITA-SAAAAN!!
バク
MUNCH

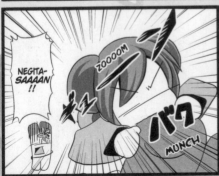

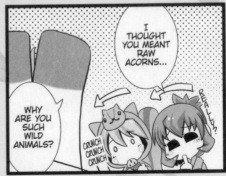

BOOM

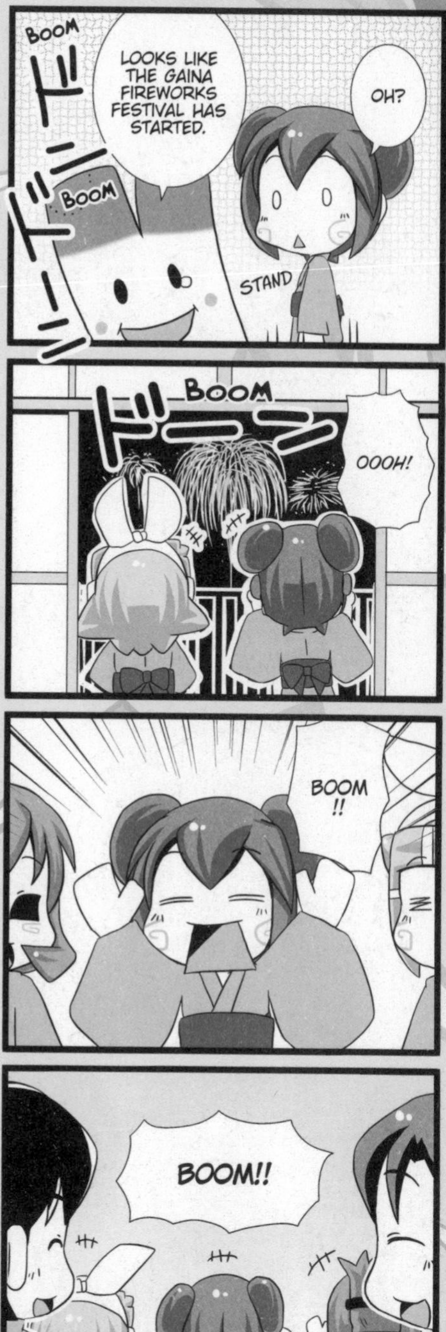
OH?
LOOKS LIKE THE GAINA FIREWORKS FESTIVAL HAS STARTED.
BOOM
BOOM
STAND
OOOH!
BOOM
BOOM!!
BOOM!!

PROMISE

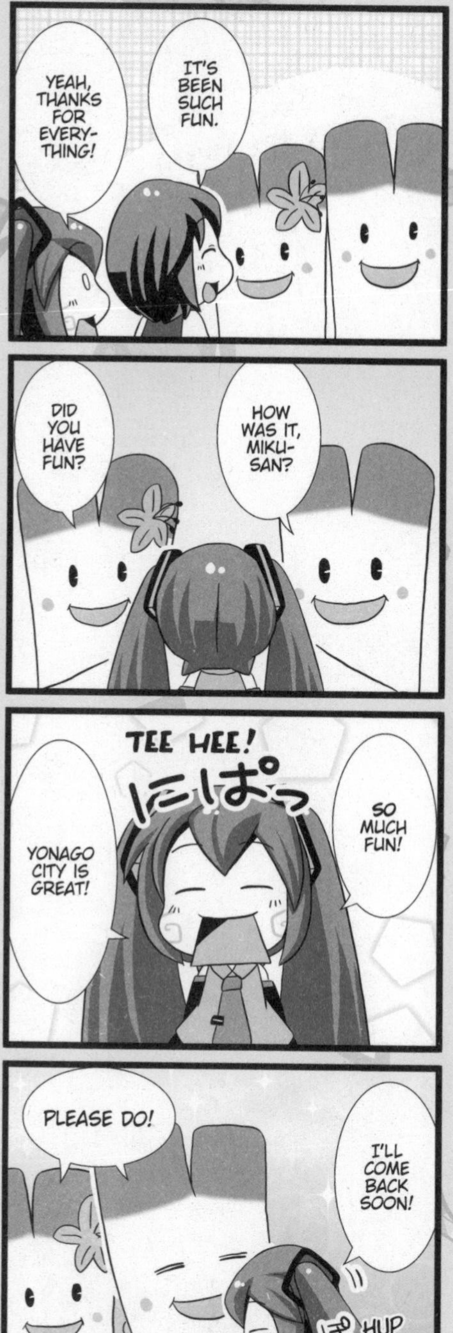
IT'S BEEN SUCH FUN.
YEAH, THANKS FOR EVERY-THING!
HOW WAS IT, MIKU-SAN?
DID YOU HAVE FUN?
SO MUCH FUN!
TEE HEE!
にぱっ
YONAGO CITY IS GREAT!
I'LL COME BACK SOON!
HUP
ぽふっ
PLEASE DO!

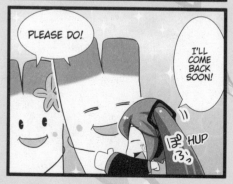

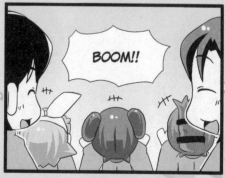

MOBILE VERSION LoiPara! BAND EDITION #11

ALL RIGHT, LET'S MAKE SOME NOISE!
YEAH!
SOUNDS GOOD!
GUITAAAR ~!!
PLOOING
WHY'S IT SOUND SO CRUMMY?!
IS IT BROKEN, OR WHAT?!
SQUEEEEEZE
DON'T TAKE IT OUT ON ME!

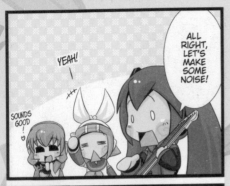

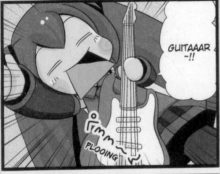

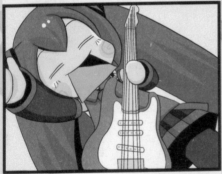

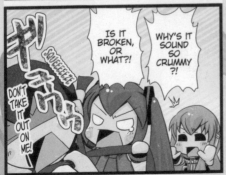

ELECTRIC GUITARS HAVE TO BE PLUGGED IN TO AN AMP...
HERE YOU GO.
ARE YOU SURE?
OOOH!!
ジャラーン
BZOWWWW
THIS IS SO FUN!!
PLUNK PLUNK
ぴょんぴょん
THAT FEELING IS WHAT YOU NEED MOST TO MAKE MUSIC!
OOH, NICE!
WOW! WOW! WOW!
AH HA HA!
SEE, I TOLD YOU IT JUST NEEDED AN AMP.
にぱー
AH HA HA!
YOU LIAR!!
TEE HEE!

MOBILE VERSION

LoiPara!

BAND EDITION

#12

TO BE CONTINUED...

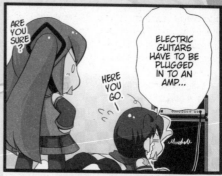

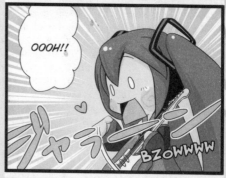

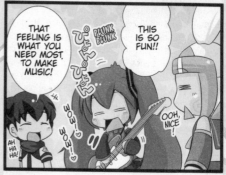

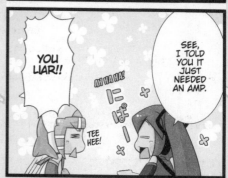

AFTERWORD

Hello, everyone. This is Otomania. Thank you for picking up *LoiPara Volume 3*. So much has happened in our lives from the time LoiPara started serialization up until its third volume. Personally, my life has changed in a lot of ways: I've moved, quit smoking, and cut back on alcohol. I think the fact that I managed to quit smoking is pretty big. I used to smoke so much every day, so it's a strange feeling to have that habit literally gone up in smoke.

Hachune-san's come a long way, too. She's been made into figures, keychains, and giant *papier-mâche*, and featured in game CGs, illustrations, and graphics. Between all this and the collaboration with Yonago, we have so much to be happy about.

However, life can't be good all the time, and there were certainly a few shocking events. The biggest shock, which we also mentioned in our 4-koma afterword comics, was that S-matsu-san, who's been our editor since *LoiPara* began serialization in *Comp Ace*, will be stepping back from his role as *Comp Ace*'s editor. He's not quitting completely, however: He still helped with this volume's compilation and things like the comic's serialization online and in Comptiq, so luckily he won't be leaving us forever or anything.

Thinking back, S-matsu-san supplied a lot of ideas for the comic. From the time when we first met and he drew a weird doodle in the margins of the check, to the time when we got circular *kushikatsu* (A.K.A., deep-fried kebab) and he asked, "Which way do we divide this?" But the best was when we were looking at the Yonago website, which had all sorts of information about Hachune-san and *LoiPara* for our collaboration... including the release date for Volume 3, which neither of us had been told. I fondly remember the moment when S-matsu joined the two of us that make up Ontama in exclaiming "That's news to me!" all at the same time. But despite his playfulness, he's very diligent when it comes to work, and has always been patient with us when waiting for manuscripts, apologized on our behalf when we needed extra time, and given us exactly the advice we needed. It's because of his support from behind the scenes that *LoiPara* exists today. S-matsu-san, thank you for everything. And for your help in the future, too.

Aside from the aforementioned S-matsu-san, we've had the support of many other people cheering us on, which I believe is the reason we've been able to come this far. I don't think it's an exaggeration to say that everyone who's helped and believed in us is responsible for the creation of *LoiPara*, not just Tamago and me. I hope we can continue to make *LoiPara* better and better with the help of everyone who gives us their support, which in turn lets us make a better comic that they will *want* to support.

We'd also like to thank all the people who have helped us along the way, from the publishers and Crypton to Edogawa Charanbo-san and Kamui Souji-san. And of course, the biggest thanks of all to those of you who read and enjoy *LoiPara*. I hope you'll continue to support us in the future.

Presented by
ONTAMA
Otomania & Tamago

Flash anime creation: Tamago   fla3   Nobayashi Tamotsu
Editor: Sadamatsu Keita   Hareyama Tsuruko   Asatani Sachino

Japanese cover/book design: ATOMIC DESIGN

Special Thanks

Crypton Future Media Inc.   wat-san kuri   ken-san   Wasshoi-san/Smith Hioka-san
CAFFEIN-san/Tottori Yonago-sama/ChoudenjiP-san/Good Smile Company   Mikatan-san

...and you!

AMMUNITION

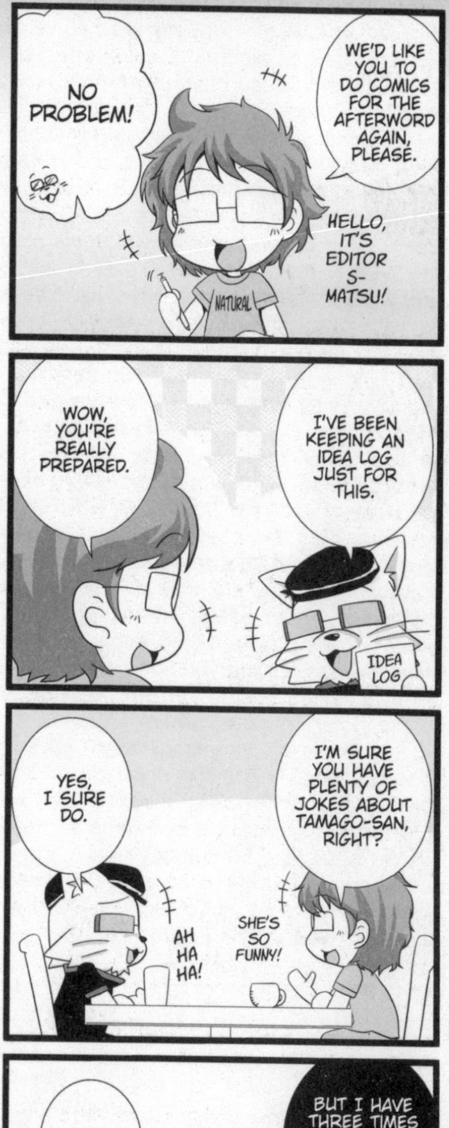

HELLO, IT'S EDITOR S-MATSU!
WE'D LIKE YOU TO DO COMICS FOR THE AFTERWORD AGAIN, PLEASE.
NO PROBLEM!
NATURAL
I'VE BEEN KEEPING AN IDEA LOG JUST FOR THIS.
WOW, YOU'RE REALLY PREPARED.
IDEA LOG
I'M SURE YOU HAVE PLENTY OF JOKES ABOUT TAMAGO-SAN, RIGHT?
YES, I SURE DO.
SHE'S SO FUNNY!
AH HA HA!
BUT I HAVE THREE TIMES AS MANY ABOUT YOU, S-MATSU-SAN...
HUH?
SMIRK

RESPONSE

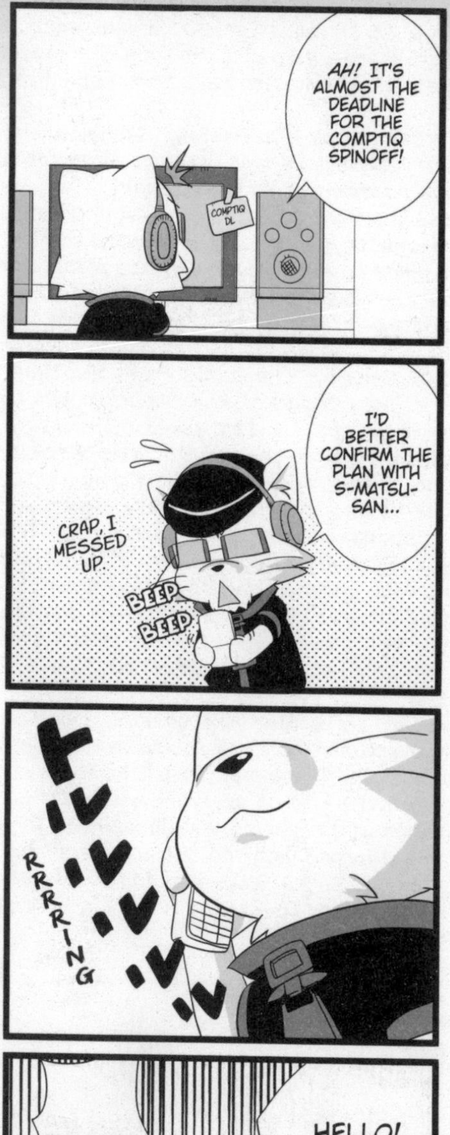

AH! IT'S ALMOST THE DEADLINE FOR THE COMPTIQ SPINOFF!
COMPTIQ DL
I'D BETTER CONFIRM THE PLAN WITH S-MATSU-SAN...
CRAP, I MESSED UP.
BEEP
BEEP
RRRRING
HELLO! I'LL PUT HIM ON!
WHO?!

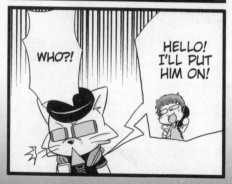

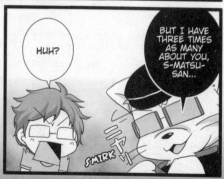

EDITOR-IN-CHIEF

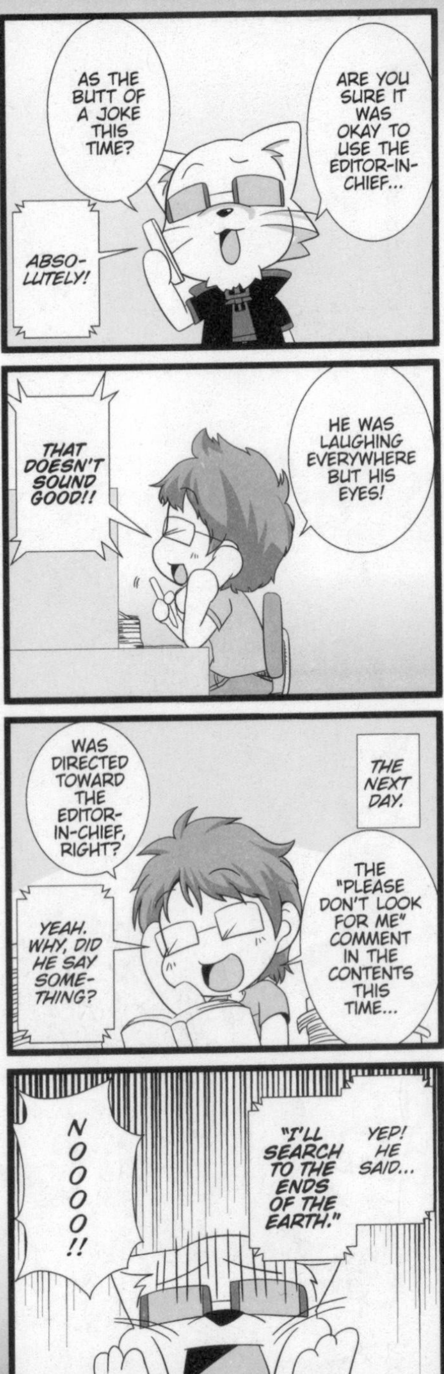
ARE YOU SURE IT WAS OKAY TO USE THE EDITOR-IN-CHIEF...
AS THE BUTT OF A JOKE THIS TIME?
ABSO-LUTELY!
HE WAS LAUGHING EVERYWHERE BUT HIS EYES!
THAT DOESN'T SOUND GOOD!!
THE NEXT DAY.
THE "PLEASE DON'T LOOK FOR ME" COMMENT IN THE CONTENTS THIS TIME...
WAS DIRECTED TOWARD THE EDITOR-IN-CHIEF, RIGHT?
YEAH. WHY, DID HE SAY SOME-THING?
YEP! HE SAID...
"I'LL SEARCH TO THE ENDS OF THE EARTH."
NOOOOO!!

READ THE ROOM

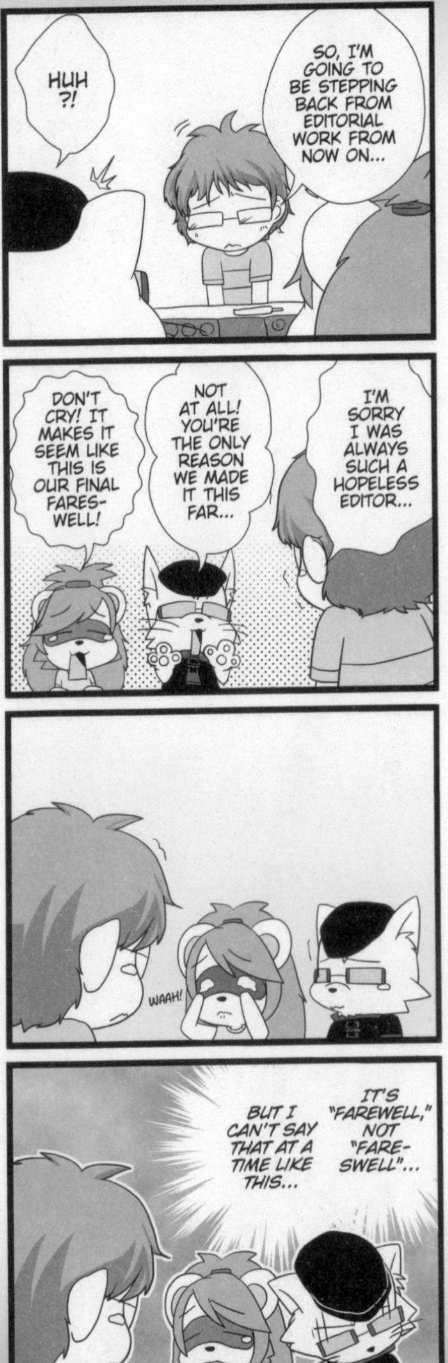
SO, I'M GOING TO BE STEPPING BACK FROM EDITORIAL WORK FROM NOW ON...
HUH ?!
I'M SORRY I WAS ALWAYS SUCH A HOPELESS EDITOR...
NOT AT ALL! YOU'RE THE ONLY REASON WE MADE IT THIS FAR...
DON'T CRY! IT MAKES IT SEEM LIKE THIS IS OUR FINAL FARES-WELL!
WAAH!
IT'S "FAREWELL," NOT "FARE-SWELL"...
BUT I CAN'T SAY THAT AT A TIME LIKE THIS...

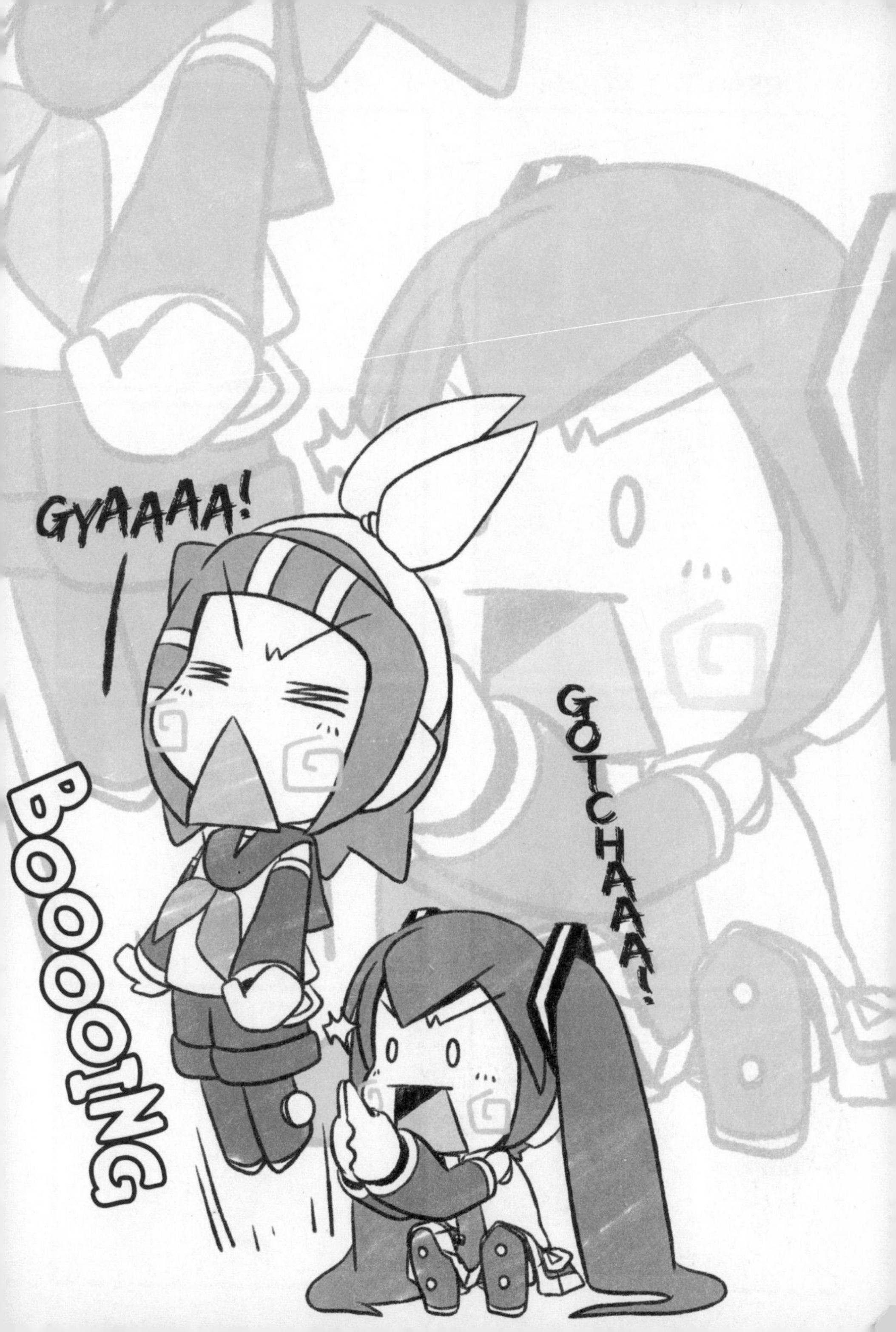

GYAAAA!
GOTCHAAA!
BOOOOING

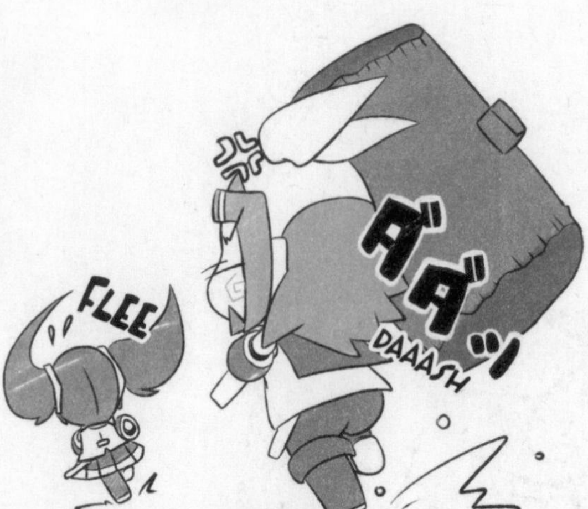
ダダッ
DAAASH
FLEE

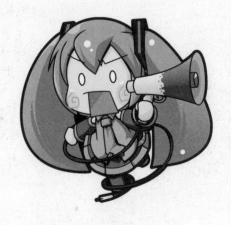

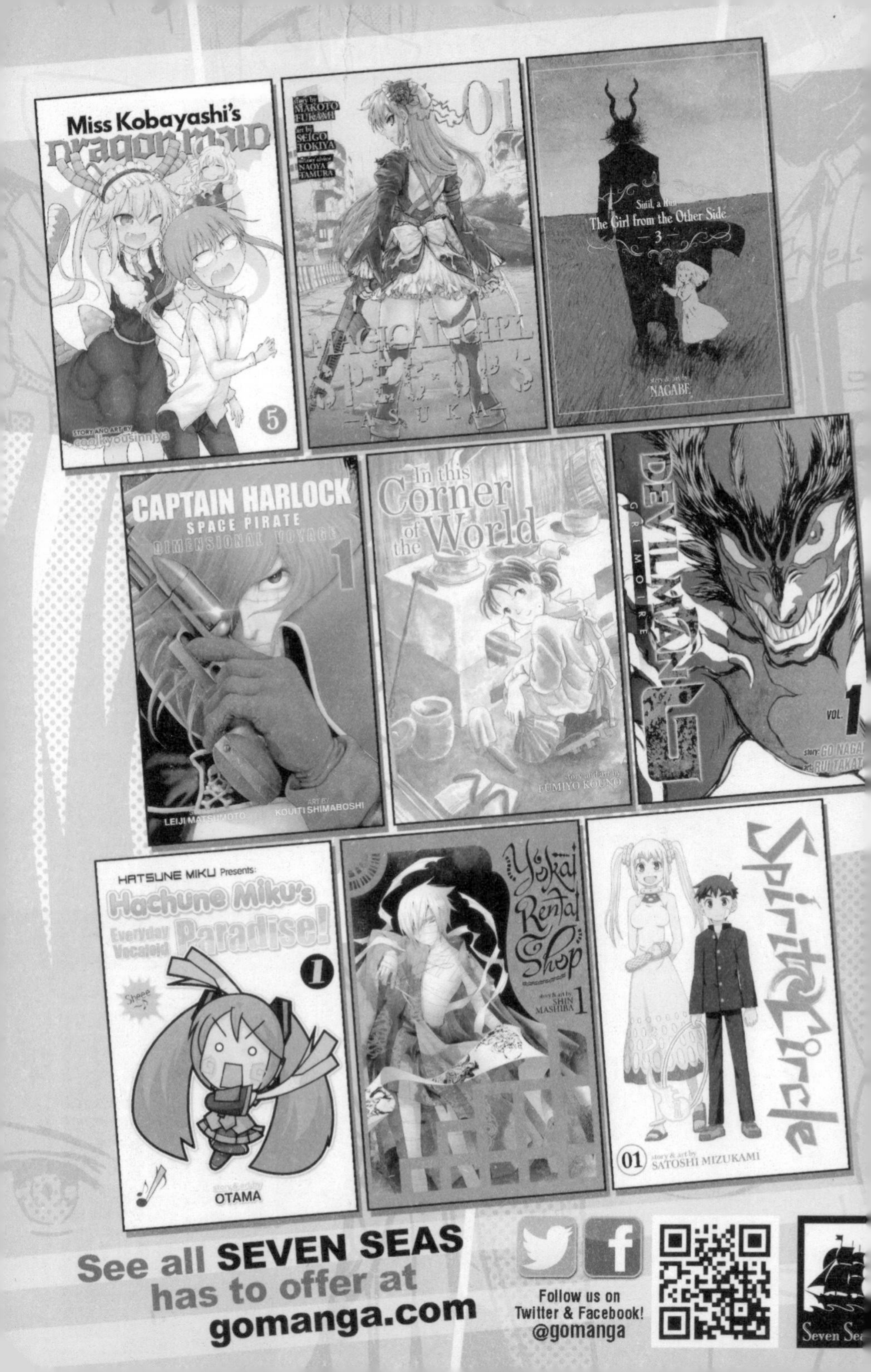
Miss Kobayashi's Dragon Maid
5
STORY AND ART BY coolkyousinnjya
story by MAKOTO FUKAMI
art by SEIGO TOKIYA
01
MAGICAL GIRL SPEC-OPS ASUKA
Siúil, a Rún
The Girl from the Other Side
3
story & art by NAGABE
CAPTAIN HARLOCK
SPACE PIRATE
DIMENSIONAL VOYAGE
1
LEIJI MATSUMOTO
ART BY KOUITI SHIMABOSHI
In this Corner of the World
story and art by FUMIYO KOUNO
DEVILMAN G
GRIMOIRE
VOL. 1
HATSUNE MIKU Presents:
Hachune Miku's Everyday Vocaloid Paradise!
1
OTAMA
Yōkai Rental Shop
story & art by SHIN MASHIBA
1
Spirit Circle
01
story & art by SATOSHI MIZUKAMI
See all SEVEN SEAS has to offer at gomanga.com
Follow us on Twitter & Facebook!
@gomanga
Seven Seas

SEVEN SEAS ENTERTAINME

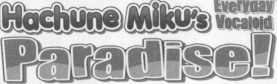

Hachune Miku's Everyday Vocaloid Paradise!

story and art by ONTAMA

VOLUME 3

TRANSLATION	**Jenny McKeon**
ADAPTATION	**Rebecca Scoble**
LETTERING AND RETOUCH	**Rina Mapa**
COVER DESIGN	**Nicky Lim**
PROOFREADER	**Shanti Whitesides** **Kurestin Armada**
EDITOR	**J.P. Sullivan**
PRODUCTION ASSISTANT	**CK Russell**
PRODUCTION MANAGER	**Lissa Pattillo**
EDITOR-IN-CHIEF	**Adam Arnold**
PUBLISHER	**Jason DeAngelis**

FOLLOW US ONLINE: *www.sevenseasentertainment.com*

READING DIRECTIONS

This book reads from *right to left*, Japanese style. If this is your first time reading manga, you start reading from the top right panel on each page and take it from there. If you get lost, just follow the numbered diagram here. It may seem backwards at first, but you'll get the hang of it! Have fun!!

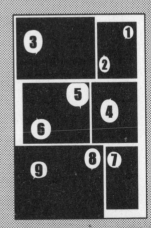